GREEK BY OSMOSIS

GREEK BY OSMOSIS

My Life on a Small Greek Island

(with Mama Kikí's recipes)

LAURA ARISTIDOU CANDRIS

For permissions or inquiries, contact: laurainnaples@outlook.com.

Cover design by Muhammad Arslan @arshgfx

Interior design by Danna Mathias Steele (Reedsy)
Revised Edition
Identifiers: ISBN 979-8-218-74561-5 (paperback); 979-8-218-74562-2 (eBook)
Published by Laura A. Candris
Printed in the United States of America

To Aris, the love of my life, who gave me summers on the Island, his parents, and every other good thing in life.

CONTENTS

PREFACE

I'm not Greek, but I had the good fortune—and good sense—to marry the love of my life, a Greek national, over my parents' objections fifty years ago. I have a Greek name because, in keeping with Greek tradition at that time, I took the possessive form of his first name as well as his surname on marriage.

I began writing the stories that became this book in 2012. This memoir reflects my personal perceptions and recollections of actual events. I have changed or omitted all names except for Laura (me), Aris (my husband), Cousin George, Mr. Lazárou, Anita, and the following deceased relatives: Mána/Kikí, Babás (though Spýros is a pseudonym), aunts Flóra, Kaíti, Frangíski, and Renoúla, and uncles Vasílis and Stamátis. In some cases, I've also changed identifying details and timelines to protect privacy. I reconstructed dialogue from memory, and sometimes changed it for clarity, pacing, or dramatic effect. I have no intention of defaming or harming anyone. Except as noted, any resemblance to real people, living or dead, is coincidental or used fictitiously. I do not represent and have not been paid to mention any company or product.

After folks on the Island started making a fuss over the foods I prepared, I decided to include recipes, especially those passed down by my angelic mother-in-law, Kikí. She would love that her recipes continue to give pleasure. They're collected in the Appendix.

The narrative includes many Greek words, but—with two exceptions—they're written in the Latin alphabet, since the Greek script would be meaningless to most readers.

Writing this book has been a labor of love—a love letter to the Island, Aris, and his mom. I hope you'll enjoy reading about my summer life on a small Greek island under the light of Apollo.

PROLOGUE

It's almost sunset. We sit on our veranda, gazing at a brilliant blue sky infused with pink and mauve. The sea shimmers like satin, shading from aquamarine to ultramarine, and a picturesque, startlingly white church perches on a peninsula of layered rock. Behind it lies an arid landscape dotted with boxy white buildings and dusty olive trees. On the horizon, the shadowy shapes of neighboring islands hover. We're pleasantly tired, having walked home from our second swim of the day.

The table is crowded with ouzo, olives, tomatoes, local cheese, crusty bread, *tzatzíki*, and octopus. Honeybees drone lazily among the caper blossoms and roses, and partridges call softly to their chicks. We wave to a farmer driving by on his way to feed his goats penned across the narrow valley.

It's the beginning of our first summer of retirement on a small Greek island in the Cyclades. We plan to live here every summer from now on.

This is the story of how, from roots in Kentucky, I made a home in this magically beautiful place.

CHAPTER ONE

―――――◆―――――

In the Beginning

First Arrival

I fell in love with the Island the first time I saw it.

It was August of 1978, three and a half years after I married Aris. We boarded a ferry bound for the Island where, at long last, I would meet his beloved parents. Although Aris and his parents were from Athens, his maternal grandmother was a native Islander, and from the age of five, he had spent every summer of his youth here on the Island.

His nanny, Aikateríni, was also from the Island, and much of Aris's time here as a child was spent with her future husband, Manólis, and other farmers, assisting—or perhaps impeding—their work. A city boy with a mischievous streak, he loved escaping to country life on the Island.

As the ferry approached, I was both excited and apprehensive—thrilled to be in this exotic place and to finally meet the parents Aris loved so dearly, but worried they might not be able to love me.

When the Island's rugged coastline came into view, I forgot my anxiety. Cliffs rose up, some almost sheer, others tumbled with geometric scree at their feet. Beyond them, low mountains loomed, steep and stony at their pinnacles but clothed further down in a thin coat of pale dirt, dotted with jagged outcroppings of rock and wild green bushes.

On slopes enjoying partial shade, oregano (*rígani*), thyme (*thymári*), and fuzzy-leaf sage (*faskómilo*) grew wild, giving the Island a lovely aroma as the wind blew seaward—a scent that always takes me back to that first arrival.

Further on, the mountains softened into weathered hills, their gentler slopes terraced for cultivation with fieldstone retaining walls laid dry. Silver-leafed olive trees (*eliés*) and scatterings of white cubical structures punctuated the hillsides. Beneath the *eliés*, where barley once was grown, weeds baked to a golden brown.

In the larger bays indenting the coastline, small white villages clustered by the sea. But most Islanders lived inland, in villages nestled above the terraced farmland, where white, flat-roofed buildings climbed the hills beside ancient stone streets and glowed in the Aegean sun. I was enchanted.

The ferry glided into the deep port bay, flanked by steep, desolate mountains, two of them capped with whitewashed churches and related structures attesting to their former careers as monasteries. The narrow road from the dock threaded past restaurants and shops on its inland side. On its seaside, the restaurants' tables, chairs—and cats—huddled under pergolas, where diners amused themselves by tossing bread to the fish and watching them compete for it.

By the time I arrived, the dock in the port had been enlarged to accommodate ferries, so I didn't have to clamber down a rope ladder into a *kaïki* (a traditional wooden fishing boat), as travelers had to do when Aris was growing up, and were still enduring just a few years earlier.

Waiting for us at the dock was Aris's dad, Babás—a man who could charm crying babies into laughing by just talking to them. He immediately swept me into a big, welcoming hug, giving no hint that he'd been unhappy that Aris had married a *xéni* (female foreigner)—something I learned much later from one of his first cousins. Delighted, and tremendously relieved, I hugged him right back.

We boarded a bus that was ancient even then. The driver's son collected fares and dispensed change while adroitly avoiding the rusted-out hole in the floor. Hugging the mountainside, the bus lumbered up the twisting road, a narrow ribbon above a steep drop to the cultivated valley. The trip to the main village was jostling and nerve-wracking. The road was badly built, and the bus, lacking functioning shocks or struts, groaned around the sharp curves without the benefit of a guardrail along the cliffside.

Our destination, the main village, boasted the only post office, pharmacy, and medical clinic serving the Island's year-round residents (then roughly 2,000), plus its many summer residents and visitors. It also featured bakeries, confectioneries, tavernas (casual dining establishments), bars, and a variety of small shops.

The bus dropped us at the village plaza. My trepidation returned—and increased with every step—as we trudged up an ancient stone-step street toward the small house Aris and his sister had inherited from their maternal grandparents, where he and I would lodge with his parents.

The wheels on the luggage weren't much help. We lugged the suitcases up the uneven, stone-paved path, passing small, pristinely whitewashed homes, their verandas bursting with colorful flowers potted in oversized tin cans painted bright Aegean blue.

When we reached the little house, I finally met Aris's mother. Her kind and gracious welcome put an end to my anxiety at last. Known to most by her nickname, Kikí, and called Mána by me, she was an angel who lived to please the people she loved. How many women can say that about their mothers-in-law? Her exceptional intelligence and intuition went a long way toward enabling us to bridge the language barrier. Over the twelve winters she and Babás later spent with us in the States, she became one of my dearest friends.

She hadn't met us at the ferry to cook the first of many delicious meals she prepared for us in the tiny, sweltering kitchen.

Meeting and Marrying Aris

The Island is a very long way from the modest suburb of Louisville, Kentucky, where I grew up, the daughter of a schoolteacher and a letter carrier who was also a Protestant lay minister. The story of how I got here begins in the fall of 1972 with my first-year orientation at Transylvania University, in Lexington, Kentucky, where I met Aris, a senior student leader. Neither of us had planned to attend Transy—but we're very glad we did.

When he graduated from prep school in Athens, Aris earned a full scholarship to Swarthmore, but his parents understandably balked at him going so far away to a place where they knew no one. He landed at our alma mater because his uncle was then a visiting professor at the nearby University of Kentucky—he'd left Greece due to the junta.

Three years later, I was awarded a full scholarship to Northwestern, which I wanted badly to accept, but my parents refused to let me go out of state at age seventeen. Transy also gave me a scholarship, so I enrolled there instead.

But for our parents' interference, Aris and I would never have met—and I'd never have known the Island.

We started dating that fall. With no money and no car, our dates were at free campus events. Although his family was well-to-do, Aris refused to sign the papers to allow his folks to send him money because he wanted to prove that he could succeed on his own. We both worked, but he worked almost full-time—tutoring, staffing the computer room, even cleaning toilets—while completing a triple major, including physics, in three years. I fell deeply in love with this brilliant, proud, urbane man, and dreaded the separation his graduation would bring.

Aris was headed to Carnegie Mellon University in Pittsburgh for graduate school, where he had a fellowship—but first, he went home for the summer.

During the first half of that summer, I received wonderful love letters week after week. I read them over and over (I had to—deciphering his handwriting took time).

Then midsummer came, and the letters stopped.

I knew that Greece was under a military junta, and that letters destined for the States could be censored or confiscated. But I didn't know whether his letters stopped arriving because of the junta or because he'd lost interest in me. In the last letter I received, he'd written that he'd been assigned to Mudge House at CMU and begged me to visit him at the start of the semester.

Hearing nothing more, when September came, I rashly decided to spend what little was left of my summer savings after school expenses to go to Pittsburgh—and either embrace or slap him. I was eighteen. I'd never been on a plane. I knew no one in Pittsburgh, except Aris—if he was even there. No one knew my plans except my roommate. It was irrational, but I was determined.

Having little money, I booked a flight from Cincinnati to Pittsburgh and took a Greyhound bus to Cincinnati. Disembarking

7

at the bus terminal, I was aghast to learn that the "Cincinnati" airport was back across the river in Kentucky! A frantic taxi ride got me there in time but left me with only three dollars—and no way to get to CMU when I landed. I refused to turn back.

On arrival at the Pittsburgh airport, I camped out in a phone booth (remember those, before cell phones?) and started calling, trying to reach someone—anyone—at CMU who could give me a number for Aris. Just when I was almost out of dimes and had resigned myself to spending the night starving at the airport, I reached a graduate student at Mudge House, who found Aris for me! He was overjoyed that I'd made it to Pittsburgh, but he had no way to get to me, and I was helpless to get to him.

The Fates were on our side. During my sojourn at the airport, I met a woman keeping vigil for her husband's delayed return from Brazil. Being desperate, I poured my heart out to her, and she offered to drive me to CMU after her husband landed. I was ecstatic! We stayed in touch for many years.

When I returned from my impetuous trip to Pittsburgh a few days later, I found my mailbox crammed with Aris's letters, delayed by the junta. Finding them was better than winning the lottery—pure joy! I laughed, cried, and kissed them (I've kept them to this day).

We got engaged not long after our happy reunion in Pittsburgh. We originally planned to marry when I graduated in May of 1975. But at Thanksgiving of 1974, immigration concerns forced us to change that plan. It suddenly dawned on us that Aris had only a student visa and couldn't work off campus. If he didn't get a work permit by the summer, we wouldn't have enough money to live on. We decided to get married before Christmas and immediately apply for a green card and work permit for him.

As you can imagine, there was a lot of speculation that we were marrying five months early for a different reason.

Aris's parents couldn't come for the wedding on such short notice as there wasn't enough time for them to get the visitor visas required then, and mine weren't at all happy that I was marrying a foreigner, one baptized in the Greek Orthodox Church at that. So, we had a very small wedding and honeymooned in my garage apartment. It wasn't much of a venue, but that didn't matter to us. We were together.

After the Christmas break, Aris returned to CMU, and I finished my degree at Transy. I didn't wait for graduation. I joined him in Pittsburgh when classes ended and enrolled in law school. Except for a few years in Jacksonville, Florida, Pittsburgh—Go Steelers!—was our home until we retired.

Why didn't I go to Greece and meet Aris's parents until three and a half years after we married? The Greek military.

Although the junta was overthrown a few months before our wedding, all young Greek men still had to serve in the military for two years. So even if we'd had the means, Aris couldn't have returned to Greece without being conscripted into military service, which would've been a major disruption to our lives and his career. When an exception to the law was enacted, we were free to travel to Greece at last.

The Village House

When Aris's maternal grandparents bought the village house as a summer retirement home, it was already more than a century old—and small. In addition to the tiny kitchen, it had: a single narrow bedroom, holding two twin beds placed foot to foot; a petite living room jammed with two single daybeds, a couple of small chairs, a small buffet, a little display cabinet, and a rotating bookcase; and a dining room so tiny it was completely consumed by a daybed that opened into a double bed, a China cabinet recessed into the wall, and a minuscule closet.

Thankfully, the house also had a decently sized bathroom—a significant upgrade added in anticipation of my visit, as well as a miniature side yard with a cypress tree having cones like tiny soccer balls, and a geranium the size of a large bush. A covered front veranda with a table and chairs offered a charming view of the village.

The space was tight with just us and Aris's parents. Later, when Aris's sister, Faní, her husband, Dimítris, and their son (our elder godson) came too, quarters were seriously cramped. Try to imagine six adults and a child in a house with a single bedroom—and, more importantly, a single bathroom!

As our careers matured and our vacation allowances increased, we started considering other options, with an eye toward spending more time here, especially in retirement. The house couldn't be enlarged to hold all of us comfortably because the side yard was too small, and adding a second floor would have blocked the view of the village that the houses higher on the hill enjoyed—something neither allowed nor neighborly.

In the late 1990s, we started searching for a property to buy in order to build our own home. We first lived in the new house in 2003, and I spent my first summer on the Island in 2007, as I began sauntering toward retirement in 2012.

CHAPTER TWO

Buying the Lot

There were no real estate agents for Island properties, so finding a building lot was something of a quest.

Over two summer vacations, we searched with Leonídas, the excellent cab driver (*taxitzís*) we always used, as our guide. He drove us all over the Island, sharing the news and gossip along the way. What Leonídas didn't know about properties for sale wasn't worth knowing. Apart from Leonídas, property for sale could be discovered by hand-painted signs, word of mouth, or a grocer in the main village.

The property we bought was the first we seriously considered. It was owned by Manólis, husband of Aikateríni, who had been Aris's nanny and helped raise him. When Aris was just ten years old, he was the best man at Aikateríni's and Manólis's wedding. Manólis's family had extensive property on the Island, and because Aikateríni had been "in service" to Aris's parents, they looked down on her and disapproved of the marriage.

To his credit, Manólis defied them all—and got the last laugh: Babás had invested Aikateríni's earnings for her, so when she "retired" to marry, she bought beachfront and other property on what became the Island's second-most touristed bay. Some Islanders ridiculed her for buying worthless sand instead of cultivatable fields. But when tourism on the Island exploded, they envied her foresight.

⋯⋯◇⋯⋯

When I first saw our bay in 1978, the road from the main village to the church on the rocky peninsula was a dirt road (*chomatódromos*), and there was only a donkey path (*monopáti*) from the church down to the bay. Behind the bay, steep hills formed a narrow valley, which widened to embrace the sea as the hills approached the shore. The shoreline on either side of the bay was rocky, but the bay front had a sandy and pebbly beach dotted with tamarisk trees, known on the Island as "salties" (*almyríkia*).

On the far end of the beach, rocks formed a shallow cave, which was home to a one-legged duck with no scruples about thieving from a taverna's adjacent vegetable garden (its owner wasn't amused, but we were).

At that time, the sand on that side of the bay had solidified at the shoreline, its uneven surface trapping sea puddles and the occasional juvenile crayfish and giving children places to carve their names in the soft stone. The bay faced south and was very much in the country (*exochí*), five miles from the main village.

There were two tavernas on the beach, which remain. Now, the bay also holds a few houses and some rental rooms. One taverna has been open since 1967 and is owned and operated by *Kýrios* (Mr.) Pétros and *Kyría* (Mrs.) Évi, who is a fantastic cook of traditional Greek dishes. We eat there for lunch almost every day, from our arrival, typically in early June, to our departure, normally in early October.

Aris and Kýrios Pétros played together the summer Aris was eight and stayed in a family-owned house on the bay. Years later, after we retired, when Kýrios Pétros was asked how late into the year he would remain open, he replied, "Until Aris leaves."

In 1978, the only structure on the hill where we would later build our house was Manólis's *themoniá* (rustic hut) on the top of the ridge. We hiked up to visit him as he was making the local hard cheese. Manólis was widely acknowledged as the expert on local horticulture. Like many native Island men, he was short and wiry, with short, wide hands and thick fingers. Most native Island women were sturdily built.

I can't tell you anything Manólis said during that visit. Aside from my near-ignorance of Greek then, Manólis spoke the local dialect with a heavy accent—they speak rapidly and seem to chew the ends off their words. I never could understand him. I did understand his offer of a slice of his homemade cheese and enjoyed it very much. I also enjoyed the panoramic view of the valley and the sea, the sprig of small-leaf basil he gave me to tuck behind my ear, and the ride he gave me on his donkey.

Aris keeps a photo of me on that donkey with Babás (a sprig of basil behind his ear too) holding the reins. He dubbed it "the three donkeys." Seeing it always makes me smile.

Aris had loved our secluded bay ever since he'd stayed here the summer he was eight. But he didn't rush to buy Manólis's property when it was first offered. I didn't understand that at all but kept looking with him. One place we looked was the bay of Vathí. A dirt road to that bay had been built just a few years earlier, and it was still only lightly developed.

Deep and circular, Vathí Bay had a wide sandy beach stretching between the village on one end and the fishing boats and ceramic kilns at the other. At that time, a donkey loaded with supplies was led across the beach by a dog tugging its reins, and the dock area near the village churches was chock-full of octopuses. I found the bay charming—so did a shipowner who later built a lovely resort hotel there. But the bay's distance from the main village and port was a drawback, and Aris loved the bay where he'd stayed as a child.

After spending two summer vacations looking at other properties that didn't appeal to us nearly as much as Manólis's, I finally asked Aris why he didn't buy the property he really wanted. Sighing, he explained that Manólis wanted too much money for it.

I thought the solution was simple and said, "So, offer what you think it's worth."

The crux of the problem finally came out when he replied, "How can I negotiate with someone who carried me around on his shoulders?"

Understanding at last, I said, "Then pay what he wants—and be glad that you can contribute to his comfortable retirement."

That was that. So, I take some credit for our having this property, even though Manólis probably wouldn't have sold it to anyone but Aris.

Before Aris signed the contract to buy the lot—or, rather, authorized Babás to listen to the reading of the contract by the *symvolaiográfos* (a kind of legal notary) and sign it as his attorney-in-fact—we had to undertake various investigations. Greek law at the time required the contract to be read aloud to the parties by the notary, an archaic requirement left over from a time when relatively few people were educated.

The investigations were necessary because you could write an agreement that said, "I agree to pay X to buy the described property, provided that it has a clear title, public water, and electricity, and hasn't been declared to be a forest which cannot be developed," but writing those contingencies didn't mean anything. Once you signed an agreement to buy real estate, you were bound to buy it, whether the contingencies were satisfied or not.

The possibility that the arid piece of steep, stony hillside we wished to buy might have been designated a forest because of its handful of scruffy junipers seemed preposterous, but it was a real risk at the time.

We also had to establish title, in other words, that Manólis was the sole owner of the property and had the right to sell it to us. In those days, Greece didn't tax undeveloped property and kept no records of its ownership. Consequently, proving title was interesting—and important—because a great deal of land had been taken from absentee owners via adverse possession. Without ownership records, establishing title was essentially a process of assembling oral (and any written) evidence, for example:

Lawyer: "How did you acquire the property?"
Seller: "My father gave it to me on his deathbed."
Lawyer: "Were there any witnesses to that bequest?"
And so on.

Eventually, everything was settled, and the sale was finalized. The property description in the deed to our lot includes boundary references to stone walls, rock slabs, and fir trees. That deed unlocked the door to the next phase of our Island adventure: building our home.

CHAPTER THREE

Building the House

Designing a Dream

Building any home entails drama—we knew that from our experience in the States. But building on the Island generated far more than we'd anticipated.

The only access to our property was (and still is) a not-always-dry riverbed. The first architect we consulted told us we were crazy to buy and build there. He didn't get the job.

Although it's sometimes a waterway during the rainy season, the riverbed is a recognized road with streetlights all the way to our place. We weren't troubled by the prospect of having it as our road since we'd be building many meters above it and had no intention of being here in the winter.

Typically, there's nothing to do on the Island in the winter. The sea's often too cold for comfortable swimming and too rough for boating, and the weather's often too wet and cold for comfortable hiking. By "too rough for boating," I mean that, in the winter, a week can pass without a commercial ferry being able to travel to or from Athens. Although the temperature rarely falls below 30° Fahrenheit, the cold is damp—the kind that goes right to your bones.

To be sure, there are some disadvantages to having a seasonally dry riverbed for a road. One year, when we returned to the Island after early September rains, the taxi we hired to take us to our place—Leonídas wasn't available—stopped short of our driveway. Large stones had been turned up in the road by the rain, and there was standing water.

I was really glad that we traveled with just carry-ons. We took off our shoes, rolled up our pant legs, grabbed our bags, and walked the rest of the way home. But there are also advantages: since our road doesn't lead anywhere except to a donkey path to the main village, we see almost no traffic on it and—absent a wedding or similar event at the church—it's usually very quiet here.

The second architect we consulted, one of Aris's childhood friends—whose name, interestingly, means "well respected"— insisted that he had to have the final say on all design elements. That wasn't the right thing to say to two Type A personalities who had renovated one house and built another from scratch. He didn't get the job either.

We ended up hiring a civil engineer from the Island, who had good command of English and was tech-savvy. He was recommended by one of Aris's cousins and had the ability to email CAD drawings, photos, and documents, which was very important to us. We also liked the house and guest house he'd built for a Dutch couple in a neighboring bay.

He proved to be a mixed blessing.

We liked the first design he produced for the house but struggled to understand how it would fit on our steep lot. So, we asked him to stake it out on the property before we arrived. It was a good thing we did: that design involved cantilevering a sizable portion of the house over the hillside and would've required extensive blasting of rock. We nixed it and told him to come up with one better suited to the topography.

Here, you're only allowed to build a collection of cubes, which must be painted white or faced with stacked stone to preserve the Island's color and character. Roofs must be flat to catch water for cisterns. Windows and shutters must be wooden and in an Island style. No picture windows are allowed—though that rule seems now to be honored more in the breach than by compliance.

Windows and shutters must be a color that already exists on the Island. But if you care about pleasing your neighbors, it's courteous to choose a color already used in the vicinity. Failure to comply with these rules meant that you'd be denied an electrical connection, unless, of course, you bribed the right people or changed things after you got electricity.

From the beginning, we intended our house to look completely traditional on the outside and have many traditional interior features, including ceilings of pine planks and chestnut beams with natural stain, varying in height from ten to fourteen feet, and stone floors. The wood is imported as it has been for centuries. However, traditional Island homes have small rooms, and we wanted a sense of space.

The public rooms of our house—the entrance (*eísodos*), living room (*salóni*), dining room (*trapezaría*), and kitchen (*kouzína*)—are larger than customary and are open to each other through wide archways traditionally used in exterior walls. We also insisted on walk-in closets in the two bedrooms, although the engineer—and just about everyone else—thought we were nuts to waste so much space on closets.

The engineer's second design had multiple levels, with the guest suite sitting atop the kitchen, accessed via external stairs.

That design suited the terraced land well and was attractive from the sea and the sides—with the sad exception of the front, which faces north. Approaching our bay from the southeast, our house looks like giant white steps climbing the hillside.

The second design also met our primary goal of ensuring that every room has a view of the sea and the church on the rocky peninsula. To maximize the view without the prohibited picture windows, the southern wall of each room was designed with two large traditional windows and a balcony door.

Various proposed changes to the front face of the house yielded no improvement. Concerned about losing more time, we gave up and told the engineer to apply for the building permit. Then we waited . . . and waited . . . and waited. Our application just sat there.

The engineer told us that a moderate "gift"—also known as a bribe—would solve the problem. Aris adamantly refused to contribute to the prevailing culture of corruption. The engineer then told us that he, not we, would be responsible if we began construction without the building permit and that he was willing to take that risk, so we agreed to start.

We finally got the building permit just before we moved into the house, three years later. Two weeks after that—to the chagrin of Manólis's son and daughter, who own property there—the government declared that no further construction would be allowed in our bay because of the significance of the church on the rocky peninsula. As the saying goes, "Timing is everything." We were lucky.

Construction—and Confusion

Anticipating visitors from the States who are accustomed to flushing their toilet paper, Aris specified a gigantic septic tank. And, unusually for the Island, he wanted a small basement.

Because water is a serious issue in this arid place, he also specified a huge cistern, able to hold ninety tons of water, as well as access to public water. With the cistern, septic tank, and basement, there was a lot of excavation work, which produced the stone to build our many retaining walls.

To my surprise, not long after the excavation began, it stopped. The Greek Archaeological Service had to inspect the site for ancient relics before the work could proceed.

If you're so unfortunate as to have archaic artifacts on your property, construction halts until they're removed—which may take decades. If, like one of Aris's cousins, you unknowingly purchase an ancient gravesite, you're entirely out of luck: You will never be able to build, and you'll receive no compensation for your property. We'd looked at that site too!

Concerned that I would worry if I knew, Aris didn't tell me about this quirk of Greek law until the property was cleared for construction. He hadn't been troubled about it because the lot had been terraced for cultivating olive trees and barley and was a good distance from any ancient site.

There are other peculiarities of building on the Island. Even though you've hired a contractor who hired the construction crew, you, the property owner, are responsible for paying into the workers' pension and healthcare funds. And if they're injured on your property, you're accountable for that too, even though you have no control over the work or them.

When we arrived during the first summer of construction, we found the workers pushing filled wheelbarrows over two worm-eaten boards laid across a deep trench. They were in flip-flops and shorts, with no gloves, helmets, or eye protection. I'd never been a fan of OSHA before, but I was appalled by the lack of safety precautions and told the engineer to stop the work

until the workers had proper safety equipment, including helmets and steel-toed boots, which we'd pay for. He replied that
it was too hot, and they wouldn't work if they had to wear such
gear. At least I convinced him to replace the boards.

You may have noticed that I referenced the *first* summer of
construction. Nothing is hurried on the Island. We joked that
we'd told the engineer we wanted the house to be finished in a
year—we just forgot to tell him which one.

Part of the issue is that there were only so many construction workers on the Island. If an Islander needed to build rental
rooms for the next season, that took priority, and your project
would be pushed back. I also suspect that no one believed that
we really wanted it built in a year.

Most homes here were built in installments because there
were no American-type mortgages. Here, if you had 90% of the
funds, you could get a mortgage for the remaining 10%. So, folks
would excavate their cisterns and septic tanks one year, then do
something else a year or two or three down the road, and so on.
Building in stages is feasible on the Island because all buildings
are reinforced concrete or stone, which can withstand the ravag-
es of the relatively mild weather without being finished.

Once our cistern, septic tank, and basement were finished,
construction of the skeleton of the house began. The reinforced
concrete ties were about a foot square. The spaces in between
were filled with mortared stacks of ceramic bricks with multiple
cylindrical holes. The resulting walls were then coated in cement
and are also about a foot thick.

Before the walls were finished, conduits for electrical and
phone wires were inserted a foot or so below the ceiling and, for
the outlets, a foot or so above the floor. Flat white access covers
for the conduit, about three inches across, were left visible in the

walls so the concrete doesn't have to be broken every time the wires need to be repaired, as is often required after a wet winter. When finished, the walls were painted white, mimicking the traditional whitewash, inside and out.

One of the most interesting things I watched during the construction of our Island home was the installation of the stone floors. The stones were rectangular, in many different sizes, and about two inches thick. The mason smacked a trowel of cement down in the center of the room, set a stone on top of it, and worked out from the center to the edges, fitting the stones together as if he were completing a puzzle, eyeballing the sizes needed. If he ever cut any stones, I didn't see him do it. His skill was impressive.

When the stone floors were fully installed, thin white lines (*armoi*) were painted down the middle of the narrow cement grout, outlining the stones in white in the tradition of the Island. After that, the floors were coated with stone sealant.

I don't know who did that work initially, but when we needed to redo the sealant on the stone floors in 2013, I stripped the stones—a job I do *not* want to do again—and we hired two women, one of them quite deaf, who were known to be very skilled in painting the traditional thin white lines between the stones. They were amazing. One in her eighties, the other in her seventies, they knelt, crouched, or sat on the hard stone floors, painting fine white lines around every stone throughout the house and the guest house, all while chatting loudly.

When they finished that work after lunching on our veranda in mid-afternoon, they asked what else we'd like them to do since we'd paid for the whole day. They absolutely insisted on also sealing the floor of the new guest house. Small islands are the ultimate small towns, and over lunch, we learned that one of these women was the aunt of a man we had hosted for several dinners in Pittsburgh while he was doing post-doctorate work at Carnegie Mellon University!

Broken Walls, Moldy Cabinets, and Other Headaches

If you ever contemplate building a home on an island in a foreign country, understand that constructing (and owning) such a house necessitates compromise—lots of compromise. Even though we hired a recommended, licensed engineer, and Aris is an engineer and a native Greek language speaker with deep connections to the Island, we still faced significant construction issues.

We ordered our kitchen and bathroom cabinets, interior doors, shutters, windows, and balcony doors from a Greek company in Athens. Without checking with us (or the company), the engineer decided that it would be "quaint" to use two pieces of schist stone for each windowsill and balcony door threshold. Schist isn't a very smooth stone, and using two pieces made the surface even more irregular.

The window crew threw a fit and refused to install the windows or patio doors on such uneven surfaces and returned to Athens without getting anything done, after we'd paid for their trip. Then the northern, western, and southern exterior walls of the house were broken, and all twenty-three of the schist windowsills and door thresholds were removed.

Kárystos stone—a smooth, heavy-duty type of slate—was installed, and the walls were patched back together. The engineer promised the repairs would be invisible. They aren't, and they continue to crack and sometimes leak during the winter— the primary reason we have the house repainted every summer.

When the new windowsills and door thresholds were installed, the engineer forgot to check the slant; several tilt slightly toward the house, trapping rainwater against it. The worst offender is the threshold of our bedroom balcony door. Every winter, trapped rainwater slowly seeps into the stone floor, causing it to stain, flake, and reject any sealant. It also penetrates the adjacent walls, causing the paint to peel (another reason for the annual painting).

To my chagrin, when we moved in, I discovered that the backs of three of our brand-new kitchen cabinets were stained with mold—and smelled of it too. The wall above them also had a thick, black ribbon of stain. When I confronted the engineer, he laughingly told me that he forgot to seal the steps connecting the different levels of the roof before the winter rains, so they leaked. I was not amused. Not at all. It took four years to get rid of the smell, even leaving the cabinet doors open all winter.

Since the only closets are in the bedrooms and only one of these is in the main house, I repeatedly asked for a broom closet in the kitchen. I didn't get it. I would put that down to chauvinism, but the Island has a long history of strong women running businesses, such as restaurants and hotels, in the absence or after the deaths of their seafaring husbands.

With no broom closet, the vacuum cleaner replaces shoes in the back corner of our bedroom closet, while the broom and dustpan lean on the wall outside the kitchen door, providing prime nesting opportunities to spiders.

The engineer convinced Aris that we didn't need windows on the eastern wall of the master bedroom, arguing that the two windows in the southern wall would be enough. He was wrong: Cooling winds blow from the north, not the south. The only way that room can be tolerably cool without air conditioning is by opening both the north-facing bathroom window and the door between the bathroom and our bedroom. Even then, it's the warmest room in the house.

Someone decided that we didn't need screens on the north-facing windows in the entrance. Since refreshing breezes blow predominantly from the north, those windows need to be open for the living room to be reasonably cool. And because we don't care for mosquitoes, wasps, or creepy crawlies, we had to have ugly wood-framed screens made for those windows (well, they didn't *have* to be ugly, but they are).

In fairness to whomever made that decision, window screens were quite unusual on Greek islands. We visited one of Aris's prep school classmates at his beautiful, recently built home on Páros, and there were no screens anywhere. They left their windows and doors wide open and didn't seem to mind the many wasps, mosquitoes, and other invading insects. That's the norm here, so visiting Greeks often forget to close our doors.

Construction was considerably behind schedule when the kitchen and bathroom cabinets were ready to be installed. The truck with the materials and installers arrived from Athens, again. We'd paid for their transport a second time, and we were paying for their daily room and board. Racing to catch up, the engineer stopped the work on the stone floor in our bedroom and diverted the versatile stone mason to setting the tile in the master bathroom so the cabinets could be installed.

The stone mason/tile setter sloped the bathroom floor toward the drain in its middle, as is standard practice in Greece. Consequently, the bathroom floor ended up half an inch higher than the bedroom floor where they meet, the perfect difference for stubbing toes. To solve the problem, the engineer built a concrete "ramp" between the surfaces. It saves our toes, but we have an ugly strip of naked concrete in our bedroom (at least it's the same color as the stone). The difference in the heights of the two floors also kept the door between our bedroom and the bathroom from closing—a problem eventually solved, thankfully.

The engineer also neglected to build the *pentzoúles* (stone-paved benches) we'd requested outside the dining room, which are characteristic of the Island. When he finally had them built the following winter, he allowed the pipe from the roof to the cistern to be blocked, causing the living room to flood with two inches of standing water, which poured out of the electrical conduit.

As you can imagine, the electrical wires, the feet of our brand-new furniture, and the sealant on the stone floor were damaged. The leak also caused mildew on the undersides of our raffia-woven chair seats, all of which had to be set upside down in the sun for several days when we returned. The basement flooded, too. (The engineer didn't offer to take care of any of the damage.)

We later discovered that the *pentzoúles* on the upstairs balcony hadn't been built properly either, so that large sections of the walls above our bedroom walls had to be demolished and rebuilt.

Although I lost several battles over the construction of the house, I won one important one: the rocks jutting from the hillside on the eastern side of our home, carved by wind and rain into shallow caves. Everyone said they should be blasted away, but I put my foot down and they weren't. Not only are they quite picturesque, they're also a haven for birds.

Last Words

You might think that, given these experiences, we'd give up on building. We didn't give up, but we didn't use that engineer again (and later came to miss his square corners and straight walls).

Despite everything—broken walls, slanted thresholds, stains, and setbacks—we have a beautiful home in a remarkably beautiful place. In the end, it was worth it.

CHAPTER FOUR

Furnishing the House, Round 1

Buying furniture for the Island house turned into an unexpected mission.

When we decided to build a house on the Island, I had the foolish notion that we could order furniture for it online. Wrong! None of the websites featuring furniture I liked offered a way to buy it. The only option was to request a catalog. I asked for several; I got none. I guess they didn't take inquiries from the States seriously, or they didn't want to incur the cost of postage.

In the winter of 2002–2003, Aris detoured from a business trip elsewhere in Europe to see his folks in Athens. I charged him with scouting for furniture there and bringing back photos. He tried valiantly but returned frustrated and told me I was just going to have to do this myself.

There were decorators in Athens, of course, but we weren't interested. We'd built an island-style house and intended to purchase island-style furnishings. The walls were white, the stone floors were gray, and we needed neither rugs nor draperies. How hard could this be?

In March of 2003, I was en route to Athens to buy furniture (*épipla*). I met Aris at the Frankfurt airport, and we traveled together to Athens. We had one week to accomplish this mission, travel included. He'd diligently canvassed his friends and relatives for leads on island-style furniture. Unfortunately, several recommended stores had closed. Others didn't offer anything I wanted for the living room (*salóni*) or master bedroom (*kýrio ypnodomátio*).

Finally, late in the week, we arrived at Mr. Lazárou's store. There, we found the perfect sofa and armchairs. A lovely bedroom suite was also on offer. I was thrilled! According to its website, this company had been making traditional (*paradosiaká*) furniture since 1898. It offered hand-carved, wax-finished furniture, treated against woodworms, and warranted for twenty years.

The sofa and armchairs have camelbacks, curved arms, and carving. They're not upholstered in the traditional sense but have seat and back cushions on wooden frames. As with many European beds, they're significantly lower than the seats of dining chairs. The bedroom pieces have raised panels and white marble tops.

When we found this furniture, we had barely three hours to choose a fabric, close the sale, get to the dock, and board the ferry to the Island to check on the construction of the house. So, there we were, two Type A personalities with a deadline, and Mr. Lazárou, the very epitome of an older Greek gentleman, inquiring after Aris's father and offering us orange juice and sweets. Greece had not long been part of the Eurozone, and he patiently converted prices from drachmas to euros and described in detail the hand-woven linen fabrics available for the cushions.

The niceties, small talk, and slow progress made me very nervous. Finally, without consulting Aris, I told Mr. Lazárou (or tried to tell him) that, if we couldn't get this done in one hour, we wouldn't be able to give him the sale. My message must have gotten through because the poor man became so flustered that I feared he was going to have a heart attack!

Despite everything, we completed the sale and chose fabric for the cushions in time to board our ferry. I left the store uncertain whether the fabric pattern I wanted (a modification of one displayed) was what we would get. I'd underestimated Mr. Lazárou: I got exactly what I wanted.

In ensuing years, we purchased many other articles of furniture from the Lazárou family, including a headboard carved with our initials, a magnificently carved drop-front secretary desk, and an equally impressive buffet that resembles the antique in the village house. We've never been disappointed. This furniture is so beautiful that I've had to disabuse more than one visitor of the idea that our home is filled with antiques.

Elsewhere, we bought a rustic dresser and nightstand for the guest room, a small dining table, dining chairs, and stools for the kitchen peninsula. The chairs and stools have woven raffia seats and lathe-turned spindles. The engineer waxed eloquent about how such chairs were unique to the Cycladic Islands.

Buying furniture and appliances is one thing. Getting them to a house on a small island is quite another. Furniture and appliances for homes on little islands like ours aren't delivered to your door by the stores where you bought them. Instead, the stores deliver them to whichever warehouse or trucking company you hire to take them from there to your island home. At that point, the stores' responsibility ends.

You can never be sure when your purchases will reach you. In the summer, ferryboats that accept trucks as well as passengers may have too much weight to be able to board the truck with your items, so it may have to wait a day or more. In other seasons, there are days when the sea is too rough for ferry traffic.

Once our furniture and appliances reached the Island, they needed to be delivered to our house via the riverbed road and our steep driveway. Aris's sister, Faní, warned us that the road was in poor condition from the winter rains. She'd tried unsuccessfully to get the Island's municipal government, the *dímos*—the whole Island is one municipality—to bulldoze the road. We decided to hire a bulldozer on our own to flatten the road, only to discover that there was but one bulldozer on the Island, and it was broken.

Our furniture and appliances were well wrapped in layers of bubble wrap and cardboard, but even those careful preparations were inadequate for the condition of our road that year. The furniture suffered various bumps and scrapes, including a series of deep indentations on the top of the dining table, but the worst damage was to the refrigerator.

The finish of the door was marred, but that was the least of our worries. The real problem was that it would not close. No matter how we adjusted the feet of the fridge, a quarter-inch gap remained between the top of the door and the body, causing it to frost up constantly. Eventually, we bowed to the inevitable and changed the door to open on the other side. The door sealed then but opened away from the work area of the kitchen. Oh well! As I said, owning a house on a small island means compromise.

The most remarkable delivery I witnessed occurred a few years later when the buffet cabinet for the dining room arrived. A substantial piece of solid wood furniture, it came on a truck with a single driver and no helper. The driver carried it alone on his back up twelve steps to the dining room. I don't know how he managed it. I gave him a cold glass of water and a well-earned tip, asked if he'd like anything else to eat or drink, and invited him to sit and recover.

I shouldn't complain about our riverbed road or steep driveway since delivery vehicles reach our house. The sole access to the village house is an ancient stone pathway composed of multiple steps, and delivery of furniture and appliances there is via donkey! Such deliveries are facilitated by a traditional architectural feature of homes in Island villages: a chamfered roadside corner with the lower part nipped off at a forty-five-degree angle and capped with an arch, designed to help laden donkeys turn corners more easily.

Of course, furniture is only the beginning of the process of making a house into a home. In Athens, we made multiple trips to a home goods store, shopping for glasses, flatware, pots, pans, sheets, and all of the other essentials for a new home— well, all that we could remember to buy. Despite several trips to that store, we forgot some necessary items, which led me to the "Little of Everything" *(Lígo ap' Óla)* store on the Island.

CHAPTER FIVE

The Little of Everything (*Lígo ap' Óla*) Store

In the main village, on a narrow, ancient, stone-paved road lined by shops, houses, restaurants, and churches, sat an utterly amazing store, run by the same family for generations. The Little of Everything store was jam-packed, from the floor to its very high ceiling, with embroidery thread, work boots, pots, small appliances, hair shears, glassware, snorkel masks, curtains, yacht flags, clothespins, baskets, fabric, and almost any other non-perishable item you might imagine. I even found a crystal ice bucket there. I always took guests there, because it was so remarkable.

Among the things we hadn't bought in Athens was a dish drainer. I hadn't thought to get one since I expected to be using the dishwasher. But it was inoperable the first year. I asked Aris what the Greek words for "dish drainer" are as this was long before translation apps. For that matter, this was before internet access reached the Island. He couldn't remember (in case you're curious, it's *strangistíri piáton*). Nor could he recall the Greek terminology for "bathmat" (I later learned that it's *patáki bániou*).

Undaunted, I headed to the Little of Everything store, where the proprietress was clever, patient, and helpful. With my rudimentary Greek, I explained that I needed the plastic thing for dishes to dry on after they're washed. The proprietress looked perplexed for a moment, then her face brightened with understanding, and she showed me a dish drainer located on the top of the highest shelf. Success!

I then explained that I needed the thing for the floor by the shower, that's not a towel and not a rug. Another stare, another visible "aha!" moment, and I was shown a stack of bathmats. I also managed to buy a set of coasters, using the French word, but couldn't convey the concept of a soap dish. I ended up purchasing small ceramic bowls elsewhere for that purpose.

The Little of Everything store also offered rag-woven mats. A bit like colonial American rag rugs, these brightly colored mats (*kourelóudes*) are rectangular and used to cover *pentzoúles* (stone benches) for sitting. I bought two and later went back for more.

Bit by bit, our house was becoming a home.

CHAPTER SIX

One Dishwasher for the Price of Two

Hope springs eternal, they say. The engineer boasted that the house would be finished in 2002. Wanting to believe him, we ordered appliances to arrive well in advance. Disappointingly, the house wasn't usable until the summer of 2003, so the appliances sat in a warehouse while their warranties expired.

When we first occupied our new house, Aris and I stayed in the upstairs guest suite and installed his folks in the master bedroom so they didn't have to deal with so many stairs. Mána and Babás had spent twelve winters with us in the States, and I'd become close to them both, but especially Aris's bright, selfless mother.

On our first morning in the house, I came downstairs and found Mána washing coffee cups and saucers at the kitchen sink by hand, using a bar of olive oil soap. Dishwashers weren't common on the Island—or even in older apartments in Athens at the time—but Mána had used mine in the States with no problem. So, I was perplexed.

I asked, "Mána, why don't you put those in the dishwasher?"

"There are just a few things; it's nothing to do them by hand."

"Wouldn't you prefer to wash them with liquid detergent?"

"Ah!" she said. "I meant to ask if we had any."

"Forgive me," I replied, "I should have told you; it's right here under the sink."

The next morning was a very eerie *déjà vu* experience: I came downstairs and again found Mána washing coffee cups and saucers by hand with the bar soap—and had exactly the same conversation with her. After that, I left the dishwashing liquid on the counter.

More importantly, this repetition came on the heels of other memory lapses I'd noticed. I was very worried and had a serious conversation about it with Aris. He then had equally serious conversations with Babás and Faní about getting Mána evaluated and started on appropriate treatment when they returned to Athens if she had dementia as I feared.

———◆———

A day or two later, I tried to run the dishwasher. I carefully added the salt—dishwashers here don't run without it—the detergent, and the rinse agent, then pushed the button. The lights came on, but nothing else happened.

European appliances typically come with thick manuals in multiple tongues. We consulted both the English and Greek versions of the dishwasher manual and suspected that the water hose was blocked. When we couldn't find the problem, we called the plumber. He checked and assured us that there was no issue with the plumbing.

The next call was to the electrician. After uninstalling the dishwasher, he solved the puzzle—apparently, while it sat in the warehouse, one or more rodents ate the insulation off the wiring. Because of this, the machine wasn't getting enough power to pump the water. How the installer failed to notice the naked wires, we'll never know. We were lucky that a fire didn't start when I turned the machine on. This wasn't repairable, so shortly before our return the following summer, we ordered another dishwasher and had it installed in time for our arrival.

Dishpan hands for a summer, and problem solved for the price of another dishwasher. Too bad all problems can't be remedied so easily.

CHAPTER SEVEN

Laundry as an Adventure

A mundane chore in the States, doing the laundry on the Island is always something of an adventure.

Our washing machine here is supposed to be the Maytag of Europe. Unfortunately, while it works very well, its German manufacturer had no conception of convenience. This machine has so many settings that it took me a long time to use it without checking the manual each time. Mána was afraid to touch it.

It's a big machine by Island standards, but by U.S. standards it's almost a toy. I can wash *one* set of sheets and a *few* pieces of underwear at one time—all of which will be stiff as a board, by the way, since we don't have an electric clothes dryer (with electricity being so expensive and the dry climate, almost no one here does). Anyway, the washing machine is parked under the counter next to the kitchen door, with a cabinet door installed on its front so that it looks like a cabinet. But it's not "built-in" the way the dishwasher is built in; it just sits under the counter, hiding behind its cabinet door.

When I first used this machine, it made a truly hideous racket and *walked* out from under the counter every time. You read that correctly—the machine stomped a foot or so across the stone floor. It vibrated so badly that the steel hinges connecting the cabinet door *sheared off.*

I do not exaggerate when I say that this machine sounded like a jet engine. Worse, or at least as bad, every time I reached in for the wet laundry, I got an electric shock. Appliances here run on 220 volts, so that shock was a real zinger!

Naturally, we called the service people for the brand. The "local" service center is on a different island, and they said they could do a service call in *November* (it was June when we called). We called a plumber, who couldn't find anything wrong. We called an electrician. Ditto. Aris looked at it. Nothing. A visiting engineer friend made it his mission to sort this out. He failed. *A year and a half later*, a service person for the brand found the problem—the restraining bolts on the tub hadn't been removed when it was installed. It's been as quiet as a mouse ever since.

For some time after that service call, I felt no shocks when taking wet things out of the washer. But after four weeks, and multiple loads of laundry, I got a good jolt when I started to remove the last load one day.

We asked the electrician, who was here working on the water pump, to take a look. He explained that the washing machine was properly grounded, but since our house was the last one on the line, *we* were the ground, and there was nothing he or we could do about it.

For several years afterward, I turned the circuit breaker off before unloading the wash to avoid getting zapped. I was *really* glad that it was near the washing machine! I finally got relief when Manólis's *themoniá* (rustic hut) up the hill from us was sold, converted into a house, and wired for electricity. It then became the ground at the end of the line, and I got no more shocks.

Another surprise that first summer in the house: Every single thing I washed had gray speckles. Everything! I was at a loss. Mána was at a loss. When I complained about this to a friend visiting from Barcelona, she told me it was caused by the salt, and I needed to add anti-salt powder. So, salt for the dishwasher and anti-salt for the clothes washer—nothing was intuitive.

I wash with rainwater collected in the cistern *(stérna)*, and couldn't believe that she was right, but she was. Apparently, our lovely rainwater gets contaminated with salt due to our proximity to the sea. There's not one word about this in the machine's manual—a rather surprising omission, given its length—but I haven't had a single gray speck since I started adding the anti-salt powder.

Although I solved the "gray specks" issue, I remained perplexed as to why the colored towels and sheets developed pale spots since I never use chlorine in the washing machine. Years later, after we retired to Naples, Florida, I finally solved the mystery. The water there is extremely chlorinated—and the turquoise towels I bought for our bathroom there got white spots the very first time I washed them. Eureka! My towels and sheets on the Island developed light-colored spots because the rainwater in the cistern is treated with chlorine.

As you might imagine, I stopped buying towels or sheets of any color but white for the Island. Our linens are now sadly monochromatic (why Aris's previously acquired French blue pillowcase bleached out so much more than mine is a mystery unsolved to this day).

Despite its initial problems, my washing machine is a major improvement over the one in the village house. There, we did the wash in a plastic portable machine, which we connected with hoses to the faucets. We added another hose to drain the water out. It handled considerably less of a load than my machine does, so when Faní, Dimítris, and our nephew stayed in the village house with us and Aris's parents, doing the laundry took most of the day.

———◆———

Most days in the summer, laundry dries very quickly in the sun, which may be the reason why clothes hung out to dry here are very stiff, regardless of how well I shake them before hanging—and regardless of fabric softener. On the Island, I iron almost everything—clothes, sheets, towels, and underwear. Otherwise, we could use our towels to exfoliate!

There's an advantage to hanging things out to dry in the Aegean sun: No matter how stained something is, the sun can almost always bleach it out. It's only a matter of time. After a relative stayed here with a girlfriend, he left badly stained dish towels behind. I hung them in the sun for a while, and the stains largely disappeared.

He must have inadvertently put washed bed sheets away while they were still a little damp, because the sheets were streaked with pink mildew (yes, we have pink mildew on the Island). Even so, I confess that, at first, I thought that he and his girlfriend must have had kinky sex involving lipstick. After some days in the Aegean sun, the mildew was dead, and the sheets were almost as good as new.

Hanging your laundry out to dry here can prove to be more interesting than you might expect. Grasshoppers, green crickets and leafhoppers like to sit on light-colored sheets, towels, and clothes. And they can be quite stubborn about staying aboard the selected items. I must check the laundry very carefully before bringing it in and folding it to put away. One year, when we arrived at the house, I unfolded unironed sheets to find a desiccated grasshopper. Yuck!

When we return to the Island each year, we have travel wear to wash, a day or two of clothes we wore but didn't wash before we left, and the sheets and towels we last used before departing. So, I always have a good bit of laundry to do on arrival. Before starting the wash, we bring the drying rack up from the basement, clean it, and weigh the bottom rails down with flagstones so the wind doesn't blow it over.

Plastic deteriorates in the Aegean sun, and as I was cleaning a drying rack that had been used for only two months, its plastic cords disintegrated, leaving me with a load of wet laundry, three more loads to go, and nowhere to dry anything. Fortunately, Aris had gone shopping to begin replenishing our bare larders. I was able to reach him by cellphone. My personal problem-solver returned with an all-aluminum drying rack.

Not having a clothes dryer is not a problem as long as the sun shines, which in the summer on the Island, it almost always does. When we get rain—usually early or late in the season—the only option is to bring the drying rack inside and live with it in the middle of the dining room, along with the sound of water dripping on the stone floor.

I pretend it's installation art.

———◇———

Arrival at our home on the Island always entails a surprise or two. We find out which of the bathing suits that seemed to be in great shape when we left have lost their elastic, making them unwearable. The same thing happens to the elastic in socks, waistbands, jacket cuffs, and bottom sheets. Rubber bands turn into goo and rubber kitchen gloves disintegrate over the winter.

One year, my surprises included finding tiny holes in my cotton underwear. There were no holes in other cotton items—sheets, towels, or shirts—just my underwear. I'm still trying to discover whether cotton-eating insects, with discriminating taste, exist in the world.

On the Island, even laundry refuses to be boring.

CHAPTER EIGHT

Shop Owners Falling Off Their Stools

Like all houses, our Island home requires regular upkeep. The first maintenance we did was in the summer of 2007, when I stayed in it for eight weeks testing whether I'd be happy living on the Island every summer. We lacked television and internet, but I had my Kindle, stocked with many books, a radio, and the magnificent Aegean Sea.

I started with small jobs, staining the chestnut beams guarding the walkways around the house, staining and finishing the interior handrail we'd added for Mána, and using the duct tape I brought from the States to seal gaps around the stove vent and elsewhere. I then decided to take on bigger tasks.

To keep the warranty on the painted shutters, we needed to treat them with teak oil. The Island-made doors also needed to be repainted. Aris told me to just get started and he'd do the rest when he arrived. But since he'd have only two weeks here and I had eight, I decided to surprise him and do it all myself so he could spend his time here relaxing.

I asked Leonídas (the taxi driver) to drop me off at the hardware store. Curious, he asked why. When I told him, he was so alarmed at the prospect of my lugging cans of paint and teak oil back to the plaza that he insisted on waiting to collect my purchases and store them in the trunk of his cab for my later trip back to the house.

The hardware store was . . . an experience. I needed teak oil, acrylic paint for the doors, a paintbrush, and sandpaper. Getting the teak oil was easy, as the word "teak" sounds the same in Greek. As for the rest, I knew versions of the words for sand (*ámmos*) and paper (*chartí*). I *thought* I knew that a brush was a *voúrtsa*, and Faní told me that I could get water-based paint by asking for "watercolor" (*ydróchroma*). Armed with those words, I thought that I'd be fine.

Wrong!

My request for "sandpaper" was met with utter bafflement. I explained that I wanted to paint doors, and I mimed sanding, adding that there was old paint on the doors. That worked. He understood and told me that I needed *glass* paper—*gyalócharto*.

As for the brush, when I confidently asked for a *voúrtsa*, the store owner nearly fell off his stool laughing. Leonídas tried hard to keep a straight face but couldn't. I'd asked for a hairbrush! A paintbrush is a *pinélo*. When they explained, I had to laugh too. Fortunately, I don't often make shop owners fall down laughing—at least not in my presence.

I still thought of myself as a kid, so it never crossed my mind that when you're more than half a century old, you can't just start sanding and painting six hours a day for twelve straight days without consequences. Because of this folly, I soon learned all about repetitive motion injury.

In addition to damaging my shoulder, I stepped down hard from the ladder onto the edge of the wooden sole of a Dr.

Scholl's exercise sandal—remember those?—and partially tore the plantar fascia of my right foot. That put an end to my days in high heels—a tragedy for someone who is five feet nothing.

Lesson learned. After that, I left the big jobs to the professionals!

CHAPTER NINE

Heat Wave!

In 2007, while I was repainting doors and treating shutters with teak oil, the Island endured two brutal *káfsones* (heat waves), a few weeks apart.

The first one began around mid-June, just days after we were shivering under blankets at night. During the second, our cool Aegean Sea became so warm that I had to swim out to very deep water to find refreshment. Unfortunately, the southern wind that brought the *káfsones* also brought stinging jellyfish, which we seldom have—almost never until late August.

I often told prospective guests that the sea in our bay is so calm, salty and buoyant that anyone can float without the bother of treading water—all you have to do is sit in the water and you'll float. I also *used* to say that, because of this, a person would have to work to drown in this sea.

Once again, I was wrong.

During that second heat wave, while backstroking quite far from shore in search of cool water, I swam right into the tentacles of a jellyfish and got stung. Naturally, I swam away as fast as I could. In my panic, I got a charley horse cramp in my calf, along with new insight into how a person might drown without trying.

At that time, we had air conditioners (heat pumps) only in the bedrooms. During the second *káfsonas*, the huge, wind-carved rocks on the east side of the house absorbed and radiated the heat, as did the flagstones around the house. By 10:00 a.m., our dining room was over 90 degrees Fahrenheit—and climbing. Athens reached 113°F, and even on the Island we hit 106°F inland.

I worked on the shutters very early in the morning until, after days of this, I gave up and camped out in the bedroom with my Kindle and the heat pump going all day and night. I developed a habit of waking in the wee hours to open the windows in the rest of the house for a few hours to try to cool it down. Then, before dawn, I closed all windows and shutters to keep the heat out.

Late one night during the second *káfsonas*, I noticed bushes on the north side of the house moving in the wind. I rushed to the kitchen to throw the windows open, anticipating a cooling breeze.

I was met by a blast furnace! The air that blew in was scaldingly hot and filled with sand. I've never experienced anything like it before or since.

An American family returned to the Island that summer, after vacationing here the year before when the wind never died down. Expecting the same weather, they'd packed blue jeans, long sleeves and fleece—and were miserable.

We've had other *káfsones* bring temperatures over 100°F, but none equaled the misery of the two in 2007.

CHAPTER TEN

How Many Greeks Does It Take to Install an Air Conditioner?

You don't install air conditioners on the Island; you install heat pumps, which can warm rooms as well as cool them. The process here involved a surprising number of workers.

As I mentioned earlier, we originally put heat pumps only in the bedrooms. Before we retired, Aris always managed to miss the *káfsones*, but I finally convinced him that we really did need air conditioning in the rest of the house. He'd been reluctant to have a unit on the roof because he worried it would spoil the traditional exterior.

On installation day, two workmen arrived to do the physical installation of the unit—one to do the technical work and yell at the other, the second to do the heavy lifting, fetching and carrying.

After a while, the electrician arrived with *two* helpers in tow. Again, one did the heavy lifting, but I've no idea why he brought the other, who did nothing at all. At that point, we had five workers—or four workers and an observer—at the house. While the electrician and one of his helpers were working, the two who arrived first sat on our veranda, enjoying the view, drinking our coffee and eating our cookies. Here, you're expected to feed folks who work at your home. The others joined them later.

We got not only a new heat pump, but a new joke: How many Greeks does it take to install an air conditioner?

CHAPTER ELEVEN

Wind!

Aegean winds are legendary.

When we told Islanders we were buying this lot, they warned us that we wouldn't be able to live here—the wind would blow us off the mountain. We confidently pointed out that the house would act as a windbreak and let us enjoy the view of the sea and the church on the rocky peninsula from its south side. As it turns out, the Islanders weren't too far from wrong, and we soon discovered just how fierce the north wind can be.

We have episodes when the north wind blows at six Beaufort for days on end and then blows at seven Beaufort for a day or two or three (the wind has reached 12 or 13 Beaufort some winters). At seven Beaufort, the wind whistles and sounds as if it's trying to fulfill the Islanders' prediction and blow the house right off its foundations. When we open the front door, our things blow off the tabletops. And the fig tree is stripped of its fruit.

To give you a better idea of this wind: We had a heavy wooden "gate" built to block our front steps from goats—and from folks who occasionally came up our driveway to picnic on our verandas in our absence. This gate is not hinged but slides into wooden slots built into the walls on either side of our front steps.

Before departing for the States one fall, I brought the gate (about fifty pounds) up from the basement and laid it flat on the north-facing front porch to be slotted into place when I left the next morning. The wind, blowing six Beaufort from the north, *tossed the gate into the air and flipped it over* as if it were nothing at all.

The wind played havoc in the house too. We have two narrow windows on each side of the north-facing front doors. Like windows all over the Mediterranean, ours are hinged on each side and open inside the house—something that has to be taken into account in placing furniture and art. One side of each window, which is not quite a foot wide, can be tilted so that the top is open about two inches, while the rest of the window remains closed.

I told you all of that in order to tell you this: We had a large, heavy decorative platter I hand-carried back from Istanbul and displayed on a stand on a low table in the entrance between two armchairs. One night, I left one side of the window above the armchair slightly tilted open. The top of that window is more than a meter above the height of the little table where I displayed the platter. The next morning, I found the platter smashed to smithereens on the floor—it had been picked up and thrown down by the wind. Weirdly, the acrylic plate stand was still upright in its place on the table!

The garage wasn't exempt either. Our garage has a very small window in its northern wall. We leave it open but keep the shutter of the window closed. Like electric garage doors in the States, ours here has a pull cord with a small weight on the end suspended from the mechanism on the ceiling so the door can be opened manually in case of a power failure.

One evening, I opened the garage door and backed our Forester out. The garage door wouldn't close. When I got out of the car, I could hear the motor running, but the door wasn't moving. It took me a bit, but I figured it out: Raging in through the narrow slats of the small shutter, the wind had wrapped the pull cord around the car's roof rack, so when I backed out, the mechanism was disengaged!

The wind's worst mischief was at sea. We took our cabin cruiser to the island of Tínos, where our younger godson was vacationing with his family. The wind was only three or four Beaufort here, but when we arrived at their bay, it was easily seven Beaufort. We shouldn't have tried to anchor there, but we'd come a long way to see them.

When we dropped the anchor, the wind whipped our yacht around so hard and so fast that the big, heavy steel anchor guide on the prow *twisted*. Manufactured in Italy, it was no match for Aegean winds. After we returned, we had a much heavier, stronger replacement installed.

I later learned that Tínos is the home of *Aíolos*, the mythological god of all winds.

The ancient Greeks named the winds. Each significant wind direction was attributed to a particular god, ruled by *Aíolos*, keeper of the winds. *Zéphyros*, the kindly west wind, lives on in the word zephyr, a gentle breeze. *Voréas*, the north wind, was strong and bad-tempered, bringing blasts of cold air. *Nótos*, the south wind, was feared for thunderstorms. From the east *Eúros* blew, the least defined wind—sometimes considered unlucky.

The *Meltémi* is the wind most often experienced in the Aegean in the summer, especially in July and August, as a dry northern wind. Typically, it blows during the day, commonly reaching four or five Beaufort, dies at sunset, and resumes the next morning. However, it can reach seven or eight Beaufort and continue into the night for several days in succession.

Nótos is sometimes associated with the desiccating *lívas* wind—the hot southwestern wind I experienced during the 2007 heat waves, which blows up from Africa and can carry sand. It's impossible to imagine this wind unless you have experienced it yourself.

CHAPTER TWELVE

Dust, Dirt, and More Dirt

An old Greek saying goes something like this: "When God made the world, He saved Greece—the best—for last. But when He got to southern Greece, all He had left were rocks, dirt, and dust." Since, with rare exception, it doesn't rain here from May until September, the Island has an abundance of dust and dirt. The relentless wind in our valley makes our home especially dusty.

I can smell dirt. When I mentioned this to Aris, he corrected me, saying, "You mean that you smell dust."

"Same thing," I replied. Here, the dust *is* dirt—and I can smell it in a room.

When the wind is dry and blowing from the north, I need to wipe down the kitchen and bathroom counters every morning to clean away the film of dirt. We vacuum the upholstery and clean the window screens every week without fail. In midsummer, we hose down the north side of the house to rid it of the brown dirt blown onto the white surface. And we keep remote controls in plastic wrap.

There are a lot of motorbike accidents here every summer. Most, but not all, involve tourists. Part of the problem is that drivers are careless, and Island roads are narrow, hilly, curvy, and not in the best condition. But another part of the problem is that the dirt makes the roads slippery.

We need signs saying, "Slippery when dry!"

CHAPTER THIRTEEN

Ants, Capers, and Woodworms

Invading Ants and Creeping Capers

Not all ants are created equal. Ants here look like ordinary sugar ants, but they eat through concrete. Don't scoff as I did when Faní first told me this. It's quite true. One day, we came home from a hundred-year rain—meaning it rained for an hour in July—and found a whole colony of ants in our bedroom, on the march.

The dense, black column of ants started at a corner of an *interior* wall from a tiny hole between the concrete wall and the stone floor, proceeded under our bed, continued straight up the wall behind the headboard, and finally exited by another tiny hole in the concrete near the ceiling. The rain must have flooded their nest. It was like a demented version of the hiking song: *The ants go marching six by six . . . and they all go marching . . . through . . . my room . . . to get out . . . of the rain, bom, bom, bom.* This episode launched the ant wars.

From the time we built this place, we were plagued by ants. Somehow, they seem to know when we'll be having a guest come to our home for the first time because they inevitably choose those times to invade. I've never seen an ant hill here. The ants swarm around and nest in our stone retaining walls, particularly near capers.

I should probably explain about capers. The capers you may enjoy in a salad or with smoked salmon are the buds of a plant that grows wild all over the Cycladic islands. It grows out of stone walls and, amazingly, out of sheer rock. I was told that caper plants are not cultivable, that they simply grow where they like, and because of this, having capers grow in your yard is an omen of good luck (I later learned that this local wisdom isn't true—at least some caper plants can be cultivated).

We had one caper plant growing twenty feet above ground out of the middle of a large living rock. That one, which was here before we built the house, was the mother of all of the capers that later started sprouting out of our retaining walls.

The caper plants didn't grow in any acceptable location. Instead, with minor exception, the dozen or so caper plants that grew in our yard chose to take up residence in the stone stairs, presenting major tripping hazards. And two of them were growing right beside our bedroom wall, threatening to damage it with their powerful roots. Naturally, Aris decided that most of the capers had to go.

Before destroying most of the plants, we decided to harvest the buds. According to a local source, preparation starts with soaking the caper buds in water for four days. This resulted in many caper blossoms and some mushy buds. So, I re-harvested and, on the advice of an experienced friend, washed and dried the buds and smothered them in coarse salt. Incredibly, this simple process yields delicious capers.

Caper salad (*kaparosaláta*) is one of the traditional Island dishes. This is made—only here, I'm told—with dried caper buds, sweet onions, vinegar, and olive oil. I've included the vegan recipe in the Appendix.

Removing the capers close to the house and in the steps didn't deter the ants. They still periodically invaded my kitchen. Initially, I was inclined to blame them on Aris's preferred breakfast of Island *koulourákia* (a sort of donut-shaped biscotti), which inevitably generates crumbs. However, it wasn't his fault. The ants came whether he ate his *koulourákia* or not. I brought ant traps from the States and watched the ants walk in and out of them with no apparent effect. I think they were giggling.

Since ants are a common problem here, I consulted friends and acquaintances. One friend recommended putting oregano around the kitchen. It had no discernible impact, but I liked the smell. Another recommended lavender, which had the same effect—none.

In case you're wondering, there were no exterminators on the Island then; you either imported one from the mainland or a larger island, or dealt with ants and woodworms yourself. So, I armed myself with insecticide powder—oddly purchased at the pharmacy, not the hardware store. I applied it liberally around the outside of the house.

A large ant-like insect with an enormous last segment came staggering out of one of the retaining walls. I crushed it ruthlessly and believe that it was the queen. Several years passed without another ant invasion. They continued to swarm outside, and

I attacked them again with the insecticide powder or doused them with ammonia, whatever seemed to work.

Woodworms: More Uninvited Houseguests

If you're a fan of antique or even old furniture, you may be familiar with the tiny holes made by woodworms, which are not worms at all but the larvae of a type of beetle. Such woodworms live here too, but the ones we really worry about are their super-sized cousins, which are so large and voracious that they make a rather loud and very annoying "scritching" noise as they munch away on your wood.

When a relative of Aris's cousin George visited with her family from the States, she told me that one of these bugs was in a chair in her bedroom at Cousin George's house—and the noise was driving her to distraction and keeping her awake. She tried to eradicate the bug, using a knife to cut away the damaged wood. She never found it, she said, but by the time she gave up, the chair was demolished.

You may recall that our house has ceilings made of pine planks and chestnut beams. We were assured that the wood for the ceilings had been treated against woodworms. Nevertheless, for the first several years after we moved in, we found several piles of "sawdust"—the waste product of the woodworms—on the floors when we arrived.

Treating woodworms in your ceilings entails balancing on a ladder to reach the ten-, twelve-, or fourteen-foot-high ceiling, attempting to identify the affected area by "sawdust" and sound, and painting or spraying it with poison. Then repeating . . . and repeating . . . and repeating, while hoping you don't fall off the ladder.

Using this method, we were able to kill all of the woodworms—except one. This audacious creature started an excavation in a chestnut beam in the kitchen ceiling. The hole it made is about the diameter of a dime and more than two feet long.

We know this because after repeated eradication failures spanning a couple of years, Aris gouged away the surface of the wood to open the hole and hit the bug directly with the poison. That worked. Afterward, we had the painters treat the ceiling beams and planks throughout the house with poison again over the winter.

Having your ceilings treated for woodworms doesn't stop the critters from attacking other wood in the house. In the winter—the rainy season here—we must leave some windows of the house open to prevent mold and mildew. We don't leave the window screens down because they would be battered to shreds by the winter winds and are *very* difficult to replace. Leaving unscreened windows vented means that insects can, and do, fly in through the slats in the shutters.

Before you decide that we're foolish, let me assure you that we tried an electric dehumidifier. More than a decade ago, we bought—for the ridiculous sum of €300—the kind of dehumidifier you could buy in the States for $100 and use for twenty years. We left one circuit breaker on and left it running over the winter. It broke once during the first winter, was repaired, and broke irreparably less than two weeks after its warranty expired.

So, we're relegated to leaving windows vented and pots of chemical dehumidifier around all winter. Even with those precautions, we sometimes find mildew on the upper walls of the upstairs guest bedroom.

———◇———

Based on the scritching noise I kept hearing, I thought that we had another woodworm in a ceiling beam in the kitchen. I asked Aris to listen, too, and we were debating which beam was the source of the noise when, leaning down, I realized that it was coming from one of the kitchen counter stools.

The wood of those stools is finished, matching the dining room chairs, and we checked carefully for a hole without finding one. However, the stools have woven raffia seats, and the wooden rails under the raffia are unfinished. I suspected that the raffia concealed the hole. Since the last thing we wanted was for a stool to collapse under a guest enjoying breakfast, I attacked the problem with all the insect poisons in our arsenal.

Just when I thought that I'd eradicated the bug, I heard it again—louder than ever—less than two weeks before we were leaving the Island for the winter. The Greek gods were laughing at me! It was time for desperate measures. First, I painted and sprayed the stool with woodworm poisons; then I stuffed it into a huge plastic trash bag, squeezed out as much air as I could, and sealed it with duct tape. Next, I shoved the whole thing into another giant trash bag, squeezed the air out again, and sealed that one too. I set the double-bagged and sealed stool in the sun to cook for several days, left it in the sealed bags for the winter—and crossed my fingers!

Almost as soon as we returned the following year, I opened the bags. Nothing. No sawdust. No noise. Success!

The next year's woodworm took up residence in the old wooden frame of a lovely watercolor we inherited from Aris's parents. I'd compliment its taste, but I don't think it stopped munching long enough to admire the art. Since that frame had already been damaged, I wasn't sorry to have an excuse to replace it.

Despite our efforts, nature's pests are as relentless as we are—the squatters inevitably return, igniting new battles.

CHAPTER FOURTEEN

Cleaning—Help!

As you might suppose, the dirt, wind, ants and woodworms pose some challenges in keeping the Island house clean.

I managed the better part of our first full summer on the Island with no cleaning help at all. This isn't ideal when you have a herniated disc because, to clean properly, you absolutely must move the furniture, and sliders don't work well on irregular stone floors. An Albanian man who was building more walls around our verandas to block the goats from our garden saw me cleaning one day and volunteered that his wife cleaned for people who rent rooms and could clean for me if I liked.

Thinking that help would be very welcome, we arranged for her to come. Our first surprise was that, despite living here for years, she spoke only Albanian. Her husband said he'd stay to translate and took up a position on our veranda (with our coffee and cookies) where he could enjoy the view.

I don't know whether his translations left a lot to be desired, or she just wasn't a very good cleaner, but I was sorry that I'd hired her. I showed her how the vacuum works—it has only two buttons: on/off and cord retract. She used it in the kitchen but then abandoned it and switched to the broom everywhere else. When using the broom under furniture, she kept it in midair, not on the floor. Attacking cobwebs, perhaps?

I don't think she'd encountered window screens before; she had no notion of how to clean them. She used my Swiffer duster to barely tickle the furniture. She was eager to wash windows, but I stopped her when the ones she washed looked worse than before. I assigned her what I thought was the easy task of sweeping the verandas. I found her sweeping the vertical fronts of the rocks on the side of the house. Whoever heard of sweeping rocks? Not wanting to offend the couple, we paid too much just to get them to leave.

Eventually, through Faní, we engaged Nicoleta, a Romanian woman with a college degree, who worked as a cleaning woman on the Island for fifteen years until she finally found a job in Romania as a librarian. She said she'd earn less in that job than she made cleaning on the Island, but she needed to acquire credits for retirement benefits.

Nicoleta was also an artist and had some English as well as fluent Greek. She was knowledgeable, honest, diligent, and pleasant. She taught me a lot about cleaning and maintaining an Island house. I was glad she found work appropriate to her education, but deeply sorry to lose her.

Before she left, she gave me one of her paintings and arranged for a woman who had helped her do the deep cleaning at the beginning of the season to clean for me and her other clients the next season. The replacement was okay but was no Nicoleta. When she became generally unavailable, we were lucky to hire Lira, an Albanian woman, who, as we later learned, is the sister of a man who'd done quite a bit of work for us over the years. It's a small island.

Even apart from the endless dirt, cleaning on the Island is different than cleaning in the States. After vacuuming, every floor is also mopped. A tool like a horizontal bottle brush on a very long handle is used to clear cobwebs and spider webs from between the chestnut beams of the ceilings. One tool Lira hadn't used before that I brought from the States is a battery-powered implement like a giant electric toothbrush for cleaning tile grout. She loves it!

Lira has the rather unusual task of looking for ants and the locations of their holes every week. When she does the deep cleaning at the beginning of the season, she also looks out for and reports on any "sawdust" generated by woodworms she finds. Lira says the worst aspect of the deep cleaning at the start of the season is the spiders that move into the house over the winter. At least they're not scorpions!

On the Island as elsewhere, cleaning women are not always treated well. Unbelievably, Lira—a lovely, intelligent, honest, and very hard-working woman—was instructed by owners of other properties she cleaned not to use their toilets. She told me she wasn't drinking water while she worked so she didn't have to. I was appalled and gave her strict instructions that, at our house, she's to do both.

In the summer of 2020, the first year of the pandemic, we were five weeks late getting to the Island because our tickets were canceled twice and Greece, like most of Europe, was closed to most Americans. We were able to come only because Aris is a Greek citizen and I'm his duly registered wife. With the delay, I worried that Lira was missing the income she'd expected to earn from working for us and told Aris that we needed to arrange to pay her for that period.

He was concerned about the cultural differences and that we not insult her or her husband by offering what they might perceive as charity. We settled on giving a gift of money for her son equal to what we'd have paid her had we arrived as planned. That worked; she was thrilled.

Lira and her husband have become our friends, and we're very fortunate to have them take care of our place when we're gone. Having our home in their honest, capable hands gives us great peace of mind.

CHAPTER FIFTEEN

The Plumber and the Drunk Electrician

A man was sitting on top of my upper kitchen cabinets, one leg dangling over the crown molding. I worried that the cabinet would break. The man was a plumber (*ydravlikós*). We'd called him because, when the upstairs guest bathroom was in use, water was running out of an outside *light fixture* on the front corner of the house. This, obviously, was not good—especially in a house with 220-volt electrical current.

The plumber explained that, when the electrician had drilled into the concrete wall to install that light fixture, he'd accidentally punctured the drainpipe from the upstairs bathroom—twice. Apparently, after enough use, hair had accumulated in the drainpipe, partially blocking it and forcing water out through those holes, through the light fixture, and into the wall. He added that this was why the cabinets in that corner of the kitchen were always rather damp.

I caught my breath when the plumber said that the cabinets would have to be removed to effect the repair. He'd already broken the outside corner of that wall and couldn't do the work from there. Cabinet removal and reinstallation would mean bringing workers in from Athens—and it would almost certainly damage or destroy the trim moldings. New trim moldings would never match the cabinets, as they had changed color after ten years in the sun. We urgently explained all of that. He was unmoved.

We then told him that we had guests coming and we really could not have the kitchen torn apart. That resonated with him more. We asked him—begged him really—to do his best to make the repair with the cabinets in place. He promised to try, provided that we ran the air conditioner.

So, there we stood, watching the plumber work from his precarious perch atop the upper cabinets, keeping our fingers crossed that he could make the repair, that he wouldn't break the cabinets, and, especially, that the cabinets wouldn't collapse and break him.

After what seemed like an eternity, he announced that he'd replaced the damaged section of the pipe. He instructed us not to use the upstairs shower for a day and, after that, to check that no water leaked out before repairing the broken walls and reconnecting the exterior light fixture. We were ecstatic—and delighted to reward him and his helper with slices of chocolate torte, served, at their request, with beer. The repair held.

⸺⬥⸺

Even before this happened, I was convinced that the electrician who wired our house had been drunk when he did the work. Because we wanted American current as well as European for the convenience of our American guests, we hired an electrician in Athens who had worked with Faní. Unfortunately, after we paid him, the man we hired didn't do the work. Without telling us, he sent someone else.

We do have dual current wiring, but we also have light switches that control nothing and an exceptionally strange arrangement of switches. To this day, we have trouble remembering which controls what. Worse, I couldn't use the broiler setting on my oven without shorting out the entire kitchen! One kitchen light was installed so close to a cabinet that the cabinet door can't open fully, and the whole house once shorted out due to an unknown cause.

To top it off, the presumptively drunk electrician threatened to sue us. Not because of anything we did, but because the electrician we hired and paid, who had secretly hired him, allegedly didn't pay him. Eventually, Faní was able to get that sorted out. And we got a good story.

CHAPTER SIXTEEN

The Snake, the Cat, and the Scorpion

Our relationship with the cat began because of the snake.

There's a venomous viper on the Island (and elsewhere in Greece), known as the *ochiá*. The bite of this snake can be fatal. The good thing is that it's not aggressive. Farmers walk the countryside on the ancient stone paths that crisscross the Island with walking sticks (*mátsa*) tapping the stones as they go, so that the *ochiá* will know to stay away. They do, I'm told, except in the spring when they're hungry and mating.

Despite our many hikes in the countryside to saints' day festivals (*panigýria*), I never saw such a snake until after we retired. One was reported once when I was hiking with a friend to the Prophet Elijah monastery. When we were fairly close to our destination, we encountered a sizable group of French hikers descending from the peak. One said, "*Mauvais serpent*" as they passed. It took me half a minute to conjure up my rusty French, but I called after them, "*Quelle couleur*?" I didn't get an answer, only a faint, "*Bonne chance*."

I consulted my friend about her wishes in the face of this news. I explained that the *ochiá* is dangerously venomous, and that medical care on the Island leaves a lot to be desired, but that the snake was not known to be aggressive and was unlikely to still be around after the racket made by such a large group. She wasn't a timid person, and had done a lot of hiking, so she was game to continue. We did and saw nary a scale.

* * *

We saw a rat snake at our house once, sunning itself on our lower veranda shortly after the house was finished. It was thin, with an oval head. I was glad to have it since they compete with and deter the *ochiá*. But Aris's folks were staying with us, and we feared that it might traumatize Mána, so Aris applied snake deterrent—moth balls—and drove it away.

Since then, I've seen a few *ochiá*: three smaller ones, dead, on the dry riverbed road, and two live ones on our driveway! The adults are dirt brown, with a darker, zig-zag pattern on their backs, and, like other pit vipers, they're thick-bodied and have evil-looking triangular heads.

Early one summer, when the weather was still cool, we were walking back from dinner in Fáros (the neighboring bay), when we encountered an *ochiá* stretched across our sun-warmed driveway. When she perceived us, she lifted her head and about six inches of her upper body, hissed her warning, and took off as quickly as she could.

Another night, we came home with houseguests to find a hatchling *ochiá*, ten or twelve inches long, resting on the paving stones near the top of our driveway, which were still warm from the day's sun. It was so young that its skin was still pale. Coming home in the dark to find a venomous snake between you and your front door isn't on anyone's bucket list—but we'd enjoyed a lovely meal, with plenty of local wine, and were quite mellow. Aris quickly dispatched it with a well-thrown stone.

Promptly after these incidents, Aris put moth balls around the property again. Greek friends recommended that we get a hedgehog (*skantzóchoiros*) or, failing that, a cat. We hadn't seen any hedgehogs that year, but there were several feral or semi-feral cats in our valley. Early on, I was reluctant to feed them as I thought it cruel to let them become accustomed to being fed and then leave them to their own devices for the rest of the year.

Most cats on the Island are attractive, with a slender oriental body type, angular heads, and long ears. This was not true of the cats in our vicinity—they were all homely. *Mavroúla* (Blackie), as we called her, was no exception. She wasn't entirely black but had odd flecks of pale hair on her face, and her fur from her shoulders to her rump was rusty. But she was friendly, well-mannered, and smart.

She first appeared one evening as we were sitting on the veranda. She came right up to us, rubbing against our chair legs and softly mewing. We gave her some yogurt. She curled up on one of the *pentzoúles* (stone benches attached to the house) and spent the night, asking for breakfast the next morning. It's hard to resist a gently begging skinny cat, and we fed her again.

That evening, we went to dinner at the home of our good neighbor, Kóstas. And there was Mavroúla. His wife told us that they had been feeding her whenever she showed up, summer and winter, for a couple of years. Once we knew that she wouldn't be left to starve all winter, we had no more compunction about feeding her. We bought cat food and flea treatment.

A routine developed. Mavroúla would come to visit from time to time in the evening when we were home, and was on the *pentzoúla* every morning, mewing for breakfast. So, every morning, I went out in a loose caftan, bent over, and filled her dishes.

This led to disaster.

One morning, Mavroúla begged for breakfast as usual. And as usual, I went out in a long, billowy caftan and bent down to pour food into her dish. This caused the front hem of my caftan to drop onto the flagstones. I didn't see the scorpion Mavroúla had been playing with—and I didn't know that it had taken refuge inside my caftan.

After I returned to the house, I felt a very sharp pain, like that of a yellowjacket sting—times twenty. Realizing that something was in my caftan, I pulled it off. I got another sting in the process. One was on my left side, just below my ribs—it had climbed that high, and the second was on my left lower arm.

I didn't know what had stung me. I watched as my skin turned red and puckered in a very large area around the puncture wounds—eight inches long on my side! I immediately washed the wounds and applied ammonia. I then grabbed one of my trek poles and poked around in the caftan puddled on the floor. There he was: reddish brown, nearly three inches long, pinchers and stinger up, ready for battle. He took off at a run, but I got the better of him and killed him with my pole.

Aris was out, so I called Faní and asked her for the number of the local pharmacist. She asked why. When I told her, she insisted on calling the pharmacist herself. Ammonia was recommended and I was told to come in if I experienced swelling or hives or if the pain was too severe.

I also checked the internet and found an immensely helpful recommendation to ice the sting sites. I used Aris's beer cans from the fridge, clamping them between my side and my arm, and trading them off whenever one became warm. The stings were every bit as painful as I'd heard—I rate them right up there with a seriously abscessed tooth and worse than a root canal. Having anything other than ice touch the affected areas was intolerable. I couldn't imagine the possibility of sleeping.

But, suddenly, after about seventeen hours, the burning pain stopped! Completely! I could sleep! And, except for the small puncture wounds, all evidence of the stings disappeared overnight. There was no lingering redness, swelling, tenderness, or pain. I went about my usual activities.

In the States, cats bring you dead birds and mice as presents. This one brought me a live scorpion.

I should have been more careful, of course, since scorpions are not rare here. But we'd never seen one on our property before. We'd seen scorpions regularly in the village house before it was renovated, especially around the toilet. Over 100 years old, it was built of stones cemented with mud, and its walls were literally alive.

On the very first morning of my first visit to the Island, Aris took his robe off the hook on the wall of the village house and started to put it on. I noticed something orange on his sleeve, but without my glasses, I couldn't see it well and asked what it was. He jumped half a meter off the floor and knocked it off. It was a three-inch-long scorpion. He killed it with a shoe.

So, there really are serpents . . . and scorpions in paradise!

CHAPTER SEVENTEEN

---❖---

Of Figs and Fáros

Fig Lust

It's been said of other things, but I believe that fresh Island figs are the real proof that God loves us and wants us to be happy. I had no experience with fresh figs until I came to the Island in 1978. I tolerated dried figs and had no interest in fig cookies. When, in high school, I read the passage in *Siddhartha* in which the courtesan's mouth is compared to a fresh fig, I puzzled over the analogy. Once I tasted a fresh Island fig, I understood.

During my first trips to the Island, we often went with Aris's parents to a sheltered bay, Fáros (which means lighthouse), to swim when it was windy. At one time, Fáros served as the main port of the Island. The adjacent small, sandy beach was reached from the main road by walking past the dock occupied by fishing vessels and through part of the town, which was built on a rocky outlier from the mountain.

At the time, that beach was completely undeveloped, and it was not uncommon for fruit vendors to go there, hawking watermelon (*karpoúzi*) and figs (*sýka*), which you ate out of your hands.

My first fresh Island fig was a revelation. I was reluctant to try it; the outside of a fig, whether green, purple, or both, looked rather unappealing. Peeled and opened, the fig reveals a fuchsia and white interior, and the taste is fantastic—incredibly rich and sweet!

We have a fig tree on our property, which produces small, green, and absolutely delicious figs, normally beginning in late July. The tree was not here when we started construction on the house and we didn't plant it. It may have been an inadvertent gift from a worker who tossed a fig he didn't care for. Whatever the source, it took root in one of the most unlikely places, a patch of rocky dirt—to call it "soil" would be an exaggeration—two feet wide between the concrete driveway and the cliff. It's grown there contentedly, with no care whatsoever, ever since.

Most of the figs on our tree are inaccessible because they grow on its cliffside, so we wanted another fig tree. For years, during fig season, when birds left half-eaten figs and overripe figs were blown off by the wind, I collected the discarded figs from the driveway and tossed them into one of the areas where we wanted another fig tree. I had no success. We tried planting the figs—no luck. We also tried rooting cuttings in water and in potting soil, but that didn't work either.

In desperation, we appealed to our neighbor, Kóstas, who has a magnificent vegetable garden, orchards, grapevines—and figs. When we described our various efforts to him, he tried not to laugh. He didn't succeed. Once he regained control of himself, Kóstas told us that nothing was going to grow in midsummer, in peak heat, and with the rains at least two months away. He also told us that our methods wouldn't work. "Wait until the fall," he said, "then find and transplant a sapling."

We did that, and the transplanted sapling survived for several years but didn't thrive. We knew that this often happens with such transplants and were optimistic that the sapling would eventually take off. We were optimistic, that is, until the pandemic of 2020 delayed our arrival by over a month. We hired someone to water our plants in our absence, but he didn't notice the little fig, never watered it, and it died. However, two volunteer fig saplings have since sprung up.

———◆———

Cousin George has houses across the narrow valley from ours. It often happened that his daughter arrived with her family right before Aris left for a meeting. And we often had the whole crew over for dinner: George, his daughter, her husband, her in-laws, and her three children, all of whom are a pleasure. I figured that I was morphing into my dear mother-in-law, because I got such a kick out of watching the middle child (then a seventh grader) eat with gusto every dish I prepared.

Cousin George brings figs as a hostess gift when they're in season. One year, he and his grandkids brought us *three* baskets of figs—enough figs for an army! Since Aris was leaving the next day, I gave some to his sister and some to our cleaning woman, which still left me with a heaping basket of figs. I hated the idea of throwing them out and so ate nothing but figs for two whole days. It was my fig diet.

I'm not the only person who's crazy about fresh Island figs. Ordinary people are converted by their fig lust into unabashed fig thieves. One day during fig season, as I walked past Kóstas's place on my way home from the beach, I saw a young woman with a plastic grocery bag half filled with Kóstas's figs. She was standing on his five-foot-high stone wall, picking his figs, right beside his house, with his car clearly visible.

I told her in Greek, "What you're doing isn't right; that isn't your fig tree."

She insisted, "The tree is overhanging the street, so the figs belong to everyone."

I replied, "But you're not taking a few figs from the road. You're filling a bag and taking figs from inside the wall. It's not right."

I guess I managed to shame her with my ineloquent scolding, since she climbed down from the wall and left.

A few days later, Aris was walking up our concrete driveway and was well past the stone posts we had built at its base to deter trespassers when he came across two women in bathing suits standing on our driveway picking figs from our tree—in clear view of our house and garage. When he asked why they were picking our figs, they smiled sheepishly and said something stupid about having thought it was a public road. They then left—with our figs.

A day or so after that, Aris found two men picking figs inside Cousin George's fence. They'd climbed a six-foot padlocked gate to steal figs!

Fáros

Fáros Bay is connected to our bay by a stone-paved path—complete with lights, courtesy of the EU. I enjoy going there to watch the fishing boats and yachts enter and leave the bay, and to eat the fresh fish and seafood prepared from a fisherman's daily catch. It's a walk of only twenty-five to thirty minutes, and while it has multiple uphill and downhill steps, it's not strenuous, or so we thought. One houseguest complained for three days about that walk.

Swimming to the beach by Fáros from our bay is my favorite activity on calm days. There are more schools of fish just past the furthest point of the peninsula between our bay and Fáros than anywhere else we swim nearby, and few people swim there. On that swim, we eventually pass sunken mining structures where I've seen an octopus hunt. The swim through crystalline waters to Fáros and back is a mile of utter peace.

———◆———

Many years ago in Athens, I saw and coveted an incredibly beautiful painting of Fáros Bay. This was the work of an artist from the Cycladic Island of Tinos, whose name was Poukamisás, which means "dress shirt maker." I'm told that his works are now included in art history books in Greece.

We'd earlier purchased two of his smaller oils depicting village scenes, one of which featured a scene on this Island, and I was eager to buy his painting of a quaint, traditional fishing boat anchored in Fáros near the hour of sunset. As the Aegean sun declines toward the horizon, the sea in the bay reflects the surrounding arid landscape, temporarily infusing its aquamarine and ultramarine hues with browns and greens. Consequently, the sea in this painting was depicted with brown and green, as well as blue. Aris didn't like that, and we didn't buy the painting.

Over the course of the following winter, we discussed this painting several times—yes, I nagged him about it—and he graciously agreed that if it remained unsold when we returned to Greece, we'd buy it. It was still unsold when we returned, but we did *not* buy it.

The painting had traveled to New York and won first prize in a competitive exhibition. The price was then raised—this was in the '80s—from a non-trivial thousand dollars to a quarter of a million dollars, the price of a very fine house in Pittsburgh at that time and way, way, way beyond our means.

I still remember it: the one that got away.

CHAPTER EIGHTEEN

Much Ado About Planting

The two most prominent characteristics of our property are rocks and height.

Our lot is *very* steep, with large outcroppings of stone, in addition to the wall of wind-carved rocks on the eastern side of the house. The seaside verandas to the south are on three levels, like the house, with planting areas on each—all in full sun almost all day.

Our rugged piece of hillside hosts a few scraggly junipers, many wild green bushes (*skínos*), capers, and an interesting bush of unknown name with leaves that are red in early summer, fall off in the heat, and sprout green in the fall. Fuzzy-leaf sage, thyme, and oregano grow wild all over our lot. When we've had a wet winter and the summer doesn't get too hot too fast, the thyme retains its purple blooms deep into June and attracts scores of pale yellow and black butterflies (*petaloúdes*).

Semi-wild, we have the large volunteer fig and a new volunteer fig that has sprung up in a crevasse below it. Strange as it may seem, clearing a pathway to that fig when it becomes productive will be easier than trying to grow another one. Another fig sapling is trying to grow out from under a large stone next to our lonely grape vine.

Our property also has a wealth of weeds. We have no ambition to tackle all or even most of them, but we have those near the house and along the driveway cleared to reduce fire risks and remove cover for venomous snakes. This is no small task, since our driveway is both long and steep. In some years, even this minimal yard work is impossible due to the wind.

Before we retired, having the weeds whacked was the extent of our "landscaping." Once we started spending entire summers here, the planting areas around the house became a priority. The first step was buying topsoil because the dirt was so poor that even the weeds struggled. Several tons of dirt were delivered in canvas bags to the front veranda, where the wind blew it against the house, turning it from white to brown. Moving this dirt—something accomplished via wheelbarrow—was essential and urgent.

As I watched the worker spreading it in the planting areas, I was struck by its light color and many small stones. Having grown up in the Ohio River Valley with rich, dark, loamy soil, I couldn't believe it was topsoil.

I asked Aris, "Did you pay for topsoil or fill?"

"Topsoil," he said.

"They gave you fill—just look at it."

He looked at it and shrugged, "Here, that *is* topsoil."

Next, we tried to goat-proof our planting areas. Many stone walls were built or increased in height, and sections of (unfortunately ugly) fencing were installed. This continued for quite some time, but the clever goats continued to be unimpressed and undeterred.

A big challenge for us is that we're here only in the summer, when there's little rain, and it's almost impossible to dig. One spring, our good neighbor Kóstas installed a fence around his vineyard next to our lot. A small section of it encroached on our property because it was already too hard to dig in the ground on his side. He told us he'd move it when the ground softened, and he did—two winters later (it took that long for the ground to allow digging).

Kóstas was of invaluable assistance in our efforts to re-place bare dirt with growing things. Over the first winter after we retired, he supervised the planting of eight oleanders, four on each side of our upper driveway, as well as a dozen grape-vines (*ampélia*). The oleanders were branches cut from Cousin George's bushes.

The cuttings were just stuck in the ground during the rainy season. Most prospered quickly, but two looked like sticks—dead sticks at that—for two years before they sprouted leaves. Kóstas also gave us a crimson rosebush (*triantafylliá*) and plant-ed it as a surprise.

Given the conditions, I never envisioned a lush garden, but I'd hoped for more than just oleanders. Known here as *pikrodáfnes,* meaning "bitter laurel," they grow readily without needing much water once they're established. They're also poi-sonous, so goats don't eat them. Because of that and our mixed success with other plants, we now have twenty oleanders, half fuchsia and half white, and may plant more. Granted that ole-anders are highway-ish, they're infinitely better than bare dirt.

Several plants grow all over the Island and are not sold here for that reason. One of these is the prickly pear cactus. If you want one, you need to find an accommodating friend to donate pads of the cactus, which you stick in the ground, as is, and water. They grow well—when not eaten. With donations from one of Faní's friends, we planted three prickly pear segments on the western (valley) side of our house, where it's hard to get anything to grow due to the combination of poor soil and high winds.

One summer, we returned to find one of those cacti blown flat down onto the ground. We watered it anyway, and it took off again. The cacti did quite well until the goats found them and ate big chunks. We now have an unattractive wooden pallet tied upright next to our front steps to block access to them. It was meant to be temporary—just until we got other fencing installed—but, since we're on Island Time, it's still there, years later.

We planted one prickly pear pad in the southernmost planting area of the property, quite near the edge of the cliff. It lived but failed to thrive. Chunks were missing; something had been eating it. We first suspected the crows, but Aris saw a big, fat rat climb up from Kóstas's orchards and gnaw the poor cactus. He built a mesh fence around it, which did its job so well that the cactus started growing right into the mesh.

Another plant you see everywhere but can't buy on the Island is the four o'clock. Called *deiliná*, these flowers grow like weeds. They're tenacious, need relatively little water once established, and even grow out of cracks and crevices. Best of all, goats don't like them. Faní gave me some seeds to plant many years ago so that we'd have a flower to enjoy. That one spawned many offspring.

New four o'clocks would have been a very welcome change from dirt in empty areas of our beds. Naturally, the seeds didn't germinate there. Instead, they grew among the grape vines—the one place we did *not* want them. We've transplanted many *deil-iná* but have yet to have good success. We'll keep trying!

⋄

I mentioned to a friend that I wanted to plant a particular ground cover we were walking past but hadn't been able to find it at a plant store. She grabbed some of the vines, broke them off, and presented them to me, saying, "Here! When you get these in, come back for more. No one *buys* these things here."

The ground cover was for an area where we can't plant anything with height without blocking our view. It spread nicely until the spring when the goats found a new path to our planting areas. They ate some, trampled the rest, and looked at us smugly. After that, the poor ground cover became weedy.

I was on the verge of having the whole bed dug up the next winter and starting all over when we got two days of rain, back-to-back, soon after we arrived. I spent six hours on each of the next two days on the ground, hands in the dirt, pulling and digging weeds out of the ground cover bed. Watching me, the house painters thought I was nuts to spend so much energy on plants we can't eat. They recommended growing arugula instead.

I'd hoped that the ground cover would be substantially restored by the time we returned the following year. Of course, I was disappointed. That winter was extraordinarily wet. Retaining walls in this normally arid place are built to hold water, not to drain it. The roots of crops rotted, and so did the roots of most of the ground cover—leaving us, once again, with dirt.

Faní kindly hired a gardener on our behalf to replant the ruined beds with other things, including lavender. The new lavenders thrived, though other plants the gardener put in withered away. When he returned to weed, he inexplicably destroyed much of the remaining ground cover that had been doing well! We nurtured the last of it, which has since spread beautifully, and we found someone less clueless.

A friend donated some aloe plants, which have been happily growing against one of our stone retaining walls and by the rocks on the side of the house. Weeding them is a different matter! Roses grow very well here too, and we have several, though they're just as susceptible to mildew and bugs here as they are in the States. We also planted lilac and bougainvillea below the lowest veranda to climb its stone retaining wall—we both love the scent of lilac.

Among our most successful plantings are rosemary bushes, though getting these established also took some doing. It grows well on the Island—if you find a spot it likes. Our first two attempts with standard rosemary were failures. But we found places that made three spreading rosemary bushes happy!

With that success, we planted another standard rosemary bush, but in partial shade instead of full sun. That one was surrounded by sage and thyme—we lacked only parsley. The herbs made the entrance to the new guest house fragrant. But—isn't there always a "but"?—the gardener forgot to water it, and it died. So much for the fragrant welcome we had planned for our guests.

The worst casualties of the goat invasions were Aris's grapevines. Planted under Kóstas's expert supervision, he started with a dozen plants, and devoted many, many hours to watering and fertilizing them. But—despite the walls and fences—the goats had their feasts, and he's now down to one lonely survivor. After many years, it produced a cluster of grapes. We sadly watched as they shriveled and died, wondering how we'd offended Dionysus.

Goats weren't the only unwanted intruders in our garden. We abandoned all efforts to grow tomatoes, even though I love them, because the minute they show the least bit of yellow color the crows are on them.

Aris had great success growing eggplants one summer. They looked like ordinary purple eggplants but had almost no seeds and were sweet. They were perfect for slicing thin and frying with a light coat of flour mixed with salt and pepper. They're served with a potato and garlic paste, known as *skordaliá*, which is equally delicious with fried zucchini, fried cod, fried baby shark, and fried skate wing. *Tzatzíki*—another garlicky spread made from yogurt—is often spread on fried eggplant and zucchini slices instead. Mána's recipes for both are in the Appendix.

Our efforts to trade bare dirt for green plants have given us some hard lessons in patience and persistence—and taught us to appreciate small victories. Despite everything, we have oleanders, roses, other flowers, and one stubborn grapevine. We lost some rounds, but the fight isn't over yet!

CHAPTER NINETEEN

Cooking!

The kitchen in the village house was something of a torture chamber—tiny, rudimentary, and sweltering. The stone and chestnut beam ceiling was quite low, as was the small, shallow sink hollowed out of a thick piece of white marble. It broke your back to work at that sink, and I suspect that using it contributed to Mána's dowager's hump.

The oven was just big enough for a single sixteen-inch pan. There was no stove, just a hot plate with two burners. The remaining features were a rather small refrigerator, a petite table, and shallow shelves for storing dishes in display mode. It had no cabinets or counter space. How Mána managed to prepare delicious meals in it was beyond me. My voluntary job in that house was cleaning the kitchen and washing the dishes after we ate.

When we built our house here, I insisted on having a big kitchen by Island standards, with lots of countertops and plenty of cabinets. At thirty-nine inches tall, our upper cabinets provide abundant storage. But, for reasons we'll never know, the installers put them too high on the walls. Being five feet nothing, I can't reach much beyond the bottom shelves without a step stool.

Possibly the first of its kind on the Island, our kitchen has a peninsula with an overhang for casual eating. And, unlike traditional homes here, it's not closed off from the rest of the house but open to the dining room through a wide archway.

Before we retired in 2012, the kitchen was largely decorative. Once we started spending a third of our lives here, I settled down to the business of making it functional. I helped the economies of Greece and the United Kingdom—pre-Brexit—by ordering such kitchen essentials as a food processor, a panini maker (in lieu of a toaster), pots, mixing bowls, and good knives (one of the Island's mysteries is why knives dull so quickly here). Seven years after we retired, I even ordered a microwave oven. A German design, this microwave surprisingly requires—not prohibits—putting a metal utensil in any liquid to be heated.

I ordered quite a bit from Amazon UK because I could search for items in English, a major advantage. Having left Greece when he was nineteen, Aris had forgotten some mundane Greek terms like "stock pot." He only remembered *katsaróla*, the generic Greek word for pots.

Searching Greek websites for a stock pot using "*katsaróla*" yielded only squat pots. Translation apps gave me gibberish. Hence, the resort to Amazon UK. It turns out that this is one time when literal translation works—more or less: I saw a filled stock pot at our favorite taverna and asked Kyría Évi what it was called. "*Katsaróla gia zomó*" (pot for stock or broth), she replied.

Aris likes to tell people that I don't cook here. This annoys me because, while I don't cook every day, I cook quite often. We frequently have folks here in the evening, and I regularly prepare *mezédes* (hors d'oeuvres): Greek meatballs, eggplant salad (a spread similar to baba ghanoush), *taramosaláta* (another spread, made from tiny pink or white caviar), *fáva* (similar to hummus, but made from Greek split peas), a dish called *strapatsáda* (made with tomatoes, eggs, and local cheese), spinach-leek-cheese pies, and a pie made with *pastourmá*—a meat similar to prosciutto, but cured in fenugreek, paprika, garlic, and cumin. I'm known for my eggplant salad and spinach, leek, and cheese pies.

Greeks put a lot of food on the table when entertaining, and so do we. If we invite folks for dinner, I prepare a main course in addition to the *mezédes*. Like most here, we almost always entertain outside so our guests can enjoy the view.

To make eggplant salad that's worth eating, you need to start with grilled and blistered eggplants. The first time I tried to make this here, I turned the broiler on and blew the circuit breaker for the whole kitchen. That problem—another legacy of the drunk electrician?—wasn't solved until we replaced the oven. But all was not lost.

The burners of electric stoves here were solid, and a friend, who is a very accomplished cook, told me I could grill the eggplants on the largest one. This works but makes the whole house smell of scorched eggplants. It also makes a mess of your burner and requires vigilance so the eggplants don't catch fire. But the wonderful smoky flavor is worth it! My recipe, starting with broiled or grilled eggplants, is in the Appendix.

Finding the spices I wanted was more of a hunt than you might think. One store had only whole nutmeg. When I asked for grated nutmeg, which wasn't available, the shop owner couldn't understand why anyone would want it rather than grating it yourself. (Just thinking about grating nutmeg makes my fingers hurt!) For a while, I brought some spices from the States. Then Nicoleta told me where I could find the more exotic ones. Aris even tracked down saffron and chicken broth when I wanted to prepare Risotto alla Milanese.

However well-prepared you think you are, it isn't until you start cooking that you realize what you don't have. Early on, I promised Faní and Dimítris a spinach-leek-cheese pie, *spanako-prasotirópita*. But when I finished making triangles to freeze for later, I realized that I had neither an oil sprayer nor a pastry brush to use on the phyllo for their pan pie. I scratched my head, and improvised: A small glass jar, plastic wrap, and a rubber band turned into a makeshift oil sprinkler. They said the *píta* was excellent.

Understanding product labels is another challenge—being able to read Greek doesn't always mean that I fully comprehend them. Shopping for the ingredients for spinach-leek-cheese pie triangles one day, I noticed that one of the many boxes of phyllo dough said that it was for "traditional pies" (*paradosiakés pítes*). Perfect, I thought.

Wrong! It was very thick phyllo, not at all suitable for folding into triangles. I switched to Plan B, froze half of the filling mixture (without the egg), and made the rest into a pan pie.

Unlike traditional spinach pie (*spanakópita*), I add leeks to cut the bitterness of the spinach, and I use a lot more cheese than is traditional, as well as a dash of red pepper and some nutmeg—ingredients Mána never used. If you want a more traditional pie, leave out the leeks, red pepper, and nutmeg, and use less cheese. But the spinach-leek-cheese pies made with my recipe consistently get high praise and disappear rapidly. It's in the Appendix, with instructions for both triangles and pan pies.

Baking needed to be done early or late in the day because our first oven made the whole house blazingly hot, causing me to wonder whether the rodents that ate the insulation off the dishwasher's wires had feasted on the oven insulation too!

Like the rest of Europe, Greece is on the metric system, so I need to pay attention when grocery shopping here. But there are times when my brain decides to take an unauthorized vacation. One such event nearly ruined my meatballs.

Wanting a pound and a half of ground beef to make meatballs, I rotely grabbed a package marked 1.5—*kilos,* of course—instead of the roughly two-thirds of a kilo I needed. My excuse is that I was listening to *The Soul of a Woman* by Isabel Allende. Still listening, and still oblivious, when I returned home, I mindlessly mixed all that meat—three and a half pounds of it—with ingredients meant for just 1.5 pounds.

You'd think that looking at the amount of meat I bought would've clued me in that I had much too much, but it didn't. I realized my mistake only after I put the mixture in the freezer—and turned the audio book off.

I then drove five twisty, patchy miles back to the store for more breadcrumbs, onions, mint, parsley, and garlic to add to the freezer bags—ready to mix in when it was time to cook. As the Greeks say, "those without brains have legs" (*aftoí pou den échoun myaló échoun pódia*). I worried about how the meatballs would turn out, but I served them to our painters, who said they were delicious. One ate more than a dozen! You can find Mána's recipe for Greek meatballs (with my tweaks) in the Appendix.

Lunch is the main meal here and we eat it almost every day at the restaurant below us on the beach, owned by Kýrios Pétros and Kyría Évi. That's why Aris likes to say that I don't cook here. We're really lucky that one of the best traditional restaurants on the Island is in our bay. (Actually, both restaurants in our bay are excellent.) We have a reserved table and eat there after swimming, Aris in a dry bathing suit (and, typically, nothing else), me in a caftan.

Kyría Évi's *dolmádes* (stuffed grape leaves) and lamb fricassee are every bit as delicious as Mána's were. Sadly, her recipes for these dishes went with her to the grave, but she left me a rough outline for stuffed grape leaves. With significant experimentation and some input from Kyría Évi, I gradually filled in the blanks. My step-by-step recipe is in the Appendix—I hope you'll like the result.

I knew almost nothing about cooking until I started learning from Mána, who had learned to cook from her mother-in-law. I had no interest in the kitchen at all when I was growing up—there weren't many cooked foods I liked. My own dear mother, who put a hot meal on the table every night after teaching all day and before doing her lesson plans, her homework for her master's degree classes, or both, wasn't much of a cook then.

I used to call the type of food she prepared "British Southern"—first boiled to death, then covered with gravy. My mom became a much better cook when she didn't have three kids, a full-time job, homework, a house, and a husband to manage.

When Mána wintered with us in Pittsburgh, she spent a significant part of the day, while we were at work, preparing our evening meals. This helped me tremendously, but I felt guilty about it until Aris told me that cooking was her hobby. When he was growing up, there were maids and nannies in the house, but no cook. Mána did the cooking. Years later, Mána confessed that—despite Aris's belief— she didn't particularly enjoy cooking, but she relished the pleasure the food she prepared gave to others. That was Mána.

On most weekends in Pittsburgh, I worked in the kitchen beside her. I loved learning from her. She was endlessly patient, though teaching me must have been trying, given how little I knew.

Working with her, I did the preparatory work and watched as she prepared each dish. I wrote down everything she did—the steps and the quantities of each ingredient, which sometimes varied even for the same dish. For the most part, she worked without consulting her recipes, and to this day, Aris maintains that anyone who uses recipes isn't a real cook (he's wrong, of course).

When we designed our last house in Pittsburgh, I specified two workstations in the kitchen so that Mána and I could easily cook side by side. Future neighbors visiting the construction site surmised that we were Orthodox Jews since we had two sets of sinks, two stoves, two ovens, and two dishwashers. No one imagined two cooks wanting to work together.

Although he later changed his mind, Babás once declared that they were too old to be making the transatlantic trip anymore, and we asked Mána to write down recipes for meals I hadn't made with her. When I tried to follow them, I was flummoxed. They were outlines, at best, with such instructions as "cook it enough" and "add as much water as it needs."

The first time I prepared lamb with artichokes, a dish I'd enjoyed many times, I cooked the lamb almost to shreds because I didn't know how long was "long enough." I also had to work to achieve a smooth sauce. But with lots of experimentation, I learned how to produce a result close to Mána's. The recipe is in the Appendix—enjoy!

In learning to cook Greek foods, I also learned what Mána always knew: the joy of giving pleasure to others. And every time I make a dish I made with her, I think of her—her patience, her joy in pleasing others—and smile.

CHAPTER TWENTY

To Market, To Market

Before cooking, one must shop. On the Island, that means keeping an eye on both the calendar and the clock.

Many stores close on major saints' days, and most—except in the port village and the big grocery store near the main village *during peak season*—close between 2:00 p.m. and either 5:30 or 6:00 p.m. for lunch and siesta. The beverage distributor near the main village is also an exception; it closes for the day by 4:00 p.m., sometimes earlier.

When we stayed with Aris's parents in the village house, fish from the night's catch were sold by a fisherman on a cart in the plaza first thing in the morning. Babás went there to buy red mullet (*barboúnia*) because it was one of the few proteins our nephew and godson ate voluntarily when he was young. I'm told that one can buy fish directly from a fisherman at 8:30 a.m. at the marina in the bay of Platýs Gialós, but I've never been sufficiently motivated to go there. When very fresh fish is beautifully prepared at nearby restaurants with lovely views, it's hard to get excited about shopping for it so early, never mind going to the bother of cooking it.

The Island now has fish stores, cheese stores, butchers, and general grocery stores—sometimes called supermarkets, though they're hardly worthy of the name. There are also mini-markets, and a market for Island produce. When I first came here, there was a store that offered, in addition to the usual fare, skinned hares hung from the ceiling.

Island regulars engage in lively debates about which store offers the best version of the local sheep's milk hard cheese, *manoúra*—and whether it's best coated in the waxy residue left in red wine barrels (*gyloméni*) or left white and uncoated. Manólis, may he rest in peace, made the best *manoúra*, yellow and dripping with butter. My second favorite was the coated version sold by the cheese monger at the port, from whom I also bought fresh eggs. That store closed due to illness, so I now buy buttery *manoúra* from the main grocery in the port.

Slices of this cheese, along with olives, tomato wedges, and bread are the traditional *mezé* provided when you order an ouzo. *Manoúra*, like ouzo, is a local taste. I don't know why, but even in Naples, Florida, when we have the taste of saltwater on our tongues, these flavors just aren't the same as they are on the Island.

I get two heads of *manoúra* grated and carry them to the States for use in *strapatsáda, mousakás* (the national dish of Greece), and spaghetti with meat sauce. *Strapatsáda* is made with tomatoes, eggs, and cheese: Peel, deseed, and purée very ripe fresh tomatoes and sauté them in olive oil to a thick sauce. To this, add eggs (preferably fresh) beaten until thick with grated *manoúra*, parmesan, or feta cheese, and then sauté the mixture lightly in olive oil.

I've included Mána's fabulous recipe for *mousakás* in the Appendix. The organization, quantification, and comments are mine, but I haven't changed it at all otherwise. My recipe for Greek spaghetti sauce with ground beef, *Sáltsa me Kimá,* is included too.

※ ———◇——— ※

There are also lively debates on the Island about the best sources for the local goat's milk cheese (*xinomyzíthra*), which is something like French chèvre, but softer and tart. I'm told that in the days before refrigeration was available here, this cheese was kept under grape leaves in baskets suspended from ceilings and stirred daily by conscientious housewives.

Xinomyzíthra cheese is enjoyed by itself with good bread, and in village salad (*choriátiki saláta*), which is made with tomatoes, cucumbers, red onion, green pepper, capers, oregano, salt, olive oil, and kalamata olives. Regardless of any experiences you may have had in Greek restaurants in the States, Greek village salad never has lettuce.

Greeks bemoan that, with the mandatory pasteurization required by the EU, the *myzíthra* cheese has lost some of its tang. My preferred source was Manólis's daughter Eiríni, who used to make a delicious version. When I can't buy it from her, I get it in the village at the *kreopoleío* (butcher). Eiríni also produces a wonderful olive oil and can often offer fresh eggs. I'm very fond of fresh eggs!

※ ———◇——— ※

The biggest grocery is near the main village. Two stores in different buildings, owned by the same family, share a parking lot. The larger building houses dry goods of all kinds, as well as cleaning implements and other housewares. Popular dairy products, wine, and bread are sold there too. The other building houses fresh fruits, vegetables, and meat, along with assorted frozen items, dairy products, and a deli.

Just because you don't see it doesn't mean it's not there. One day, I was disappointed by the eggplants on display, which were large and past their prime. When I asked, I was shown a carton of much fresher large eggplants. On further inquiry, a carton of fresh, small eggplants was produced. Mint is never displayed there, but it's available on request.

While checking out with the ingredients for Greek meat-balls, spinach pies, eggplant salad, and *taramosaláta*, the cashier (a member of the family that owns the store) recounted the dishes I'd be making and asked when we'd be having company. There are no secrets on the Island.

Islanders and Island regulars are tomato snobs. I've listened to lengthy and passionate debates (with much excited gesturing) about the quality of the tomatoes served in the village salads of various restaurants and tavernas. Whenever possible, I bought tomatoes from a farmer from a neighboring island who supplied the restaurant of Kýrios Pétros and Kyría Évi. He grew excellent tomatoes.

The holy grail is the traditional Island tomato, grown with very little water, thanks to its amazingly long, thick roots. It's extremely acidic—and *extremely* tasty. The first time I came to the Island, I fell so deeply in love with Island tomatoes and ate so many that I developed acid sores in my mouth! Sadly, they're hard to find now.

Locals are snobbish not only about tomatoes but also about other foods, including *fáva*, which is a dried yellow split pea, un-related to the fava bean. You can find it at Greek grocery stores.

Locals have strong feelings about where the best *fáva* is grown, and the difference in the flavors of split peas from different areas is rather remarkable. The best I've had are from the island of *Schoinoúsa*. In case you visit a Greek grocer and find fava, Mana's very easy vegan recipe is in the Appendix.

Like so many aspects of Island life, shopping is an experience and, occasionally, a triumph. Earlier this summer, at the big grocery store, a member of the family opened a second cash register for me. When an Islander who doesn't know me looked at her, eyebrows raised, she said, "*Eínai dikí mas*"—she's one of us.

CHAPTER TWENTY-ONE

The New Guest House

After hosting a family of four adults during the summer of 2011, we had another guest suite built, as a separate structure, the following winter.

While the family was with us, the adult children slept in the entrance on the daybed, which separated into twin beds, and their parents stayed in our bedroom, allowing the family to share the main bathroom. We moved into the upstairs guest room. That was the second time we'd surrendered our bedroom for guests. The first time, we slept on the daybed in the entrance—talk about feeling exposed—and we decided that this time would be the last.

The new guest house perches above the retaining wall on the mountainside of the driveway and offers views of the valley but, sadly, no sea view. We had it faced in stacked stone, so that, like the garage, it blends into the landscape. The design, which Aris drew, was simple: a large rectangular box, including a bathroom next to a walk-in closet, both rectangular, with a small veranda outside. On the drawing, Aris specified that the bathroom was to be two meters deep.

As happens on the Island, it did not turn out that way.

One day in early spring, I got a frantic message via Skype from Faní, who had returned to the Island, that she urgently needed to speak with Aris. I was working from home and called her back. She told me that there was a *katastrofí* (catastrophe) with the construction of the new guest house, and she needed to speak with Aris immediately. I relayed the message, fearing fire or a worker injury. Thankfully, it was a much smaller disaster.

For reasons we'll never know, the bathroom was built a mere forty-two inches wide—hardly wider than a hallway! There was nothing to be done. The structure was essentially finished. The windows, exterior door, plank-and-beam ceiling, and stone floors were already in place. All that remained were the bathroom fixtures, tile, and two interior doors.

Moving an interior wall would've meant redoing both the stone floor and the wooden ceiling. It would have been even more difficult to move the foot-thick exterior wall. We asked Faní to direct the builder to do nothing toward finishing the bathroom—we'd deal with it when we arrived.

(The engineer who managed the construction of the main house is looking better now, isn't he?)

Toward compensating for the lack of sea view, we'd envisioned a spacious bathroom in the new suite, but wound up with a long, skinny space with a high ceiling. It echoes like a bell tower—a "quirky" guest experience. The shower, with its glass block wall, is forty-two inches square, so it's fine, but you can't fit twenty-four-inch-deep sink cabinets into a space that's a mere forty-two inches deep and expect guests to maneuver with any degree of comfort.

After contemplating the space for a while, I told Aris that we needed yacht sinks and highly reflective tile. Yacht sinks—very small sinks—are easy to find in Athens since apartments there (like those in New York City) are small. When an apartment in Athens has a powder room (which isn't very common) it's usually tiny with an equally tiny sink.

To make up for the cramped space, we sought out lovely fixtures and found the perfect tile: a deep Aegean blue for the floor, a lighter blue for the lower walls, and white for the upper walls with a decorative band of Aegean blue—all very shiny. Ironically, this skinny bathroom has better appointments than ours—and the bedroom it serves is 50 percent larger than our own. But it has no sea view.

There are no secrets on the Island. The Islander who delivered the bathroom tile commented that the guest house was new. Another one delivering the bathroom fixtures did too. When the painters came, they asked about painting the exposed concrete portions of the guesthouse white. I asked Aris, who said no—if we painted parts of it white, the new structure would be more noticeable (he shuns ostentation). I told him that everyone already knew about it, so we might as well have the painting done. We did.

Once the tile arrived, we called the tile setter, Lira's brother. He did a wonderful job, but, *of course*, there was a problem: The interior wall separating the bathroom and closet didn't meet the back wall at a ninety-degree angle. Lira's brother had no choice but to cut floor tiles into extremely narrow triangles to fit, using up all the floor tile in the process. None remained for the bathroom threshold.

We called the store in Athens to order more tile, but it had none in stock. The store contacted the German factory, but it was shut down for the August vacation. Argh! The builder salvaged the situation with a piece of white marble for the threshold. Not my first choice, but it works.

The wall between the bathroom and the closet isn't the only one in the new structure that isn't straight. The back wall of the bedroom isn't either, and the ceiling has an extra wedge of wood plank to compensate. I'm still baffled by the apparent inability to construct straight walls and ninety-degree angles. That's one problem we don't have in the main house.

(The engineer who managed the original construction is looking even better, isn't he?)

We never received any clear explanation for why the bathroom was built so narrowly despite the specifications. Our best guess is that the builder or his crew thought it was a mistake—that no one would *really* want a bathroom that large. To his credit, the builder felt badly about it. He gave us honey from his own hives, and a *very* reasonable bill.

The builder wasn't the only one unable to follow simple instructions. The contractor hired to provide and install the interior doors in the new guest suite couldn't either. Because that bathroom is so narrow, we carefully explained that the bathroom door had to open into the bedroom, while the closet door was to open into the walk-in closet. Nevertheless, as if we'd said nothing of the kind, both doors were installed to open into the bedroom.

Naturally, we asked that the closet door be redone.

"No, no," we were advised, "It's much better this way. There's more room in the closet."

"We understand," Aris replied, "but we'd still like to have that door open into the closet, not the bedroom. Humor me."

"Ah," came the response. "It cannot be done. The holes and cuts for the hinges are already in the coated wood trim. You'll have to wait a long time for new trim to arrive if we change it. It's better as it is."

So, we shrugged, bowed to the inevitable, and left it alone. This was a wise decision because that contractor went out of business not much later (no need to wonder why).

While the door installer was busy ignoring our directions, an electrician with an Albanian helper in tow was working in the new guest suite too. We were also expecting the plumber, but he had an emergency and didn't make it. Because the plumber couldn't install the sinks, the electrician couldn't install the lights above them as he needed to see their exact placement.

Unable to finish the work in the new bathroom, the electrician took care of several small issues in the main house and, as electricians do in the States, he left bits of wire behind on every floor. Some things are universal.

Despite its quirks, guests report that they enjoy the new guest house, and we're relieved to be able to accommodate extra visitors without sacrificing our bedroom.

Do you suppose that The Rolling Stones' song, *You Can't Always Get What You Want,* was inspired by building here?

CHAPTER TWENTY-TWO

Furnishing the House, Round II: Art, Accessories, and More

The hardest part of furnishing the Island house was acquiring art. When you have white walls that are ten- to fourteen-feet high and gray stone floors, you *need* art.

I brought a few small items from the States, most notably an antique map of "Turkey in Europe" and a lovely, framed photograph of Pittsburgh's golden triangle. After Babás died and we closed Aris's parents' place, we had a few pieces of wall art shipped from their home in Athens to ours. A friend gifted us two photographs of Island scenes suitable for framing. But we needed much more—and we wanted to buy from Island artists if we could.

We were partially successful. We bought most of the art in our house on the Island, but not all of it is by Island artists. Our first purchases were two beautiful limited-edition photographs, printed on canvas, and taken on the Island by a visiting English photographer. One of these is of a farmer using a donkey to thresh wheat in an *alóni* (a wide, circular flag-stoned space with a low stone wall, open to the sky), a scene unchanged for hundreds of years. Several small watercolors and oils in our home were painted here by a Greek artist from the mainland who visited the Island several summers.

We also patronized—a lot—a local woman who paints the Island's picturesque villages and churches and has a remarkable talent for capturing the light. A friend who owns properties on the Island decided to purchase from her too after seeing her work in our home. We were delighted to share the artist's contact information with her.

Buying paintings is the fun part. When you live on a small Island, framing them is another matter. There's no framer here. A carpenter could construct a simple box, or Aris could take the paintings to Athens to be framed on his next trip there, but he doesn't take the car on those trips and transporting large canvases back and forth on a ferry without one wouldn't be fun. So, rather ridiculously, I had frames made in the States.

This entailed measuring the paintings carefully, taking good photos, and having deconstructed frames made. We then had to get them here. Since frame parts, like other sticks, aren't allowed in carry-on luggage, they must be checked into the hold.

All of this means that we have to really love a painting to be willing to go to the bother of framing it. I "framed" one painting, right on the Island, myself. It's a triptych. When I showed the photos to the framer I patronize in Naples, he kindly recommended that I forego a frame—and his services—and mount the canvases on a board covered with fabric in a background color used in the painting. I did just that and they look great!

The Island is famous for ceramics and, being fond of them, we have many decorative items, including *amphorae* with white crackle glazes in metal stands and three two-foot-high ceramic urns glazed in gold and blue. The urns solved a unique decorating problem—how to conceal the pipes intended for radiators should we ever choose to install them. The pipes protrude about ten inches from the corners of the stone floors and have unsightly red and blue plastic casings—now hidden behind the urns.

I found them, marked €40 each, in the back of a ceramics shop at the port. This wasn't a bad price for urns of that size, but in Greece, one bargains. Offering cash and commenting that they were dusty and had clearly been on sale for a while, I got all three for €75. Aris would likely have been offered a better price since he's a native, but the urns were the perfect solution for my problem, and I wasn't about to risk anyone else snatching up any of them. I was right, for once: Although I've returned to that store many times, I've never seen urns like those again.

We have some rather unusual items of "decor." Stacked on the floor by the dining room door to the veranda are six yellow floor cushions, topped by two colorful *kourelo údes* (rag woven mats). These are for the *pentzo úles,* the stone-topped benches attached to the house. In the living room, a big gray Swiss ball serves in place of a chair for the drop-front secretary desk, much better for the back. A ceramic bowl in the kitchen is filled with sunscreens for hair, face, and body. Another ceramic bowl on the dining room table captures sunglasses, chargers, and earphones.

Other ceramic bowls and platters with beautiful glazes serve simply to decorate cabinets and tables. Wanting to replace the Turkish platter smashed by the wind, I was dithering over the purchase of one of these in the shop of our favorite ceramicist. I settled on a large platter glazed in shades of blue and green. When I brought it to the counter to pay, the ceramicist's wife commented, "Ah! You have chosen both the mountain and the sea." I love this Island!

Having pride of place against the center pillar between the living and dining rooms is a meter-high stoneware vase. Its bottom half is glazed in gold, but it's topped with a crystalline glaze in multiple shades of blue. This stunning piece was made by an exceptional artisan who, sadly, lost his battle with cancer several years ago. We also purchased two smaller vases with his special glazes and exhibit them conspicuously, one on a stand near a window where the light plays on the crystals in the glaze. A couple of his stoneware platters bearing images of local fish enliven the kitchen.

The stoneware artist's equally exceptional wife is a very skilled weaver. For the shutterless window and windowed door of the upstairs guest suite, she sold me the last set of beautifully patterned, unbleached linen curtains she ever wove. Embroidered Island-style white cotton curtains cover the shutterless window of our bathroom and the two windowed doors of the main house, but we have no other curtains.

When you live on a steep hill out in the country and have working shutters almost everywhere, curtains—dust catchers susceptible to dry rot—are not wanted. We have no floor coverings either: There's much too much blown dirt here to have carpets or rugs of any kind. We have far more airborne dirt here than in Athens. But even in Athens, drapes and carpets are removed and upholstery is covered for the summer because of the dust and dirt. I'm told that this is also done in other hot, dusty places like Beirut.

Our wall art includes two large ceramic platters painted with village scenes. I went on something of a quest to find the artist who painted them. While dining in the garden of a restaurant in the main village, I was struck by two beautiful, large paintings of Island churches decorating its walls and asked the restaurant owner about them.

He gave us the artist's name and the name of his bakery—he is a baker by profession—which is in a bay near ours. We went there and spoke with him. He explained that, aside from the ceramic platters, he paints only on commission. One day, we may commission him to paint the perspective of the bay from our house.

In the main house, we have metal lamps with glass shades purchased from Mr. Lazárou to supplement the suspended overhead, empire-style lighting. Locally handmade pierced-work ceramic lamps help illuminate the guest bedrooms. One of these was offered with a lampshade and I bought it immediately. I delayed buying the other because it had no lampshade, and there was nowhere on the Island to purchase one. When I asked the ceramicist, he—unhelpfully—recommended that I get one in Athens. The port of Athens is a three-hour ferry ride away, so a shopping trip there could be a two-day excursion. Not for me. I want to be here as much as possible.

The lamp required a shade with a harp that screwed into place under the lightbulb. We checked Greek websites without success. Eventually, I resorted (again) to Amazon UK (it was still pre-Brexit) and found one! Normally, shipping all the way from there to the Island would've cost more than the lampshade, but I also ordered a chrome stand for the bathroom of the guest house to compensate for its lack of cabinets, so shipping was free.

Absurdly, the lampshade was shipped, unboxed, in the same container as the chrome stand. To no one's surprise, it was smashed on arrival. I went online and submitted packaging feedback with photos of the crumpled lampshade. Before I even finished typing the replacement request, Amazon UK issued an apology and said a replacement was on the way. You've got to love the Brits!

We have several clay pots on the verandas for Greek small-leaf basil and mint, but the decorative prize belongs to two meter-high, unglazed, wide-mouthed, two-handled ceramic pots, with ridges up the sides, known as *kioúpia* here and *pithária* elsewhere in Greece. (We also have a large painting of a *kioúpi* against an old lime-washed stone wall, on prominent display in the dining room.)

Making large ceramics is a special skill because they're prone to exploding in the kiln. We ordered the *kioúpia* from an Islander specializing in such pots and waited half the summer for them. In true Island fashion, he didn't call us when they were ready. He simply showed up with them.

Fortunately, houseguests had returned to our place after lunch ahead of us and were there to take the delivery. Even better, the *kioúpia* survived the rough trip on the dry riverbed road and up our steep driveway. Unfortunately for our guests, they were drafted into helping us move the big, heavy pots to their proper places on the verandas—which they did willingly.

That sort of thing happened to several houseguests in the early years of our retirement. Furniture would be delivered while they stayed with us, and they'd help move the item or items into place and carry the packaging down to the trash bins near the beach (there's no trash collection from homes or businesses here). We're fortunate in our friends—they always did this cheerfully. Furnishing the new guest house and everything that entailed were the worst test of the bonds of friendship.

We originally outfitted the upstairs guest suite with the twin beds Aris and Faní slept in when they were kids (with new mattresses of course), together with a rustic dresser and night-stand with white marble tops, a mirror, and a dining armchair with a raffia-woven seat. Fortunately, we hadn't yet purchased anything else for that room.

When the guest house was almost finished, we ordered new furniture for our bedroom from Mr. Lazárou. We planned to move our existing bedroom suite, including the queen-sized bed, into the upstairs guest room, and to move the furniture from that room to the guest house. Of course, it would've been simpler to move the existing master bedroom furniture into the guest house, but that room, though the largest, has no sea view, while the upstairs bedroom has one of the best views in Greece and is a more desirable accommodation.

Our new master bedroom furniture arrived—unexpectedly early, during grape harvesting season—when close friends were visiting from Lexington. We'd planned to hire someone to move the furniture around, but workers weren't immediately available. The new items, including a queen-sized mattress, were very inconveniently deposited in the middle of the dining room. They couldn't be relocated to our bedroom until the existing furniture was removed. Our friends very obligingly volunteered for service.

I don't think they fully appreciated what they were getting into.

First, we hauled out all the furniture outfitting the upstairs guest suite and carried it down twenty stone stairs from that room and up five more into the guest house. The mattresses—heavy, one-piece combinations of mattress and box spring—made our muscles ache. In their new home, those furnishings joined Aris's grandfather's childhood desk, which Aris also used as a boy.

Phase one over, we started on the master bedroom's weighty furniture: queen-sized mattress, bed frame, mirror, dresser, nightstands, and their marble tops. We carried them out the balcony doors, up two steps, along the side of the house, and down two steps. Then up four steps and around a turn. And, finally, up sixteen more steps into the guest room.

As you can imagine, those stairs seemed to grow longer and steeper with each article we carried! Had the marble tops been affixed to the furniture, we never would've been able to move the dresser. By the time all the new furniture was relocated from the dining room to its destination in our bedroom, we all were exhausted. But the rooms looked great! We ate and slept well that night. And I'm happy to report that, despite this experience, our Lexington friends came back.

Through art and exercise, our house became a home.

CHAPTER TWENTY-THREE

The Great Crow and Goat Attacks

Murder in the Rocks

Most of the time, we love living in the countryside—but not always.

Two years in a row, hooded crows (called *korákia* or *kourúnes* elsewhere and *káryes* here) built nests in the rocks of the cliff behind our verandas. They startled us awake every morning before six, croaking harshly and attacking their reflections in our windows and balcony doors. Not content with disrupting our sleep, they destroyed window screens—built into the window frames and the very devil to replace—and pecked holes in the wood below the glass. Some of the holes were half an inch deep and the diameter of a nickel!

The crows attacked with such force that I feared they'd break the glass or damage the seal between the double panes. Once they started, they'd attack repeatedly until about eight o'clock. It was bizarre: One crow would fly hard at the glass, slam into it, and fall to the ground with specks of blood on its face only to be immediately followed by another doing the same thing. Adding insult to injury, they pooped all over our windowsills and verandas.

Hooded crows aren't all black but wear gray vests. Despite their natty attire, I don't like them. Aside from the damage to our house, they kept the sparrows from nesting in our rocks. Normally, the wind-carved rocks beside our home teem with nesting sparrows in the summer. But, since crows eat other birds' eggs and nestlings, few sparrows were around in those years. Perhaps this is why a group of crows is called a "murder."

In the States, Aris—whom I teasingly call "Dead Eye"— shoots game birds for us to eat (I'm especially fond of quail). He's an excellent shot, but his skill didn't help with the crows. He borrowed a friend's shotgun and shot a crow or two, but the pellets weren't effective and did them no harm. The shots didn't even faze them. Was some of their cawing laughter? I bought shiny mylar tape and hung it from the tops of the doors and windows to crinkle and flash in the wind. That helped.

Bleating and Eating

As if the crows weren't bad enough, the goats struck. Morning after morning, just as we were falling back to sleep after the crow attacks, goats started bleating loudly outside our bedroom windows! It was simultaneously comical and maddening.

You'll recall that we spent a small fortune building more and higher stone walls and installing lots of ugly wire fencing to keep goats away so they wouldn't eat the plants we fought so hard to grow. We never imagined being bleated awake!

Our barriers didn't stop them. Even hobbled goats navigated the steep, rocky hillside and jumped our walls and fences to get to our verandas, where they feasted on our plantings. In case you're wondering, hobbling is done by tying a goat's front leg to its back leg on the same side with a short rope. It was illegal but widely done anyway.

For many years, goats were kept all around us—just across the road by the grandson-in-law of Aris's former nanny, beside our place by his former nanny's son, and above us by someone I don't know. The goat enclosure across the road was quite a dump. In keeping with Islander frugality, all sorts of salvaged materials were collected there—an old tire, damaged doors, wooden pallets used for freight, bits of cabinets, rusty sheets of tin, concrete blocks, and even a hot water heater. Some was piled atop the goat enclosure, some was fashioned into a hodgepodge shelter, and some just lay around, inviting snakes.

Our good neighbor Kóstas knows everyone. One day after the goats showed up in our garden, we stopped to chat with him when we passed his property while walking back from the beach. After exchanging pleasantries, I told him about the goats. He was unconcerned since they weren't in his vineyard.

The goats must have enjoyed our view because they kept loitering around, eating our roses and other plants, and pooping everywhere. After several more days of this, we spoke with Kóstas again.

"The goats are still on our verandas, eating the grapevines and everything else," I said.

"That's too bad," he commiserated. "But goats will be goats."

"Aris asked everyone, and no one claims them," I persisted. *"Can we eat them?"*

I don't remember his reply. I think he laughed. I didn't really want to eat the goats; I wanted to be rid of them. But eating is a very serious matter to Greeks, so this was a meaningful threat—far more effective than calling the police. It may have been mere coincidence, but the goats disappeared the next day. We were free of them for some years.

Billy and the Harem

Years later, as summer progressed and the goats had eaten everything in their enclosure, the former nanny's grandson-in-law started releasing them into the road. Aris spoke with him about this, explaining that the goats climbed up our driveway and ate our plants. He refused to believe that hobbled goats could get to our house.

Within ten minutes of that conversation, goats were at the top of the driveway, munching away on our fig tree. Aris chased them away and spoke to him again. This scene played out repeatedly, each time followed by calls to the former nanny's daughter, who owned the goats and the enclosure, and was distressed too.

Despite repeated assurances that the problem had been taken care of, the goats attacked. The billy goat led a harem of five females up our driveway early one morning when Aris was in the U.S., and I was home alone. I'd stayed up late the night before, engrossed in a book, *A Little Life* by Hanya Yanagihara, and after getting up at seven to check for goats, I made the disastrous decision to go back to bed—one I would soon regret. It was hot, so the air conditioning was on, and the windows were closed.

Later that morning, Cousin George's seventh-grade grandson came over to return a borrowed flashlight, only to be confronted by the billy goat. Having heard stories about an unfortunate billy goat encounter his father had as a child, he wisely retreated. I'd have done the same. The billy goat was a big, bold fellow who wouldn't back down; he put his head down and stared intently as if calculating just how much effort it would take to butt you off the cliff.

By the time the grandson left, the goats had eaten our small fig tree down to the ground and stripped every leaf and branch they could reach from the big fig tree. Strangely, they don't eat the sweet fruit of the fig, just everything else—leaves, bark, and branches. Perhaps encouraged by the grandson's retreat, the billy goat boldly led his tribe up our front steps and around our house on the flagstone walkway to the gardens.

By 9:30, when the grandson came back and successfully returned the flashlight to me, the goats were gone—after having eaten every leaf from every grapevine, three of the four rose bushes, and most of our other plantings. I was devastated.

Pot-Banging and Lock-Picking

The marauding goats returned to the scene of their crime at 7:30 the next morning. I was waiting. They hadn't made it to the garden before I chased them. There wasn't much left to protect, but I was mad! I hoped no one would see me running down the driveway after them, banging a pot with a metal spoon, and throwing stones—badly. I chased them off three times before they gave up.

Chasing goats: morning exercise in the Island countryside.

My hope to have gone unnoticed was in vain. Cousin George, his daughter, and her whole family watched from their house and found the whole scene extremely entertaining. The youngest asked if I would do it again.

Aside from making a spectacle of myself, I managed to lock myself out of the house! I'm not a morning person and had been up until 2:00 a.m. again, still engrossed in the same book. After I rushed out the front door to photograph the criminal goats and chase them away, the door shut behind me. It locks automatically, and I hadn't taken the key.

The key was still in the lock, inside the locked door.

Wearing only a rather thin caftan and sandals, I had to figure out how to get back in the house. Given my attire—or lack thereof—I didn't want to walk over to Cousin George's place to get help.

We kept an extra front door key hidden on the property specifically for emergencies of this sort, but you can't insert a key into a lock that's already occupied by another key. I scoured the yard, testing sticks, until I found a piece of fairly stiff wire some workers had left behind. After several tries, I was able to nudge the key from the inside of the lock, unlock the door with the emergency key, and re-enter the house.

At that point, I decided to go back to bed.

CHAPTER TWENTY-FOUR

Return of the Cat

The cat we fed the first summer came back the following year, looking none the worse for wear, though she was clearly pregnant. I warned her not to bring any more scorpions. We were out with friends the first night after she returned, but I left food in her dish. We didn't see her when we came home, but spotted two very skittish kittens, about ten or twelve weeks old. They took off the moment they saw us.

We didn't see either of the kittens again for several days, but another homely, mostly black female and a large orange tabby showed up to eat. Late that night, we were awakened by caterwauling. We weren't sure whether our veranda had become a trysting place for amorous felines, or a territorial fight was in progress. I got up to take a look. It was the latter.

Mavroúla was at the top of one set of veranda stairs, hissing and growling at an unseen foe. She was defending her territory and food supply. Since she wasn't the least bit shy—she'd gladly have come into the house if I let her—I opened and closed the door loudly, getting rid of the intruder or intruders. Mavroúla then curled up on the *pentzoúla* to wait for breakfast.

One of the kittens returned to our verandas two or three times a day to eat, more often than Mavroúla. He was a handsome black and tan mackerel tabby with a bit of white on his chin and enormous ears, but he was feral—and not the brightest bulb in the lamp. He kept trying to eat Mavroúla's food, even though he had the very same food in his own dish, and he batted her tail more than once. She growled at him and made other noises as if she were telling him off, but he didn't seem to get the message. His antics kept us amused.

Aftí is the Greek word for ear, and I dubbed the kitten *Aftoúlas* because his were so big. He was like Pavlov's dog. I whistled for him when I went out with food and fresh water, and he always came, meowing as he ran. He was too afraid to get close to us, but he liked to hang around whenever we were outside, and he talked to us. He meowed when he thought we were too close to him, and he meowed back to us if we spoke to him. But he wouldn't let us touch him, though he was extremely jealous—practically turning somersaults in frustration—when he saw us petting Mavroúla.

I made a toy for him out of a piece of thin cardboard folded into a fan and tied to a string. He came within a foot of me to bat at it. Otherwise, he amused himself with the lizards. There are two varieties of lizards here, one type that changes color called *sávres* (which I believe to be Aegean wall lizards), and green and brown speckled creatures, a bit thinner and with longer legs, called *samiamídia*. I'm told that they're geckos.

I never see any *sávres* during the day, but the *samiamídia* are interesting to watch as they sun themselves on the flagstone verandas in the morning. As the stones get warmer, they stand on one front leg and the opposing rear leg, lifting the others. When those get too hot, they switch. They generally disappear from late morning until early evening, as the midday sun is too intense.

Since Mavroúla was quite aggressive about defending her territory against other adult cats, I suspect that she allowed Aftoúlas to stay only because he was still a kitten. He was lucky. Not only was he well-fed by us, but Mavroúla taught him to hunt—a necessity for the winter months.

In expectation of Mavroúla's impending kitten birth, I prepared a box with a towel and a flapped opening. Mavroúla ignored it and gave birth to her three kittens on the steep, rough hillside below the house under one of the wild green bushes, known as *skínos*. We discovered the kittens' location from the sound of their mewling and put fresh water in the shade near them to keep Mavroúla from becoming dehydrated while she was nursing them.

After four or five weeks, Mavroúla brought the kittens to the house. By that time, she was tired of feeding them and wanted us to do so. The two males wouldn't come near us, but the female, a calico, was content with her mother's judgment and happily approached for kitten kibble. She also let us pet her, but I couldn't tell if she enjoyed it.

We ended up putting food and water near the back of the verandas for the male kittens and food, water, and treats, like yogurt, near the house for Mavroúla and the calico. The clever girl grew much more rapidly than her brothers.

We had a pair of ladder-back chairs on the veranda near the dining room door, one upside down on top of the other, with an old pillow on top. When Mavroúla and Aftoúlas took off for a hunt at night, the three kittens curled together on the pillow in the "cage" formed by the legs and stretchers of the upside-down chair. Once Mavroúla and Aftoúlas returned, sometimes with a dead rat for the kittens to try—yuck!—all five felines snuggled up together under the windows on one of the *pentzoúles*, making a nest from a *kourelóu* (rag woven mat).

CHAPTER TWENTY-FIVE

Other Island Fauna

It turns out that the cure for attacks by a murder of crows is cats sleeping under your windows.

Once the crows left us alone, the sparrows and partridges came back. We have many nests in our wind-carved rocks. I'm often awakened (temporarily) around 7:00 a.m. by the sound of the sparrows in our colony chattering at each other and their off-spring. The sparrows never sing early in the summer; they only sing after their progeny have left the nest (I know a few human parents who can relate to that).

Despite the mess they make on the flagstones beside the rocks along the east side of the house, I really enjoy the sparrows—with minor exceptions. At times, we've been plagued by remarkably befuddled birds. What do you call sparrows that start building nests in mid-July, for heaven's sake? Or those that choose to ignore unoccupied holes twenty feet above ground in the adjacent wind-carved rocks and try to build a nest on top of a working shutter—hardly a stable base—beside the door we use the most?

One pair broke the plastic grate covering the vent for the stove hood to nest inside—keeping me from using the exhaust fan—and persisted in rebuilding after their partial nests were repeatedly destroyed. These birds ought not breed! To keep them out, we had to cover the vent opening with layers of duct tape until the painters came with their long ladders and replaced the broken grate.

The partridges show up a little later in the morning. Large and lovely birds, they walk and hop (not fly) all in a row from the lower levels of the terraced planting areas to the upper ones—and from there, up the mountain and over the stone wall at the top. Sometimes, they take the time to "bathe" themselves in the dirt beneath the flowering plants.

There's always a "watch partridge" standing guard—absolutely motionless—over the flock, adults and chicks. Partridges have a most remarkable call. It's neither a quack nor a gobble but has elements of each—I call it a "quabble"—and at times they sound just like squeaky bed springs. I'm glad to see them thriving—and sorry when I hear gunshots in September.

From time to time, we see jackrabbits in the road or hopping up Cousin George's driveway around sunset. This is wonderful since rabbits had all but disappeared from the Island due to overhunting. Cousin George has an orchard and a vegetable garden, as does our neighbor Kóstas—major attractions for rabbits. I doubt that they're as happy to see the rabbits as we are, but I'm sure that they'd rather see rabbits than rats!

In a year of drought, the Island had lots of rats. I can't tell you how much I hate rats. On our property, the only fruits are prickly pears and figs. There are no figs when there's a drought, but the rats eat the prickly pear cacti mercilessly. In Pittsburgh, we used "Have a Heart" traps to capture, unharmed, the field mice that entered the house from the woods, but I have no empathy for rats. Aside from everything else, they attract snakes, so I'm happy when Aris puts down rat poison.

It's unnerving to open the exterior dining room door to find a rat drinking from the saucer under a pot of basil less than two feet away. The first time this happened, we were expecting seven guests for dinner. I told Aris that we simply couldn't take a chance on a rat running into the house with people going in and out that door all night—or risk a rat spooking a guest and causing a fall. He took care of it, of course. But while he was in Athens, another rat showed up to drink from the same saucer under the basil. I saw it when I was watering the plants and turned the hose on it, driving it away.

It takes a great deal of poison to kill a rat! In that drought year, after fifty pellets of poison, we found three dead rats and were hoping we'd solved the problem. Then a fat rat showed up on the driveway just as Cousin George was leaving with several other guests after dinner. The count of poison pellets used went up to 100, and the body count of dead rats—those we found—rose to eight. We don't leave poisoned dead rats lying around if we can help it. I confess that I wouldn't mind if the crows ate one, but I'd be sorry if a hawk did.

We hear and see hawks floating on the upper air in our valley. When we see three in late summer, we know that they've successfully raised that year's eyas. We suspect that they killed the *ochiá* (Greek viper) we found nearly beheaded at the base of our driveway in the middle of the afternoon—not a time when snakes are typically active. We asked Cousin George, Kóstas, and the others in the valley about it, but all denied having seen or killed the snake.

Of course, the snake killer might have been a *koukouvágia*, a small owl named after its call, though these owls are not usually active in mid-afternoon either. These petite owls say, "Coo-coo-vow," never "who." One evening, we were sitting in the *alóni*—the circular part of our veranda—watching the full moon rise, and a *koukouvágia* landed on the *alóni* wall. It stayed for a minute, watching us curiously as it bobbed its head.

We've also had an eagle owl (*boúfos*) living nearby. We heard her hooting at night, and she did say "who." We saw her once—more than two feet tall—on the road as we were coming home in the wee hours of the morning.

Late one afternoon, as we were getting ready to drive to the main village, we found a fledgling eagle owl, perhaps eight inches tall, smack in the middle of our driveway, very close to the garage door, making it impossible for us to leave. The poor thing had been worn out by its attempts at flight. Touching it was out of the question; we feared its mother would abandon it. Approaching it accomplished nothing. It was so exhausted, stunned, or both, that it didn't even try to move away from us.

I retrieved a broom and long-handled dustpan, thinking that I might be able to nudge it onto the dustpan with the broom and carry it to the side of the driveway to await rescue by its mother, but it was terrified of the broom and hopped off to the side into the dirt, allowing us to leave. We checked when we returned and were delighted that it was no longer there.

Native fauna in our valley also includes bats (*nychterídes*). I don't know what species of bat inhabits the Island, but I had a close encounter with one. One night after dinner, as we were sitting in the *alóni* watching the stars, I saw something small drop from the sky and land on the *pentzoúla* on the far side of the table. It began slowly to move, and I went over to investigate. It was quite a small bat with large translucent ears—not unattractive. I hoped it would stick around and eat lots of mosquitoes!

Rather incredibly, we once saw a flamingo standing in our road very late at night. They're not native here—it must have been migrating. Migrating blue herons and an entire flock of cranes have also paid us visits.

We often see and hear a sort of mourning dove, known as *dekaoktoúres* because their call sounds as if they're saying *dekaoktó* (eighteen), over and over. As in every other coastal area I've seen in the world, we have seagulls and cormorants. The seagulls appeared in our valley after the goats were replaced with ducks and geese. They like the poultry feed. We also see migratory ducks.

And we've had some special visitors. Once, a single swan (*kýknos*) showed up and paddled back and forth across our bay all day. Another time, we were graced with a brief visit by a hoopoe (*tsalapeteinós*), a large yellow bird with black and white striped wings and a high, black-tipped crest.

I'm told that quail (*ortýkia*) and eagles (*aetoí*) inhabit the Island, but I haven't seen them. There are thrushes (*tsíchles*) and turtle doves *(trygónia),* both hunted as game birds. Thrushes are quite delicious with a sauce made from their livers (sorry, I don't have the recipe). There are also teeny-tiny birds that say, "Tsi-tsi-tsi," known as *tsitsinákia,* but I don't know their species. Finches, perhaps? Swallows come in the fall, and I imagine there are other birds I've yet to observe.

One or more hedgehogs (*skantzóchoiroi)* live near the base of our driveway. Another hedgehog is sometimes seen in the evening, hurrying along the dry riverbed road near Kóstas's place or closer to the beach. One night we returned home to find a small hedgehog on our driveway. It ran to the dirt on the side and plopped down as if it were dead. Look up European hedgehogs—they're adorably cute! I'd been told (incorrectly) that they eat lettuce and other greens. I didn't have any, but I put some cucumber out for it. Unsurprisingly, given what I later learned, it displayed no interest.

I'd assumed that the local legend that hedgehogs kill venomous snakes was just an old wives' tale, but I researched European hedgehogs, and sure enough, they do kill and eat snakes, along with snails, mice, worms, centipedes, and frogs! Reportedly, they have a genetic resistance to certain kinds of venom. And they can pierce a snake's skin by curling themselves into a ball and rolling over it. The next time I'm near one, I'll skip the cucumber and offer animal protein. Sadly, we'll never enjoy having them in our "garden" because they can't negotiate walls or steps.

Elsewhere on the Island are frogs. Have you ever read or seen *The Frogs* by Aristophanes? In that play, the frogs say, "*Vre-keke-kéx koáx koáx.*" Very, very odd to my American ear. Before I ever came to the Island, Aris and I had an ongoing disagreement, with me insisting that no frog ever made any such sound, and Aris maintaining that Greek frogs say exactly that.

He was right, of course. There's a small footbridge over a creek bed between the main village and the one above it. In early summer, or after the first fall rain, the frogs can be heard clearly there. There's never a croak or a ribbit; they say only *Vre-keke-kéx vre-keke-kéx koáx koáx.*

The menagerie in our backyard is one of the many reasons I love this Island.

CHAPTER TWENTY-SIX

Miss Priss and William of Orange

The third summer of our retirement, we hadn't seen Mavroúla, but a very friendly white cat with patches of orange stripes approached us, purring and rubbing against our legs, as we walked to Fáros. On leaving the restaurant, we took the fish heads with us and gave them to the cat. She purred again and followed us most of the way back to our bay before turning around.

We found the same cat along the pathway the next time we walked to Fáros and stopped to pet her. On the way back, we gave her fish remains again. She gobbled them up, then raced after us. That time, she didn't turn back, but followed us all the way to our home, where we fed her.

She'd obviously been someone's pet once, as she was very friendly and affectionate. She jumped in our laps, purring, the instant we sat down outside. She had some wounds, which she allowed me to treat. She also tolerated receiving flea treatment. She was a prissy cat, so I named her Miss Priss, or Missy.

Some days after Missy took up residence, Mavroúla turned up—too late. We'd have been glad to have them both, but Missy, a larger animal, chased Mavroúla across the valley to Cousin George's place. Mavroúla stayed away and Missy ruled.

Missy soon made her preferences known. We brought her leftovers from lunch, but she wasn't interested; she wanted kibble. I tossed the rejected food over a wall. Soon after, two orange ears appeared at that spot.

They belonged to a big, old orange bullseye tabby cat, so beaten up from his battles that his face had little fur but was mostly scarred. Missy didn't like it one bit, but I felt sorry for the poor old guy, treated his wounds, applied flea treatment, and fed him separately from Missy, who swiped at him whenever she could. Because of his battle scars and color, I named him William of Orange—Willy for short.

He expressed his gratitude for the care and the food by becoming the very definition of "underfoot." We couldn't walk outside without him tripping us as he wove between our legs, making a noise like a poorly maintained motor. It took me a while to realize that the strange noise was his novice attempt at purring.

Exceptionally affectionate, Missy wanted badly to be in the house with us. I didn't want a house cat with dirty paws, but she was persistent. Once in a while, she snuck in when I was carrying the laundry, and I always found her curled on a dining chair cushion, hidden by the tablecloth.

She also worked at the window screens until she figured out how to raise one side so she could slip inside. I couldn't stay mad when she was so happy to be with me. She was with us every day, and I worried about her health.

A friend told me that a French veterinarian was on the Island for two weeks to neuter animals. I looked up how to fashion a cat carrier from a box—it's amazing what you can find on YouTube—and made one, intending to take Missy to the vet. But she disappeared, completely.

Whether by coincidence or ESP, she was gone the entire two weeks the vet was on the Island. We didn't catch a glimpse of her even once. When she resurfaced, looking thin and gritty, the French veterinarian was gone. I guess I should have tried to take Willy, but I didn't trust him to let me put him in a box, or not to spray in the car.

I tried hard to find someone to care for Missy and Willy over the winter. One of Aris's childhood friends was impressed by Missy's manners and affectionate nature. He said he'd take her to Athens as a companion for his aunt, whose beloved cat had recently died. When the time came, however, he worried that his aunt wouldn't want her and backed out.

Although I'd tried before—unsuccessfully—with Mavroúla and Aftoúlas, I tried again to hire someone to feed Missy and Willy through the winter. I had no better luck. No one lives in our bay in the winter, and no one was willing to do it. Faní agreed to feed the cats until she left the Island in December, but they stopped showing up soon after we departed.

Missy came back to us the next summer. Willy, poor old guy, didn't. A year later, Missy didn't return, but we found her in Fáros, looking fat and strong. Evidently, she found a forever home.

CHAPTER TWENTY-SEVEN

Gone Goat

In a year of drought, in the hottest part of the summer, a skinny, old, double-hobbled nanny goat showed up at the base of our driveway. She trembled from dehydration. Aris lugged buckets of water down our steep driveway for her. She drained the first in one go. He also cut her hobbles so she could better fend for herself. Then he collected fig leaves and took those to her too. After that, he asked everyone in the valley about her, but no one knew anything.

Miserably thin, she stayed at the base of our driveway. Aris kept feeding the poor thing and taking her water, so I named her Molly. Having had no luck with our neighbors, he tried the mayor and the police. No luck there either. Unhelpfully, the police promised to haul the carcass away if she died. At that point, we started telling everyone we knew that there was an unclaimed goat at the base of our driveway, free to anyone who wanted her.

In October, right before we left for the winter, Molly disappeared. I'd love to think that someone gave her a good home, but I suspect that she became a delicious meal. Bear in mind that a quick, humane death is a far better fate than slow dehydration and starvation. Though often idyllic, Island life can be harsh too.

Molly isn't the only goat to have disappeared. After years of battles, wall building and fence erection, the goats across the road were replaced with pigs. Not much is cuter—or more delicious—than a piglet. Better yet, the pigs don't jump the walls of their enclosures and attack our plantings.

Alongside the pigs are geese and ducks. Geese are very noisy and walk up our driveway, pooping everywhere—but they don't eat the flowers either.

CHAPTER TWENTY-EIGHT

Ant Wars Redux: Another Summer, Another Invasion

It was morning, late in July. It hadn't been particularly hot, but the Island hadn't seen a drop of rain since early May. As I walked to the kitchen, still sleepy, I saw something black on the rim of the sink. It was moving! I approached cautiously. The pastry brush I'd taken from the dishwasher and left there to dry was crawling with ants. Obviously, the dishwasher hadn't removed all the olive oil, and the ants were having a feast.

After several years of peace, ants once again invaded the kitchen—and our bedroom, living room, dining room, and even the bathroom. The winter had been exceptionally dry, and the ants were desperately seeking water. Teeny-tiny brown ants invaded from hairline cracks in the grout where the kitchen backsplash and counter met. The minuscule monsters also came from a hole they excavated in the concrete under our bedroom balcony door and from behind the bathroom mirror, glued to the tile wall.

Black ants—the size of sugar ants in the States—swarmed out of holes they bored between the stone floors and the concrete walls in the living and dining rooms. They even came from the ceiling! Aris was sitting at the dining room table—fortunately reading, not eating—when one dropped right in front of him. Before that happened, we'd been trying in vain to figure out how the ants were getting onto the tablecloth. The mystery was solved, but the problem remained.

I realize that I'm not talking about roaches, but it's truly disgusting to wake up, walk to the kitchen to start your tea, and find the sink and countertop alive with ants. It's even worse to finish your breakfast, go to brush your teeth, and find ants camped out on the case of your dental retainer—revolting! Nor is it much fun to start working at your desk in the living room only to find ants crawling on your laptop—and up your legs. I *had* to do something.

I scoured the exterior of the house and applied the poison Fani recommended everywhere I found ants. I applied it indoors, too—but in the kitchen, that meant scrubbing the countertops clean of poison every morning, reapplying after breakfast, and then scrubbing and reapplying over and over again.

The ants disappeared!

My victory was short-lived. After a week or so, ants returned with renewed determination from new holes. I bought and applied a poison a friend swore by, only to have the same experience. Same result with ammonia. Filling the holes with silicone accomplished nothing—they blithely excavated new ones.

Next came a syrupy concoction the pharmacist highly recommended, promising that the ants would take it back to the nest and it would kill the colony. It worked for over two weeks, but just as I was about to celebrate and relax, they returned in force.

The most maddening event was when the ants emerged from behind outlets in the kitchen wall and raided a kitchen cabinet. Bizarrely, they didn't invade the cabinet with the honey and fruit preserves. The one they overran stored olives, crackers, and other savory items.

Fortunately, due to an ingrained habit left over from living in roach-ridden Florida in the '70s, I'd sealed all the foods in Ziploc bags. So, the ants did no harm—except to my psyche. I countered the assault with a new weapon—cayenne pepper, liberally deployed. I prevailed: They evacuated my cabinet.

At the suggestion of a friend on Facebook, I also got Borax (safe for use on kitchen counters) from the pharmacy. Using it unsparingly just about everywhere, I got them under control.

Until the next time, of course.

CHAPTER TWENTY-NINE

Guests: The Good, the Bad, and the Ugly

For many years, we planned to stay in Pittsburgh when we retired, except in the summer. I loved everything about Pittsburgh. Everything, that is, except the weather and the roads. But two heavy, cold, gray winters back-to-back, one with enough snow and ice to close the airport, put an end to that plan. We decided to live in Naples, Florida, when we're not on the Island. We figured that if you live in warm and sunny places by the sea—whether in Southwest Florida or on a small island in the Aegean—your friends will find you, sooner or later.

Pandemic aside, that's true. The problem is that it's not necessarily just friends who find you. Acquaintances and less than favorite relations sometimes ambush you, brazenly inviting themselves or asking to be invited. Learning how to dodge those assaults is a fundamental survival skill for those who live in tourist destinations.

When the Island house was new, a young relative (who'd never previously shown the slightest interest in our company) asked to stay with us for *several weeks*. Alarm bells went off in my head: Hosting even the most congenial guest for weeks is a strain, never mind a teenager we barely knew.

She fancied herself a vegetarian at the time, so I first described the available foods. She was stunned that there were no McDonald's or Pizza Huts on the Island (and even today there still aren't any chains here) but conceded that she could survive on the local fare. She was somewhat more daunted when I told her—as was the case then—that we had no television. But her interest withered away completely when I told her that we had no internet, either. Brilliant sky, crystalline sea, sunshine, exotic location, and amazing food weren't enough for her—thankfully.

Out of the blue, one acquaintance asked when I planned to invite her to our place in Greece. She wasn't someone I knew well, and I was rather taken aback by such a bold approach. Recovering, I explained that one of the reasons that Aris and I have been married so long is that he doesn't invite anyone I don't know to stay at our home, and I don't invite anyone he doesn't know (I think she's been plotting to meet him ever since). I offered to help her find a hotel, pensión, or bed and breakfast, but she wasn't interested.

We also learned long ago that not everyone appreciates our lifestyle on the Island. When asked, we explain that we eat, swim, boat, walk, sleep, and read. Although we also entertain and go out with friends, it's a pretty quiet life. There are plenty of bars on the Island with throbbing music and exotic cocktails during tourist season, but we don't patronize them.

We go to restaurants and tavernas around the Island some evenings, especially before and after peak season and when we have houseguests. In the main village, we patronize some of the restaurants and tavernas along a narrow, ancient stone-paved street known as the *stenó* (the narrow). The *stenó* is also lined with shops, bars, houses, and churches. Several tavernas have their tables on or abutting the *stenó*, allowing diners to watch the passers-by and the many children playing there, often quite late at night (they're safe here).

We also take guests to a village on a hill above the main village, where large homes were built by shipowners in the classical style, with walled gardens and magnificent wrought iron gates. Aris's great-grandfather, who was one of those shipowners, is entombed in a church in that village. Additionally, we take them to the various beaches to swim and eat and always to *Kástro*, the old capital of the Island.

Every island I've visited in the Cyclades has a "*kástro*," which means "castle." The *kástro* here is a walled town, built centuries ago atop a cliff overlooking a narrow, pebbly-beached bay. The wall surrounding the town—composed of the backs of conjoined houses—is entered through tunnel-like gates, known as *loggias* (from the Venetian occupation of the Island, but pronounced here as "londgias"). Uniquely on the Island, that village has two, and in some places three, levels of houses and churches, some accessed by footbridges above the lower road.

Archaic marble columns and sarcophagi are scattered throughout *Kástro*, relics of its ancient past. Some have even been incorporated into homes there. The oldest homes have very low doorways with split doors—the top third of the door can open while the bottom part stays shut. The seaside of the village is circled by a stone-paved walking path, offering lovely views, especially at sunset.

When I first came to the Island in 1978, the road to *Kástro* was unpaved. The town was relatively isolated and had its own dialect. There were no stores there then, but a salesman with a donkey carrying a wide variety of household goods walked the streets of the village, hawking his wares.

———◆———

Folks with bad knees or hips or who just don't like physical exercise aren't very happy on our hilly Island where the streets of most towns are stone steps, never mind the many steps in our house and our twenty-degree driveway. One guest, who bragged of being fit, called the 300-meter walk back from the beach with the trudge up our driveway the "Bataan Death March!" Other guests have balked at walking for thirty minutes to go to dinner in the neighboring bay on the well-maintained and lighted stone path, which we've never thought strenuous, though it does have quite a few stairs.

With rare exception, a person who doesn't like the sea isn't going to be happy here. After many invitations, I persuaded Anita, a very dear friend, to come. Every fall during law school, I listened to her talk about having spent her summer at her pool, and much later about the pool at her new home in San Diego. I surmised that she loved the water.

When she arrived on the Island, I was dumbfounded to learn that she didn't care to swim or boat or be in the sea at all. She'd spent all those years just sitting beside her pools without going in! Fortunately, she loved the Island's quaint villages and food, and she loved sitting on the beaches taking in the view of the sea and the islands floating on the horizon. She loved being here so much that a photo taken from our veranda became the background for her Facebook page.

One of the foods Anita loved here was Imám Bayildí (meaning, the Imam fainted), which like many "Greek" dishes, originated in Turkey. There are several stories about the origin of the name, but the one I like is that the Imam was overcome by the delicious flavor of the food. I had to beg Anita to taste the dish, which Kyría Évi prepared wonderfully. Anita insisted that she didn't like eggplants, but after much prodding, she finally agreed to try it.

She fell in love at first bite and eagerly ate it all. An accomplished cook, Anita later asked for the recipe for the dish she dubbed "eggplants poached in oil." Imám is best here because the eggplants are sweeter, but it's delicious anywhere. There are other versions, but Kyría Évi helped me with the recipe in the Appendix, and it has garnered a good deal of praise, including "*eínai óneiro*" (it's a dream).

We sometimes misjudge which friends will enjoy being here. We were certain that one friend would love it, but she didn't, not really. Her husband is one of Aris's Greek childhood friends, and she'd been to Greece with him many times. She knew something of the language, and she enjoyed the cuisine. We also knew each other well and had stayed in each other's homes in the States.

But simply having a room and a beach chair in a bay with one of the best views in Greece wasn't enough. To her, vacation meant maid service, a cabana boy, and a piña colada—desires we couldn't fulfill. We enjoyed hosting her, but she'd have been happier at the resort hotel in Vathí.

Everyone who has ever had a home in a beautiful place has a "bad guest" story. This is mine. Though big-hearted, this friend talked like a magpie, often using a formal version of Greek, which posed quite a challenge for me.

One evening, Aris and I were at dinner with her and several other mutual friends when she heard that he was leaving for meetings in America. Excitedly, she announced to the whole group that this was perfect—she'd stay with me and keep me company! On learning that Aris was leaving on Sunday, she promptly asked, in a voice loud enough to be heard by all, whether he'd mind if she arrived at our place Saturday before he left. We enjoy having company, but we have a strong preference for choosing our guests—and the timing of their stays—ourselves. However, had she told me earlier that she needed a place to stay, I would certainly have invited her.

We had a previous engagement for Saturday night and encouraged her to join us. She declined, protesting that she just wanted to watch news and go to bed early. I offered to show her how to access movies on our very complicated system, but she denied having any interest in watching anything beside the news, which we left on for her. Curiosity got the better of her though, and she messed around with the controls for the TV and internet, looking for movies, and ended up crashing the whole media system!

On Sunday, I wasn't feeling great and didn't swim. She took a nap after lunch; I didn't. The painter called and said he'd be at the house just after seven in the morning. I explained these things and that I planned to go to bed early. She was still talking my ears off at 11:15 p.m. After many conspicuous glances at my watch, I gave up and told her I really needed to go to bed, and needed her to go up to her room, so I could turn off the outside lights and lock the doors.

This guest said she wanted to help me make *spanakópita* (spinach pie). Her 'help' mostly consisted of advice about what

I was doing wrong in her opinion and what I should do instead. On the last day of her visit, she decided to reciprocate and cook something for me. I should have discouraged her because, despite her good intentions, she made a mess in my kitchen. It was bad enough that I seriously contemplated letting the cat in to clean the floor. To her credit, the food was delicious.

She set drinking glasses on my wood furniture without using the coasters at her elbow and left her dirty dishes and dirty napkins on my natural linen upholstery. (Admittedly, I'm persnickety about the furniture.) To top it all off, she found the five screened windows in her bedroom suite inadequate. Not wanting to use the air conditioner, she propped open the curtained door on the east side of her room, which is like a wind tunnel. At least when the curtains blew off, she chased them down the mountain and retrieved them. I love her, but I breathed easier after she left.

———◆———

We offer guests comfortable accommodations within easy walking distance of the beach, a stunning view, breakfast every morning, wine and nibbles before dinner, and use of the Wi-Fi, washing machine, drying rack, and the extra snorkel masks and fins. We also provide transportation by boat or car around the Island. Normally, we provide an evening meal only on the night of arrival, when folks typically are tired after their trip, and most other meals are eaten out.

Two guests seemed to think that, since we were giving them free accommodations, we should also pay the full tab, including tip, at every restaurant or taverna. They came separately and didn't know each other. Coincidentally, both were divorced women who had solicited invitations to stay with us.

Aris once described someone as being so tight that he squeaked when he walked. I was reminded of this expression when each of these women visited. When it was their turn to pay (sixth meal eaten, third meal eaten out) and no indication of intent to pay was given, we resorted to handing over the bill, saying it was correct, and the waiter could take payment.

This strategy wasn't initially successful in either case. They each said, without the slightest display of embarrassment, that she hadn't brought her wallet. The following day as we were leaving the house, we asked, as innocently as possible, whether she remembered to bring it.

We also had a guest of a guest—not the first such visitor, but maybe the last—who seemed to think that we ran a free hotel. She didn't have much to say to us and showed up for breakfast long after everyone else had eaten.

With barely a word of greeting, she asked for coffee and took it and her food outside to enjoy by herself. On the last night of her visit, she preferred to stay in, which meant, of course, that I'd be preparing the meal. When I asked about her absence, I was told that she'd gone to her room, asking to be called when it was time to eat!

That experience caused me to wonder whatever had happened to manners. I was taught that an arriving guest never sits before asking what she can do to help, always jumps up to assist with serving, makes pleasant contributions to the conversation, and never leaves until she's washed—or helped wash—the dishes. It wasn't just Louisville. At least one of Aris's cousins here had the same upbringing. That guest's guest obviously didn't.

Despite these rare exceptions, most of our guests have been delightful and deeply appreciated the beauty and culture of the Island. Some have made multiple repeat visits. Several hiked with us to the top of the tallest peak (about 2500 feet) capped by the former monastery of Prophet Elijah—where on a clear day you can see eighteen surrounding islands. Others hiked with us to *panigýria* (saints' day celebrations) and got into the spirit of the event. Some have refrained from hiking, but have snorkeled happily, danced to classic rock on our verandas, or pondered the night sky.

Because these visits were lovely, there isn't much to tell about them. I will mention this: We have difficulty persuading visitors to wear shoes around our house. One morning, we had just cautioned a guest about this when a stinging centipede (*scolópendra*) strolled out of our bedroom. He got the point.

That's *not* a normal occurrence, by the way. The covers of the access points to the conduit in our bedroom had been removed to allow the conduit to dry out after the wires, damaged by humidity, had been replaced. But it was a graphic reminder of the dangers of the Greek countryside.

Good guests leave us with warm memories, but bad guests give us the best stories.

CHAPTER THIRTY

More Plumbing
Adventures

The toilet in the master bathroom broke, most inconveniently, one night when Aris was out of town and I had a houseguest. At least I could still flush it by dumping a pot of water into it. That toilet cost me my swim the next day. I'd just reached the beach with my guest when the plumber—the hero of the top-of-the-cabinet drainpipe repair—returned my call and said he'd be there within the hour. So, back up to the house I went.

He arrived about two hours later. Unfortunately, part of the toilet was broken, so he couldn't do the repair then. He said he'd return with the part *se lígo* (in a little while). I'd been on the Island long enough to understand that "a little while" doesn't mean very soon. I took the time to drive my guest to her destination.

More than an hour after I returned, the plumber arrived with the new part, installed it, cleaned up, and charged me a grand total of €40—for the work, two trips to our house in the country, and the part, which cost €23. When offered a tip, he politely declined. I told him that it would give me pleasure if he and his helper would enjoy a beer on us. At that point, he accepted.

The same plumber installed the plumbing fixtures in the new guest house. The bracket to hold the showerhead on the wall hadn't arrived when he did the rest of the work. When it finally came—at the peak of tourist season—we called him, and he came at 9:00 p.m. one night to install it. He refused any compensation whatsoever—even beer money—insisting that it was just part of the job for which he'd already been paid.

Things are generally expensive here, but services are often ridiculously cheap.

CHAPTER THIRTY-ONE

Greek Speak

Once in Greece, you get an automatic promotion: Instead of Ms. or Mrs., you become *kyría*, literally "lady." Instead of Mister, you become *kýrios*, literally "lord" or "master." (They're the equivalent of "Mrs." and "Mr." in modern usage). As in the Southern United States, where surnames are dropped once people become well-acquainted, and women are addressed as "Miz Laura," the title is often used with your given name. Though it just means "Mrs." now, I still like being called "Lady Laura."

Even better, you're returned to your youth. When speaking to a group of friends, Greeks consistently address them as "children" (*paidiá*), as in, "Children, where will we go to eat tonight?" One day, during lunch with a group of friends from Athens who came to the Island for a holiday weekend, one of the men referred to me as "*to koritsáki*," (the little girl). Only in Greece would such an appellation be applied to a retired woman.

This book isn't intended for language instruction—which is a good thing, as I explain later—but as long as we're on the subject of common expressions, you may wish to know that:

"Welcome" is *kalós órises* (in the singular familiar) or *kalós orísate* (in the plural or formal). The correct response is *kalós sas vríkame*, which means "good to find you."

"Hello" is *geiá sou* (in the singular familiar) and *geiá sas* (in the plural or formal). Those *g*'s are pronounced as *y*'s—as in "yee-ah sue."

"Pleased to meet you" is *chárika polý* (the initial "ch" is pronounced as a hard "h").

"How are you?" is *ti káneis* (informal) or *pós eíste* (formal); the typical response is *polý kalá, efcharistó* (very well, thank you).

"Goodbye" is *geiá sou* or *geiá sas*—yes, just like hello—or just *geiá*; and there is also *antío*, which is closer to "farewell."

"Yes" is *naí*—which, unfortunately, sounds negative to English speakers—or *málista*.

"No" is *óchi* (often said with an upward motion of the chin). "No" can also be expressed merely with a cluck of the tongue and an upward motion of the chin. There's an old Greek joke in which a shepherd on one hill yells across to another on a different hill, asking whether he's seen his black sheep. The second shepherd clucks his tongue and tilts his chin.

"Please" and "you're welcome" are *parakaló*.

"Thank you" is *efcharistó* (though if you say, "if Harry stole" quickly, you should be understood).

"Pardon me" is *me synchoreíte*, or you could say "sorry," which is *sygnómi*.

Finally, one requests the check at a restaurant or taverna by mimicking writing in the air or asking for it: *to logariasmó parakaló*.

In Greek, the diminutive of a noun is formed by adding "aki," "itsa," "oula," or "ouli," For example, the word for nose is *mýti* (pronounced like mee-tee). A small nose is a *mytáki, mytoúla*, or *mytoúli*. I tell you this because the diminutive forms of nouns are used *incessantly*, in virtually all aspects of life. I'm rarely addressed as "Laura" by any friend; Greek friends almost invariably call me "Loráki" or sometimes "Lorítsa." There are augmentatives, too, although they're used less frequently than the diminutive forms. For example, a large nose is a *mytára*.

The use of diminutives extends to virtually all aspects of life. No Greek dining in a taverna ever asks for bread (*psomí*); instead, all Greeks, including big burly men, request a little, small bread (*lígo psomáki*). Similarly, beer (*bíra*) becomes *birítsa*, though there's no intention of ordering "small beer," and wine (*krasí*) inevitably morphs into *krasáki*, even when ordering a liter. Listening, one would think that no Greek ever consumes more than a tiny portion of anything.

Greek speech is also rich with other colorful endearments. Some are similar to the English terms, such as "my love" (*agápi mou*), "my doll" (*koúkla mou*), my baby (*moró mou*), "my sweet" (*glykiá mou*), and "my heart" (*kardiá mou*). Others are quite unusual, such as "my bug" (*zouzoúni mou*), "my eyes" (*mátia mou*), "my bird" (*pouláki mou*), "my blossom" (*bouboúki mou*), or "my gold" (*chrysó mou*).

These endearments are sprinkled freely in conversation with children, of course, but also with many others. You often hear someone using one or more of these expressions sarcastically when disagreeing with someone, e.g., "My gold, you're speaking nonsense"—though this wouldn't normally be expressed quite so politely.

One of my favorite Greek expressions is *se lígo*, which means "in a little while." This is an extraordinarily flexible expression, as it could mean five minutes or an hour, depending on the intention of the speaker. I once waited forty-five minutes for a taxi to arrive "*se lígo*." Another of my favorites is "sit a little" (*kátse lígo*), which is the equivalent of the American slang expression "hang on"—neither of which makes literal sense.

When a Greek sees or hears something quite remarkable, she or he may say, "We are not well" (*den eímaste kalá*). If someone doesn't care to participate in an activity, the expression is, "*den écho kéfi,*" which is not really translatable, but means more or less, "I'm not in the mood for it." "*Kéfi*" is another extremely flexible expression. If a party was wonderful, a Greek might say that it had *kéfi*.

Another interesting word is *misiadáki,* which is a diminutive form of "a half" and may be applied to objects as well as people. Some say that Aris is a *misiadáki* because he's here only part of the time. Others say it's because only his mother has Island roots.

Then there are rather extraordinary expressions using the verbs for eating and drinking. Instead of saying that they suffered through a heat wave, Greeks say that they "ate" the heat wave (*fágame ton káfsona*). On the other hand, if you say, "we ate the sea with a spoon," (*fágame ti thálassa me to koutáli*) you're saying that you were in the sea for a long time and enjoyed it tremendously. If someone "ate wood" (*éfage xýlo*), they were beaten or spanked.

Once, when Aris was discussing our imminent departure from the Island with someone, he said, "our breads have come to an end" (*teleiósane ta psomiá mas*), which means that the good time is ending—or we're dying. If a Greek thinks that someone walks on water, the expression is that he drinks water in that person's name (*pínei neró sto ónomá tou*).

When someone's been gluttonous, you may hear a Greek say that "he even ate the poisonous plant" (*éfage ton agléoura*); or "he even ate the tablecloth" (*éfage to katapétasma*). Someone who eats a lot is a "strong fork" (*geró piroúni*) and one who drinks a lot is a "strong glass" (*geró potíri*). If a cook wants to know whether a dish was enjoyed, he or she may ask, "does it say anything?" (*léei típota?*)

Other expressions that are unusual to an American include:

If the summer was great, you may hear that "it was sugar" (*ítan záchari*).

To describe a heavy rain, there's *ríchnei papádes* (it's raining priests) or *vréchei kareklopódara* (it's raining chair legs).

If you got a lot done, you might say that you "made priests" (*ékana papádes*).

Eye strain may be expressed as "I see small birds" (*vlépo poulákia*).

There's also *eínai ólo kólos kai idea*, which literally translates as "he's all ass and ideas" but means that he's all talk and no substance.

And my personal favorite: *chília mastigómata stin plátí kápoiou állou den ponáne kathólou* (a thousand lashes on someone else's back don't hurt [me] at all). I think of this whenever someone eagerly proposes projects entailing lots of work—for someone else to do.

⁕

I've been exposed to the Greek language for well over forty years but never took lessons until after we retired. I began learning

Greek aurally, from Mána, during the twelve winters Aris's parents spent with us in the States. The first year they stayed with us in Florida, but the others were spent in Pittsburgh. You wouldn't think it would be attractive to people from Athens to winter in Pittsburgh, but it was.

The temperature doesn't drop very low in Athens in the winter, but the cold is a damp cold, and in older apartment buildings, like my in-laws', fuel was shared, and the owners voted on its usage. The others in my in-laws' building worked during the day and didn't want to pay for heat in the daytime. Consequently, Babás and Mána were cold much of the day when they wintered in Athens. I was the beneficiary of this because I was able to enjoy their company for several months every winter for those twelve years.

After dinner in Pittsburgh, when we had cleared the table and if I didn't have legal work still to do in the evening, Mána sat with me and patiently answered my questions while I pointed at different things and asked, in Greek, "What is that?" We also worked through verbs. I said, in Greek, "Today, I want. And yesterday? And tomorrow?" And she gave the answers. Of course, there were more than a few times when what she said and what I *thought* she said were not the same thing at all.

Unfortunately for my Greek, but reflective of my in-laws' affection for me, they never corrected my mistakes. They thought my goofs were cute, and they didn't want to discourage me. Because she was so bright and intuitive, Mána always understood me despite my multiple mistakes. I never realized how poor my Greek really was until she developed dementia.

Once Aris and I retired and started spending our summers on the Island, I started working on my Greek. This is a slow process of unlearning years of misunderstandings and correcting poor grammar. In addition to Rosetta Stone, I bought a book written in Greek, which I was assured was appropriate for an eight-year-old.

Unfortunately, it was full of slang expressions, and I had to look up two words in every sentence. By that time, we had Wi-Fi at the house, and I could access Google Translate—which, unlike a lot of translation apps, offers Greek. Although it's not perfect—none are—it's *very* useful.

One night, being frustrated, I begged Aris for help. He was perfectly willing—as long as a back rub was included. I came to a word with four—yes, four—vowels in succession, which I couldn't begin to pronounce.

Aris asked, "What's the matter? Why did you stop?"

I replied, "How can I read this? It's got all those letters strung together!"

Without missing a beat, he said, "Well, I don't know what they do in Kentucky, but here in Greece, that's how we make words."

We laughed until we cried.

———◇———

A few years after we retired, I began taking Greek language lessons at the Greek Orthodox Church in Naples, Florida (yes, I went to Greek school as in *My Big Fat Greek Wedding*). I was in a second grade-level class for adults. The classes helped with my grammar and kept my Greek from atrophying over the winter. I later took individual classes off and on.

My grammar is still lousy, though it's much better than it was. Among other things, I have a ridiculously hard time remembering and using the correct form of the future and past tenses of verbs (there are several of each). And the accusative case can provoke me to tears. A Greek polyglot friend visiting us in Naples told me that I'd never speak Greek correctly without understanding the accusative case. This hadn't come up in my classes, and I asked her to explain it. She couldn't. My teacher couldn't explain it, either. I eventually found an explanation in Wikipedia.

I understand a great deal more Greek than I can speak—the difference between passive and active vocabulary. I thought I was an utter idiot because I was always defaulting to the present tense in group conversations—until a friend of Italian ancestry, who grew up speaking it, told me that he did the same thing when visiting Italy.

At least I'm fluent in food! I do well in one-on-one conversations, as long as they don't stray too far afield, with occasional help from Google Translate (my Greek vocabulary is not broad), and I can make myself understood in shops and restaurants and purchase or order what I wish.

In addition to the different alphabet and the multiple diminutive and augmentative forms of words, the inflection of verbs and the declension of nouns, pronouns, articles and adjectives make Greek difficult for English speakers—or at least for this one. English spelling is ridiculous, but we don't inflect adjectives or articles at all: The adjective "good" is always "good" and doesn't change depending on gender or whether one is referring to a person or thing or several persons or things. So, once you have learned "good" in English, you can depend on using it correctly, e.g., good girl, good men, good food, good job.

Greek words are quite different: There are thirteen different inflections of the Greek word for "good," depending on the gender (masculine, feminine, or neuter), number (singular or plural) and case (nominative, genitive, accusative, vocative) of the noun it describes. Just saying that makes me tired!

Even proper names are inflected in Greek! And did I mention that proper names require articles too? If you speak about Aris, you say "*O Áris*" (the Aris); but if you wish to *address* Aris, say, to call for his attention, you must say, "*Ári*" or he won't understand that you're speaking to him. In the same way, Giórgos becomes Giórgo, Pétros becomes Pétro, and Chrístos becomes Chrísto. Remembering this is helpful in getting the attention of a neglectful waiter. On the Island, names are cut much shorter: Menélaos becomes Mené, Giórgos becomes Gio, and so on.

Pronunciation is another challenge. English speakers don't move their mouths and tongues in the same ways as Greek speakers. It took me a long time to be able to pronounce the word for "I forgot." That word, Ξέχασα in the Greek alphabet, starts with one of the Greek letters that doesn't exist in the Latin alphabet, and sounds something like "KSAY-ha-sa" with a hard "k". For years, I said "I don't remember" (*den thymámai*) instead. The hardest word for me to pronounce is the word for freezer, which has another of those letters. It's written, καταψύκτης and sounds something like "kata-PSEE-ktees". Even now, I must say it slowly to be understood.

On top of all of this, there are two forms of modern Greek, the spoken language, *dimotikí*, which is also used in newspapers and modern writing, and the formal version, *katharévousa,* still found in legal notices and documents. The formal version of the word for "goat" is *aíga*, which bears no relation to the word for "goat" in everyday speech (*katsíka*).

This is to say nothing of the dialect on the Island. In modern Greek, much like Italian, the word for cat is "*gáta.*" On the

Island, "cat" is "*káthis*." And then, there's the rapid-fire speech. Put it all together and it's exhausting!

———◆———

One of the oddities of the Greek language is the absence of a word for "privacy," which may explain why Greeks will climb aboard your boat in your absence, without invitation, and climb over a locked fence or a high stone wall to enter your property for figs. It hasn't happened recently—we now put wire fencing across the driveway after we leave—but in the past, we often found grease stains on the flagstones of our verandas when we returned after an absence—the product of the picnics of trespassers who wished to enjoy our view.

When Aris found a man sitting in our boat, he asked him whether the boat was his. The man admitted that it wasn't.

Aris said, "Yes, I know. It's mine."

The man responded, "I'm not hurting it; I'm just sitting here."

Aris then asked, "Did you drive here?"

"Yes," the man replied, puzzled.

Aris asked again, "Which is your car?"

"Why?" asked the man, beginning to be alarmed.

"Because I want to go sit in it; I won't hurt it, I'll just sit there," said Aris.

The man took the point and vacated our boat.

CHAPTER THIRTY-TWO

Manners

Greeks express their delight in seeing you physically. Handshaking won't do; hugs and kisses, one kiss on each cheek, are essential. Such expressions of affection are deeply embedded parts of Greek social interchange. Almost all phone calls or electronic messages with friends end with "*pollá filiá*" (many kisses).

Wishing others well is a delightful and expected courtesy on the Island, and you should be prepared to receive—and give—multiple good wishes every day:

Greeks will wish you "good day" (*kaliméra*) every day when they first see you. Courtesy requires that you do the same.

One hears "good afternoon" (*kaló apógevma*) fairly rarely, though "good noon" (*kaló mesiméri*) is frequently expressed.

As lunchtime approaches (2:00 p.m. or later), the wish is for a "good appetite" (*kalí órexi*).

After lunch, since the siesta is still common, the wish is for a "good rest" (*kalí xekoúrasi*).

After any meal, it's common courtesy to express a wish for "good digestion" (*kali chónepsi*).

You'll be wished a "good evening" (*kalispéra*) by almost everyone you meet from mid-afternoon until quite late at night when *kalinýchta* (good night) and *kaló ýpno* (good sleep) come into play. Proper manners demand that you initiate or return these wishes.

When parting in the wee hours, the wish is *kaló ximéroma,* meaning "good sunrise."

In other circumstances, the wish is *kalí synécheia*, which literally means "good continuation," but is used as a general expression of good wishes upon parting.

On the first day of the month, one should expect to be wished and to wish others a "good month" (*kaló mína*).

On Monday—never on Sunday—you should expect to hear and say *kalí evdomáda* (good week).

In the summer, expect to receive and give many wishes that the summer will go well (*kaló kalokaíri*).

If you'll be traveling elsewhere, you will surely be wished a safe journey (*kaló taxídi*).

When your summer visit to the Island is ending, expect to receive and give wishes for a good winter (*kaló cheimóna*) and a good return (*kalí antámosi*).

From time to time, when parting from friends, you'll be given, and may express, a wish to "go to the good" (*na pas sto kaló*), which is a general sort of benediction.

And then there's my favorite: When you complete a transaction, Island proprietors often express a wish that you will be well (*na 'ste kalá*). Isn't that lovely? You may respond by employing a most useful expression, *epísis*, which means "the same [to you]."

Greeks don't pay much attention to birthdays, but if you invite others to join you for a meal on your birthday, you must pay the bill. And everyone will wish that you live to see your 100th (*na ta ekatotíseis*).

Greeks have an entirely different concept of body space than I do. Like a lot of other Yanks, I want at least a foot of space all around me, and I'm unhappy when my space is encroached upon without my invitation, even kindly—as happened when I was standing in a crowded bus in front of an ancient, tiny woman dressed all in black who was seated. She might have been four feet tall. All of a sudden, she pulled me into her lap! I started to get up, but Aris said that rising would be insulting, so, very uncomfortably, I stayed put.

In what passes for a queue in Greece, everyone crowds together, jostling and pushing. Until the pandemic, there was no personal space at all. When the worst of the pandemic passed, Greeks mostly reverted to their prior habits. On the Island, this is an issue only at *panigýria* (saints' day feasts), when everyone is trying to get in to be fed. In Athens, you *must* push past others to have any hope of crossing a street on the light or boarding the metro.

Another cultural difference is that Greeks fear drafts. I once unintentionally panicked a whole bus full of Greek passengers during a heat wave. The bus had no air conditioning and, incredibly, all of its windows were closed. I gradually edged to a window and started to open it when an entire chorus rang out in protest of my creating a draft (*révma*) that would kill them all! Later, when I stood wilting in the heat in Aris's aunt's house, I asked about a fan. She had a small one and had it retrieved for me, but only after many dire warnings of the risks of the draft it would create.

"Visiting" occurs after the siesta, never earlier. You should never call anyone on the phone in the afternoon before 6:00 p.m. either. When I first came to the Island, we made the rounds, visiting Aris's relatives. Since Mána's mother's family was originally from the Island, many of her relatives had summer homes here.

When visiting someone in the afternoon, you'll likely be served a spoon dessert which may be submerged into a glass of cold water. Spoon desserts are fruits (such as cherries, baby lemons, or grapes) or vegetables (such as tiny eggplants) preserved in syrup so thick and sweet that it sticks to the spoon. You can feel your blood sugar rise as you consume the proffered spoonful.

Instead of preserves, you might be served a spoonful of a marshmallow-ish *mastícha*-flavored sweet. Mastic is the sap of a bush that grows only on a part of the island of Chíos and produces a natural chewing gum, used to flavor liquors and confections. I'm told that in ancient Greece, wars were fought over access to mastic.

When first introduced to the custom of offering spoon desserts in the afternoon, I asked Aris to tell our hosts that I couldn't eat them because all that sugar made me feel ill. He cautioned me that it would be terribly rude to refuse. I then asked him to tell our hosts that I'm diabetic. That worked. White lie to the rescue!

Among the relatives of various degrees we visited in 1978 were *Theía* (aunt) Kaíti and *Theíos* (uncle) Stamátis. Theíos Stamátis was a famous artist and political cartoonist—and quite a character. He professed to believe that he'd been a cat in a former life. Theía Kaíti was one of the kindest, gentlest souls I've ever known. She spoke English and was very welcoming to this *xéni* (female foreigner).

Babás, a hypochondriac, once scolded Theíos Stamátis for not going regularly to the doctor.

"I'm ashamed to go," Theíos Stamátis said.

"Why ashamed?" Babás asked.

"Because," said Theíos Stamátis, "the doctor will ask, 'Do you drink?' and I'll have to say, 'No.' Then the doctor will ask, 'Do you smoke?' and I'll have to say, 'No.' The doctor will then ask, 'Do you fool around with women?' and I'll have to say, 'No' again, at which point the doctor will ask, 'Then why do you want to live?'"

We also visited Theía Évi, a polyglot who retained her mental acuity and was boarding the bus all by herself until she passed away at age ninety-nine. I recall once visiting Theía Frangíski in her big classical-style house, a family seat. I wish I'd known her better. She was instrumental in bringing a program of music instruction to the Island for the children.

We also spent some time with Theíos Vasílis, who returned to Greece after thirty years in New York as a shipowner's chief engineer. He sponsored one of the main *panigýria* (church festivals) on top of a mountain and rode a donkey to it every year, enjoying the dancing and comradery. He lived to ninety-seven. His sister, Theía Flóra, lived to be nearly 106, despite having been obese. A sweet lady and former schoolteacher, Theía Flóra read the newspapers every day with the aid of a magnifying glass when she was well past 100. Aris says she made the best Greek meatballs ever.

We often visited Aris's Theía Renoúla, another character, who'd spent years in New York, where she had a difficult life after her father lost everything in the 1929 stock market crash and committed suicide. She also lost her brother and sister. I was told that she was quite a beauty when she was young and that she'd been married off to a wealthy and stern man. I met her when she was in her nineties. She had a wicked sense of humor. She loved to read Danielle Steele novels in English, which I brought to her in large print. She smoked like a chimney and favored rotisserie chicken, American tobacco, and risqué jokes.

Sadly, all of these relatives have gone the way of all flesh, but I'm glad that I had the opportunity to know them for a little while. Lest you think that Mána had many siblings, you should understand that Greeks are quite loose about the use of "aunt" and "uncle." Mána had only one sibling, a sister who lived in Australia. All of these "aunts" and "uncles" were relatives, but I never knew to what degree.

When going to someone's home on the Island for the first time, the traditional courtesy is to bring a gift for the home, typically something ceramic, such as a bowl or a wine pitcher. I learned of this custom belatedly when people started visiting our newly built house. I was upset that Aris hadn't told me about the custom earlier. He explained that it hadn't applied to us because we had just been vacationing. Although we always took something—such as wine or pastries—when visiting someone's home, we'd made many visits without taking the traditional gift, and I worried that those we'd visited earlier thought me discourteous.

When invited to someone's Island home for an ouzo or dinner, it's expected that you will contribute to the meal, by bringing a dessert, appetizer, or other food. Wine, ouzo, or *tsípouro* (a type of *rakí*) are always welcome too. We usually take wine as well as some food. (Taking wine is also a prophylactic measure in case the wine offered is not palatable—wine made on the Island is sweet, thick, and potent!) Before taking your first sip of wine, beer, or ouzo, you should raise your glass and toast to your companions' good health—*eis ygeían* or *stin ygeiá sas*—or wait for someone else to do so. It's impolite to drink before the toast.

Dishes you might contribute when dining at someone's home include: *Taramosaláta* (pink or white caviar spread), *Melitzanosaláta*, *Fáva*, Spinach Pies, *Gígantes* (Giant Baked Beans)—or whatever you prefer. (The recipes are in the Appendix.)

Food is rarely served in courses in homes here, or in many tavernas. Frequently, everything is on the table at the same time, and the table is groaning. Islanders and Island regulars offer many dishes, multiple *mezédes*, salads, and often a couple of "main" courses, as well as fruit, dessert, or both.

Some of the dining practices in tavernas and homes here take some getting used to. Greeks often eat out of serving dishes. Instead of taking a serving of salad or meatballs onto their plates, they may stick their own forks into the common salad bowl and other serving dishes. Some did this even during the pandemic, proving that old habits are hard to break.

Greeks also often dip their bread into the olive oil, tomato juice, and liquified cheese in the bottom of the common salad bowl. Known as *papára*, this is delicious and I'm sure I'd be thinner if I'd never learned to enjoy it. Of course, like everywhere else, after you taste the food, you praise it. You might say, "*chrysá ta chéria sou*," which means "your hands are golden." And you thank your hosts on parting.

One quirk of entertaining here is that friends sometimes invite us for a meal *at our place*. They propose to provide the food (or most of it) with us providing the space. One of these friends traded his share of the Island house he and his brother inherited to his brother for his brother's share of a house they jointly inherited in Athens. He was, consequently, without a space for entertaining on the Island.

A hunter and a *very* accomplished cook, he's grilled exotic meats and *foie gras* on our barbecue *(psistariá)* for us and mutual friends. Other friends, whose Island house is small and remote, brought a whole dinner to our place.

Island regulars also sometimes bring a friend, unknown to you, to your home for dinner, occasionally with no warning. More often, a relative you've invited for dinner will call or text to tell you, sometimes on the day of the meal, that they want to—or will—bring someone with them.

Normally, one more seat at the table isn't a problem, but on those rare occasions when it rains, trying to fit extra people around our small dining room table can be interesting: Ten years after we retired, faced with a series of rainy days, we had to figure out how to install the dining table extension so that we could accommodate a seventh (uninvited) guest—who then decided not to come after all!

What sounds to American ears like angry yelling is part of the Greek culture of vigorous discussion. The very first time I came to Greece and met Aris's aunt and cousins, I was appalled that they were (to my American ears) yelling at each other in front of a stranger. It was hot, and between the heat and the yelling, I developed a terrible headache—and I almost never have headaches.

I asked Aris if we could go for a walk to get some fresh air. Safely outside, I asked why they were all so angry. Surprised, he explained that they weren't angry at all—they were just discussing the rent they should charge on a property they owned collectively!

There's also the Greek chorus effect. The first time a former colleague of Aris came to the Island late in the summer, we left together (after a lovely visit) for Athens. We took the big, slow ferry because the sea was rather rough. Our tickets were in the first-class section which had couches for seats. As usual, many people placed their luggage beside them on the couches.

When the ferry stopped at another island, a large group of children boarded with first-class tickets but couldn't find seats. The pursers came around asking the first-class passengers to remove their luggage from the seats to make room for the young people. One woman protested vehemently and loudly that stowing luggage on the seats was a privilege of a first-class ticket, and the seats had been oversold.

Apparently, she called in a report to that effect to the authorities because, not long after her vocal protest, it was announced that disembarkation would be slow because someone had reported that too many tickets had been sold, so all departing passengers would need to line up to be counted by officials from the port authority. Immediately after this announcement, a number of passengers began berating the woman for having made the report and causing everyone such inconvenience. Others took her side.

The debate continued and more and more people gathered around and joined each side. The argument grew louder and livelier as time passed and hands and arms were waving everywhere. The former colleague's wife looked frightened and worried aloud that things would erupt in violence. Surprised, Aris assured her that this wouldn't happen—we were just witnessing the modern version of a Greek chorus!

Kisses, good wishes, groaning tables, and loud, lively debate are all part of social life here.

CHAPTER THIRTY-THREE

Island Time

The only way to have any peace of mind on the Island is to surrender to Island Time.

Aris once explained that since Greece was occupied by the Ottomans for 400 years, the concept of time shifted from Western to Middle Eastern. Doubtless, that's part of the reason, but I also think that Islanders simply don't share the American and Northern European preoccupation with time. Why should they? It's lovely here and whatever it is that may concern you will be accomplished . . . eventually.

Island Time affects almost all aspects of life here, including social engagements. One of Aris's cousins was invited for dinner at nine. She arrived at midnight, without a prior call or explanation. A childhood friend showed up for an ouzo (casual drinks with hors d'oeuvres), with an unexpected girlfriend, more than two hours after the appointed time.

We invited another of Aris's childhood friends and her family for an ouzo. We then collectively decided to have dinner at the fish restaurant in Fáros. Reservations were made with their concurrence. They left in their car—it's a twenty-minute drive at most—and we walked. They weren't at the restaurant when we arrived twenty-five minutes later. After waiting half an hour, we decided to order, convinced that they'd had car trouble. They arrived after we were served. No car trouble: they had just decided to stop at their place first. What's an hour or so?

It also impacts transportation. For many years, we depended on taxis. We could've taken the bus, but the bus stop is an uphill mile and a quarter away. The cab driver would arrive anywhere from ten minutes before the promised time—a very rare occurrence—to half an hour or more later. There was one important exception: Trips to the port to catch a ferry. Since ferries wait for no man, the cabbie (*taxitzís*) was *always* on time

The biggest impact of Island Time is on getting work done. When we were forced to install additional fencing against the rampages of neighboring goats, we asked the worker to return to do some landscaping. Without other conversation or notice of any kind, he showed up weeks later with his wife as his helper very early one morning—and did a fine job. They disappeared before I finished breakfast, leaving no bill. *Two months later*, after multiple inquiries from us, he finally returned to be paid.

You may recall that we were never in love with the front face of the house. For years, we debated how to improve its appearance. We finally settled on installing a small chestnut beam pergola above the kitchen windows, hoping to train jasmine to crawl across the beams. When the carpenter took the measurements, he said he'd be back to install it in mid-July. We didn't hold our breath.

Sure enough, we heard nothing from him until mid-August when he called saying he would arrive in half an hour! Aris was in Athens, and I was leaving for a hair appointment, as I explained. He was terribly disappointed that I wouldn't cancel a long-standing appointment when he decided to show up that day without prior warning.

That delay was nothing compared to this: In the summer of 2020, the wooden slats on the top of the pergola shading the sitting area outside our dining room started rotting—or at least we started noticing the rot. We engaged a carpenter to replace them with an aluminum product. We heard nothing from him the rest of that summer.

Aris tracked him down the next summer. He said he had the materials, and he'd do the installation *apó vdomáda*—which means "next week," but is a *very* flexible expression of time. It doesn't necessarily mean the following week, so much as sometime thereafter—in other words, eventually. He didn't show up that year.

In the spring of 2022—nearly two years after we hired him—the pergola slats were falling apart and falling down. It was time for desperate measures. Aris called. Lira (our cleaning woman and friend) called. Another friend called. Repeatedly. Aris would've been pulling his hair out— if he'd had any to spare. Eventually, he reached the carpenter's wife and told her to tell him that if the job wasn't done by the time we arrived, he'd hire someone else.

The job wasn't finished when I arrived, but at least it had been started. The carpenter had removed the rotted slats and two rotted supports. After Aris got here, the carpenter returned with the materials and his injured son (who had two bandaged fingers from a saw accident, perhaps emulating his father, who is missing fingertips on one hand).

They finished the job! It's not perfect—there's a two-inch square patch on the underside, but after waiting two years, we weren't going to reject it. We'd already learned that "you can't always get what you want" here. In contrast to the extraordinary delay in getting the work done, it took no time at all for the son to show up to collect payment.

———————◆———————

Living on Island Time, we've learned to slow down and measure time in months . . . or years, not minutes.

CHAPTER THIRTY-FOUR

Greek Names: Often Strange, Historical, or Both

In Greek tradition, the first child is named after the father's father or mother. Any second child is named after the mother's father or mother. This tradition is very strong. When our nephew (who is our elder godson) was to be baptized, we and his parents tried to persuade his grandfather—whose given name was Spýros, short for Spyrídon, the patron saint of potters—to allow the child to be named Alexander after his grandmother, Alexandra, since Spýros is not a name that travels well. He was extremely upset by the idea, so the poor kid ended up stuck with his name.

I started asking about the meanings of Greek names as a way of remembering them. With no memory hooks for such names, I had a terrible, horrible, miserable time trying to recall the names of Greeks I met. Through this process, I became quite enamored of the meanings and histories of Greek names, which are passed down from generation to generation following the tradition just described. In this way, a child may inherit a name such as:

Anastásios, derived from *Anástasi,* meaning "resurrection;"

Athanasía, meaning "immortality;"

Anthoúsa, meaning "blossoming;"

Evángelos, meaning "the bearer of good news;"

Elefthérios, derived from *Elefthería,* meaning "freedom;"

Níkólaos, meaning "victory of the people;"

Panteleímon, meaning "all compassionate;"

Panagiótis, meaning "all holy;"

Sevastós, meaning "well respected;"

Sofía, meaning "wisdom;"

Themistoklís, meaning "glory of justice;"

Theófilos, meaning "friend of God;"

Theódoros and *Dorothéa,* meaning "God's gift" and "gift of God," respectively;

Theológos, meaning "theologian;" and

Theodósios, meaning "God-given."

When I first learned these names, I wondered whether those bearing a name like "friend of God" felt a burden to live up to it. I've not seen evidence of this, and Aris assures me that it's not the case. I still wonder whether someone named "well respected" or "wisdom" has an edge in getting a job.

Other Greeks bear the names of Greek mythological figures, such as:

Ádonis, Aphrodíte's mortal lover;

Ártemis, the goddess of the hunt and wild nature;

Afrodíti, the goddess of love;

Athiná, the goddess of wisdom, war, diplomacy, medicine, and commerce (the accent changes when referring to the city— its name is *Athína*).

Defkalíon, the son of Prometheus, a ruler associated with the flood myth;

Dímitra, the goddess of the harvest;

Kalliópi, the muse of eloquence and poetry;

Menélaos, the husband of Helen of Troy; and

Pinelópi, the wife of Odysseus.

Dáfni, which means "laurel," was a nymph associated with springs, brooks, and streams in Greek mythology.

My name exists in some form in most languages spoken in Western Europe and is derived from "laurel" in Latin. Had I been born Greek, I likely would have been "Dáfni." There are many Flóras on the Island, but no Lauras or Loras, and it took a while before Islanders got my name right.

Greeks celebrate "name days"—the dates associated with the saint for whom one is named. In the Greek Orthodox Church, every day of the year is dedicated to one or more saints or martyrs (women named Maria get a choice of Marian feast days on which to celebrate).

Like his paternal grandfather, Aris was named for a historical Greek figure, not a saint—so he never celebrated a name day as a child. He was an adult before he learned from a friend that he actually had a name day after all. Even I have a name day—on August 10.

CHAPTER THIRTY-FIVE

Sea and Sand

Sand, Sunbathing, and Swimwear

If you're looking for magnificent beaches, this isn't the place. There are spectacular beaches elsewhere in Greece—the white volcanic rocks of Milos, the pristine beach of Elafónísos on the southern coast of the Peloponnese, and near Kastelli in Crete where we drove a dirt road to an undeveloped pink sand beach with turquoise water. The beaches here are fine, not wonderful. They have heavy, tan-colored, silica-based sand, and many are also pebbly.

The good news about the sand is that it doesn't get churned up in the sea and make it murky. The bad news is it's hot! We don't walk across the sand to the sea—we run!

When I first came to the Island, I bought a wide-brimmed straw farmer's hat and a loose cotton midi-dress from a local store to wear on the beach. I was sorry when the store closed, and I couldn't get them anymore. I then brought wide-brimmed hats and ankle-length caftans from the States. For many years, I was the only woman on the beach covered up and wearing heavy sunscreen. I was the *trelí Amerikanída* (crazy American woman) even before I started wearing sunscreen swim shirts.

Hiding from the sun like that just didn't make sense to the Greeks. Sunbathing is called sun therapy (*iliotherapeía*) and has many adherents, including very mature women and men, who stretch out on rocks jutting into the sea so they can bake better in the sun.

We keep beach mats and a beach chair for the convenience of our guests, but we never sunbathe. Greeks often marvel that, after spending months here, and swimming almost every day, I'm not very tan. I look even less tan wearing my white, zinc oxide-based sunscreen. One of Aris's friends, who's always darkly tanned—and as wrinkled as a prune in consequence—wanted to touch my face to see if it were real!

In recent years, hats, protective cover-ups, and sunscreens have become more popular in Greece, so I'm no longer the only shrouded figure on the beach (though those of us covering up are still a decided minority).

I've collected many colorful, sun-blocking wide-brimmed hats over the years. But some summers, they don't do me much good because it's too windy to keep them on my head. More than once, I'm sorry to say, I've had to chase a hat blown down our steep hillside, through thorns and weeds. I did *not* enjoy the experience. Now when it's that windy, I leave my natty hats sulking in the closet and wear one with a chin strap.

I also have a collection of caftans and choose which to wear on any given day, depending on how hot it is and whether it's peak tourist season. During peak season—normally about mid-July through August—there's always a line for the women's room. Not wanting to hang around in my wet bathing suit waiting for the restroom in order to change, I wear caftans that are as loose as tents.

Aris and others have mastered the technique of changing under towels wrapped around their bodies. I'm afraid to try that. I worry that the towel will fall off in the middle of the endeavor and reveal all my secrets. So I stick with changing under tent-like caftans. It's an act requiring balance and agility worthy of the Olympics: standing first on one foot, then the other, while removing my bathing suit without letting it touch the ground, then reversing the process to get my underwear on. It gives me great incentive to practice the yoga stork pose.

European women wear bikinis unabashedly on the beach well into their seventies. They accept their bodies as they are, and don't mind exposing the marks of life and age to the gazes of others. I admire their healthy attitude, which makes this a great place for those of us with less-than-perfect bodies to be on a beach. But I wear one-piece bathing suits just the same, though (with rare exception) I'm the only woman under eighty wearing one.

European men are the same. Big-bellied men appear in Speedos and think they look good. Like elsewhere in Europe, topless sunbathing by women is allowed on the island, though relatively few appear topless on beaches here. No Islander ever does.

Sea and Sea Life

People come to this Island for its picturesque villages and for the sea. The waters of the Aegean Sea in the Cyclades are very beautiful and the bays are normally quite calm, making swimming here much like swimming in a buoyant lake. I'm prejudiced, of course, but this sea is more appealing to me than the beautiful waters of Australia's Whitsunday Islands, Cayman, Fiji, or anywhere else I've been fortunate to swim. The Aegean is crystal clear here, and I think the words "aquamarine" and "ultramarine" must have been coined specifically to describe this sea.

When the sea ripples in the mid-day sun, thousands of tiny lights dance on its surface. And in very deep water, the color shades to lilac. "Crystal clear" is a cliché, of course, but it's apt. I won't swim in deep water unless I can see the seabed—and everything between me and it. Here, the sea is so clear that I can usually see to a depth of over fifty feet.

Fishermen report that, when the moon is full, fish can see and avoid fishing lines, so that's not the best time to patronize fish restaurants. If you go anyway, you might be served a local version of "fresh" fish—fish caught and frozen in winter. When Aris asked the owner of a taverna near the port whether the fish on offer was fresh, he drew himself up proudly and replied, "Of course! I caught it myself in February."

In Naples, Florida, the Gulf doesn't reach a depth of thirty feet until half a mile from shore. But here, the seabed falls away rapidly, and you'll often be in thirty feet of water just 100 yards offshore. Whether for that reason, the latitude, or other factors, the Aegean isn't very warm: Yells of *eínai pagoméni!* (it's freezing!) are commonly heard in early June.

You won't see colorful corals (there's almost no coral) or teeming schools of fish here. But you'll always see some fish—and occasionally, something more interesting.

The first summer I came to the Island, I encountered a small octopus (*chtapódi*) in a remote bay, not accessible by car. We hiked with friends down many ancient stone steps to the small cove. Flanked by huge stone shelves, it wasn't well-sheltered, and the sea was often rough there, but on that day, it was like glass. I hadn't become very comfortable in the sea yet. Having grown up in Louisville, with mud-bottomed rivers, I'd never learned to swim properly, so I stayed near the shore.

After paddling around for a while, I stood in waist-deep water, taking in the magical view, when a small octopus approached. I remembered Jacques Cousteau calling octopuses the "kittens of the sea," and stroked the creature, which seemed to enjoy being petted. I was so pleased and excited that I called out to the others that I was playing with an octopus.

That was a mistake.

Like most Greeks, Aris's childhood friend took food very seriously, and immediately cried out "*mezé*!" (appetizer). He swam over, grabbed the poor little octopus, and turned it inside out, killing it, and expelling its organs. He then slammed it on the rocks repeatedly to release the lactic acid in its muscles. After killing it, he cooked it. I'm very fond of octopus, but I didn't have the heart to eat that one.

The brutal process I just described is the common way octopus is prepared on the Island. After that, the octopus goes into a pot—with no water at all—and is heated, causing the muscle to release a fluid. When the fluid boils off, it may be boiled in salted water until soft. When I serve octopus in the States, I skin it—removing the suction cups—and slice the pure white flesh, which is often confused with lobster. Skinned or not, sliced boiled octopus is served cold, dressed with olive oil, red wine vinegar, and oregano.

Searching for octopuses is a favorite pastime when we're snorkeling—not to catch and eat them, but to watch them because we enjoy it so much. The key to finding an octopus is to locate its "garden." Contrary to the impression created by the Beatles song, an octopus's garden is a collection of empty shells (the remains of its meals), usually around a hole in the sea floor, which might be hidden under a shell.

Sometimes octopuses nest in open sand, but they're more often found in seaweed or rocks. I love watching them hunt. Their movements are fluid and graceful. It's mesmerizing—like watching a sea ballet.

I was thrilled to discover a large octopus hunting on open sand while a friend was visiting from the States. I excitedly called to her and Aris to come see it. After watching a few minutes, Aris dove down and touched it, thinking it would take off to deeper and safer water, and perhaps release its ink.

However, this fellow was not to be intimidated. He did neither. Instead, he curled his tentacles into a crown around his head and puffed himself up like a ball, changing color only slightly. Aris touched him again, but he "stood" his ground and never left while we were there.

A close relative of the octopus is the cuttlefish (*soupiá*) whose cartilage is used in songbird cages. I've never seen one while snorkeling around the Island, but I've seen them in a bay of an uninhabited island nearby. Cuttlefish is one of my favorite foods when prepared with its own ink.

Unfortunately, I've never found it prepared with ink at any Island restaurant. I asked Kyría Évi about this, and she said that harvesting the ink is too labor-intensive for restaurants (I suspect that buying the ink already harvested is too expensive). She prepares a lovely dish of cuttlefish in red wine and tomatoes.

I often prepared cuttlefish with ink in Pittsburgh, where the cultural diversity of the city made most foods accessible. When we moved from Pittsburgh to Naples, I hand-carried (in thermal containers) only two foods—squid ink and *manoúra* cheese from the Island. But for years, I couldn't find cuttlefish in Naples. Several fishmongers there didn't even know what it was! One did, and thought he could get it for us, but was disappointed.

During our first four years in Naples, I made cuttlefish only when visiting friends in Spain.

During our fifth winter there, it dawned on me that we knew a chef in Miami, Filippo, the husband of the youngest daughter of Kýrios Pétros and Kyría Évi. It's only two hours by car from Naples, and we often fly out of Miami for international trips. What's two hours of highway driving where good food is concerned?

I contacted Filippo, who said that he could get it frozen in a fifteen-pound bag. I asked him to do that and arranged for Aris to pick it up when he landed in Miami from a trip. So that Aris wouldn't need to park, Filippo met him with the cuttlefish on the street as he was driving from the airport. Aris joked that the exchange on the street corner felt like a drug deal—trading cash for cuttlefish!

We enjoyed the cuttlefish in batches over the winter. The next year, we finally found a source in Naples for both cuttlefish and its ink—which costs more per pound than filet mignon. Several initially skeptical neighbors have relished it too. Eventually, Aris found ink here in Greece.

In case you're adventuresome, I've included Aris's paternal grandmother's recipe for cuttlefish in black ink, with my tweaks, in the Appendix. This dish looks like sin and tastes like heaven. Aris says I prepare it better than his accomplished mother!

Aside from octopuses and their cousins, there are large orange starfish (*asterías*), as well as red ones, and some gray ones sporting seven or eight legs. I've also seen small sea rays (*saláchi*). Sold in the States as "skate wing," they're delicious when lightly floured and sautéed, or grilled. Rays are fascinating to watch. When they meet an obstacle on the sea floor, they behave much like a robot vacuum cleaner, backing up, turning, and trying again.

Edible crabs are rare here, but you can amuse yourself by looking for the Aegean crab, with plant life growing on its shell.

It may surprise you, but growing up in Louisville, where the only fish we ate were breaded and frozen fillets or sticks, it took me a long time to come to terms with fish. But I love it here. Fish fresh from the sea have an entirely different taste and texture than other fish.

My favorite is red mullet (*barboúni*), known in Spain as *salmonetta* and in France as *rougét*. They're small, white-fleshed, bony, and delectable. Bottom feeders, they're easy to spot in the sea by the feelers under their mouths. Some Greek restaurants in the States import them daily if you're ever game to try them. I like them fresh, small, dusted in flour, and sautéed in olive oil. A joke told here is, "Why don't cats eat the heads of the *barboúnia*?" The answer is, "Because people do."

Another favorite is the garfish (*zargánes*), skinny and delicious cousins of needlefish. My mouth starts watering when I spot them swimming in the sea, usually in schools near the surface in late summer. You can eat the small ones whole, bones and all, which are a great source of calcium. I love seabass too, also called branzino in the States and *lavráki* here, grilled. They're raised on a nearby island.

Other delicious fruits of the sea include spiny lobsters, which I think are sweeter than the Atlantic lobsters with big claws. A close cousin of the lobster, called *kolokhtýpa* (which translates as "butt hitter"), named after the way it moves, is also delicious. Instead of feelers, it has front flaps, as well as a flatter body and a wider tail. Sometimes we find tiny clams (*kydónia*), eaten raw on the half shell, which almost melt in your mouth.

When we find good shrimp on the Island, I like to prepare *Garídes Saganáki* (Shrimp with tomatoes, green onions, garlic, ouzo, and Feta cheese)—the recipe is in the Appendix—and offer it with Risotto alla Milanese.

———◆———

The Aegean is populated with bottle-nose dolphins (*delfínia*), though I never see them close to shore here as I do in Naples. It is also home to what I understand are the rarest seals (*fókia*) in the world, the smallish monk seals. We've seen them a few times near an uninhabited island, and one winter, a friend sent us a video of one playing with him in the Island's main port.

There are also sea turtles (*helónes*). Very large turtles! The shell of one we've swum with (followed around) several times in the bay of a nearby island is at least four feet long. She has a particular territory, is easy to find, and is utterly indifferent to our presence. We're told that she's quite ancient.

Along the shore of another nearby island, we saw a smaller turtle whose shell was badly cracked along the upper ridge. A whole collection of mussels (*mýdia*) had attached themselves to the damaged area. Neither this odd decoration nor the damage itself seemed to slow her down—a fine example of overcoming adversity.

I treasure every moment in this beautiful sea.

Sea Hazards

Hazards in the Aegean are few—careless boaters are the greatest danger. I once was hit by an outboard motorboat while snorkeling. Aris saw it and was certain I was dead or maimed. Fortunately, the boat wasn't going very fast, or I would've been pulled into the propellers. When I yelled and hit the side of the boat with my fist, the "captain" immediately sped off!

Natural perils include sea urchins (*achinoí*) on some underwater rocks, typically tucked in holes or under ledges. They're easy to spot and avoid. Sea anemones (*anemónes*), which look a lot like spider chrysanthemums and have a nasty sting, live on some rocks and in some areas of sand, but are also easily avoided by anyone paying attention. Once in the last forty-eight years, I saw a sea centipede (*skolópendra*) near the rock cliffs, and there is the rare moray eel (*smérna*).

Jellyfish (*tsoúchtra*) are uncommon around the Island, except late in the summer or during a heat wave when the wind blows from the south. It's easy to see and avoid them while wearing goggles or a mask. Most local species are relatively harmless, and the stinging purple ones, which have made appearances here about every decade (in my experience), can't kill you. I've never encountered sea lice or sand fleas . . . thankfully. There's a fish with a poisonous spine on its back (*drákaina*) that's a problem if you step on it, but they're rarely in shallow water in the occupied bays.

I've also never seen a shark (*karcharías*) while swimming or boating. Aris has seen two unidentified species, many years apart, in uninhabited bays. There are no barracuda.

The relative absence of hazards makes swimming in this glorious sea a joy.

CHAPTER THIRTY-SIX

Shelling

I love collecting seashells (*kochýlia*). I'm good at spotting them in the sea, but I have a bad ear and can't dive. Aris, who, until recently, was still free diving to at least forty feet, retrieves shells for me.

On one trip to a neighboring uninhabited island, he brought up two large and beautiful shells. One was a living conch. The peach-colored animal had antennae and red eyes and was so lovely that we hadn't the heart to kill it, even for *mezé*.

The other large shell was black and white and occupied by a black slug with white specks. We didn't have the same qualms about it. We took it back to Kýrios Pétros at the restaurant and asked whether it was edible. He told us the only thing the slug was good for was its shell and said we should hang it on a hook until it fell off. We declined and returned the slug, with its shell, to the sea. We don't mind killing a creature for dinner, but we won't kill one for its shell.

We've passed on other shells too. On an underwater rock near the peninsula between our bay and Fáros, I found a foot-long Triton shell. Excited, I swam over to get Aris and show it to him. He dove down and brought it up. It was very beautiful, but it was alive, so he took it further out to sea where it might be safe—at least from two-legged predators.

In roughly the same area near the rocks, I later saw part of a very large giant tun shell protruding from the sand. Once again, I excitedly called Aris over to retrieve it, but it was also occupied. The slug looked just like a big blob of silly putty with spots. Aris took that one out to deeper water as well.

In Vathí Bay, Aris saw something shimmering in the seaweed, dove down, and brought up a large—and unoccupied—giant tun shell in perfect condition. He's found many others since, in various smaller sizes. One of those is my particular favorite.

While snorkeling on a swim toward Fáros, Aris noticed an octopus's garden and dove down to retrieve a mid-sized giant tun shell. As he started to lift it, it was pulled back—by the octopus! The creature was using it to cover its hole and tried to keep it. Aris won the tug-of-war, so we're now the proud owners of an octopus's door.

Quite unintentionally, we also acquired an octopus's house. While anchored in a cove of the nearby uninhabited island, Aris brought me a small Scotch bonnet. I put it in a pocket of our boat, which—fortunately—had some seawater in it. When we returned to the boat to leave, we found a tiny octopus staring up at us. It had left the shell. We returned the poor little thing to the sea, happy to see it swim away.

Aris has retrieved many other seashells for me—cockles, cones, murex, tiny abalone, sea urchins, and Scotch bonnets of many sizes, as well as many sea biscuits. Sea biscuits merit some explanation. They're relatives of sea urchins and sand dollars but look like inflated versions of the latter. They're egg-shaped rather than round, and many we find here also have a gray pattern resembling a tortoise shell.

To house the abundance of shells, I've filled several ceramic bowls and platters, some quite large. The two biggest decorate corners of the living room floor, and tiny lizards sometimes take up residence in them. These geckos are always welcome in our house—they eat insects.

Perhaps the most unusual shell Aris has retrieved comes from a type of mussel that thrives in both the Aegean and Adriatic. The shells of these mussels can grow to be two feet tall or more, though they're fairly narrow, about eight or nine inches wide at the top for a shell of that length. The pointed end is typically buried in sand. The outside is the color of sand and razor-blade sharp, while the inside is a shiny pearlescent orange.

The mussel inside can grow to be two or three inches and lives with a couple of tiny crayfish that warn it to close its shell in case of danger. The mussel tastes peppery, and it's typically seasoned with salt and pepper, floured, and fried.

English speakers find its name amusing. In the singular, it's a *pínna*; in the plural, they're *pínnes* (pronounced "pee ness")—which, of course, means nothing else in Greek.

When our friends Ron and Jacki visited one year, Aris took them diving for *pínnes* in the bay of the uninhabited island nearby. While I can't dive, I'm a great *pínna* spotter, and many were brought up for lunch—so many that we shared them with everyone else dining at Kýrios Pétros's taverna that day, where we had them prepared.

A year or so later, we were at the aquarium in Monterey, California, with a sizable group including Ron and Jacki. Jacki spotted those mussels in a display and excitedly called across the room, "Aris, there's your *pínnes*!"

All heads turned. Jacki slapped her hand across her mouth and colored scarlet.

We laughed till we gasped for air.

CHAPTER THIRTY-SEVEN

Sky, Moon, and Stars

The light on the Island, sometimes called the light of Apollo, is stunning and attracts many artists. The atmosphere has extraordinary clarity, and because of that, the sun feels more intense here than it does in South Florida. Clouds are rare in the summer, and the daytime sky is intensely, flawlessly blue—azure and cerulean. The closest I've come to experiencing this light anywhere else was skiing above tree line in Summit County, Colorado, though the blue of the February sky there was not as deep as it is here in summer. The blue of the Tuscan sky comes close.

The night sky is equally amazing. *Pansélinos* is the Greek word for "full moon." We're always very aware of the moon's phases when we're on the Island. I thought this was because we often ate dinner on our veranda or at beachside restaurants, but I learned that the full moon is something of a national obsession. Entire radio programs are dedicated to it—with good reason: Due to the clarity of the atmosphere, the full moon is intoxicatingly brilliant in the Cyclades.

Full moons rise a deep orange-red, then fade to yellow before reverting to their normal silvery white. They shimmer on the placid sea like silver and are so bright that we need no other light to navigate our riverbed road or our steep driveway. They are always glorious shining on the sea.

When the moon is new, we see the Milky Way (*Galaxías*) at our house. On our very first night in our new home, we climbed the outside stairs to the guest room to go to bed, having installed Aris's parents in the master bedroom. We hadn't found the switch to turn on the lights for those stairs—remember the drunk electrician?—and Aris warned me to be very careful. The night was dark, the house was newly inhabited, and he cautioned me to be on the lookout for snakes, scorpions, and other creatures. I reached the top of the stairs, looked up, and exclaimed, "Oh my God!"—scaring him half to death. I couldn't help myself: the Milky Way arced brilliantly over our heads. I hadn't seen it since I was a child, and it quite literally took my breath away.

In addition to the white netting of the Milky Way, several constellations are clearly visible when the moon is new, including Orion, the Scorpius, and the Little Dipper. Orion is my favorite. I look for him everywhere and was disturbed to see him upside down when we were in Australia.

When the moon is new in August, we're awed by countless shooting stars during the Perseid meteor shower and sit, mesmerized by them, for as long as our necks can bear the strain of looking up.

CHAPTER THIRTY-EIGHT

Getting Around

Taxis

To get around the Island, we relied for years on one cabbie (*tax-itzís*), Leonídas, one of those Greeks who doesn't look Greek. As a younger man, he had thick, curly auburn hair and freckles. In 1984, he purchased (used, of course) the very first Mercedes-Benz taxi on the Island. He nursed that vehicle through two engine replacements for about thirty years.

What a nice man he is! When driving us somewhere, if he noticed an older Islander on the side of the road, walking or waiting for a bus, he always offered a free ride. We never objected. Even now, we always call on Leonídas whenever we need transportation, such as when I arrive on the ferry in early summer. I always ask for the news of the Island, and I'm as pleased as punch when he says there's none.

When our house was new, we brought Aris's parents with us to the Island at the beginning of our vacation, settled them in the master bedroom, spent our vacation with them, and left them at our place for the rest of the summer. Faní took them home in September. We paid Leonídas in advance to transport them daily. He didn't ask to be paid in advance, but we did it— and told Aris's parents that we had—so they'd be sure to use his services to get out and about.

Mána and Babás could manage the walk down to the beach and the restaurant, but not the return trip up our long, steep driveway. And they needed transportation to town. We thought about putting a ski lift beside our driveway to get them up and down, but after two summers, Babás said the steps in our multi-level house were too much for him. While I'm sure they were an issue, I think they found living in the countryside too boring. They were society people who went out *every single night* when Aris was growing up—except the night Mána broke her arm.

The Motorbike and the Car-Eating Wall

Before we imported our car, we bought a motorbike. Larger than a Vespa (which is Italian for "wasp"), this type of motorbike is known here as a *papáki*, which means "duckling."

When we ordered it, we thought it would be small enough that we'd both be able to drive it. Ha! When it arrived, I realized that, at five feet nothing, I was too short to operate it. When I braked and put my foot down on the road to keep it upright, it tilted more than 45 degrees—it completely toppled over. So much for my dream of driving a big purple Harley later in retirement.

As a result, Aris drove the duckling, and I was relegated to holding onto him from behind (you can imagine how thrilled I was to show up everywhere with helmet hair). But there are advantages to riding behind—the wasps hit him, not me, and it was warmer. The nippy rides back from town on the motorbike caused me to bring several jackets to the Island.

When we returned home on the *papáki*, I always dismounted and trudged up the driveway as Aris drove up carefully. He was afraid for me to be on the back of the bike while he was navigating our long driveway, with its twenty-degree incline, even though the concrete was deliberately left rough for traction.

As you go up our driveway from the riverbed road past the turn with the path to Manólis's son's property, there's a steep drop on the left and large rocks, followed by a stone retaining wall on the right. At the top of the incline, just past the fig tree, a left turn takes you toward the northern boundary of our property—where our garage is now, with a cliff wall on the right and a steep drop on the left.

A 130-degree right turn at the top of the driveway, around the end of the retaining wall—dubbed "the car-eating wall" by Faní—takes you to the part of the driveway leading to the house. That segment is paved with stones and flanked by oleanders.

We have friends (and even the occasional taxi driver) who refuse to drive up our driveway. I can't blame them. One houseguest, who stayed with us before we imported our car, hired a small rental. All rental cars on the Island were stick shifts, which are tricky on steep inclines. Turning in our driveway early one morning, she caught the rental's left side on the car-eating wall, incurring a €400 repair bill.

The car-eating wall got me too—it's too low to be visible in the rearview mirror, and our 2011 Forester has no rear camera. As I was backing up very slowly one morning, I backed right into it. Despite my sloth-like speed, its rough stones did a number on the bumper.

Importing and Housing the Car

We needed a garage to house the car we intended to import, as well as the motorbike and the motorboat. Building the garage

190

was a simple job for which we hired an Islander whom Aris had known since he was a kid. The garage is sheathed with the same stone as our retaining walls to blend into the landscape, and as you may have gathered, it's not very close to the house. That's not a problem except when it's raining—or when worrying about snakes on a dark night.

Backing out of the garage to turn around while avoiding the bulging cliff wall on the right, the steep drop on the left, and then the car-eating wall, has never been easy for me. It became harder when the *themoniá* (rustic shelter) on the top of the hill above us—where Manólis made cheese—was converted into a house, and an electrical pole was installed opposite our car-eating wall to serve it. Every year, when we return, I must relearn those tricky maneuvers. It's like an annual driving test—Island style.

◦┄┄◆┄┄◦

We bought and imported our car in 2011, the year before we retired, when we knew we'd be spending our entire summers here. To understand what follows, you need to know that Greeks are (or at least were) terrible tax scofflaws. It's been said that tax evasion is the Greek national sport. Even international corporations handed out part of their employees' pay in cash in envelopes (*fakelákia*) to limit taxes and contributions to the pension and social medicine funds.

Automobiles are taxed as a proxy for income—the bigger the engine, the higher the tax. However, there were special rules for Greek expatriates who imported used cars to Greece for personal use for less than six months per year. Aris qualified.

At that time, cars cost about twice as much in Europe as in the States, so Aris carefully researched to find a reliable small

SUV of a make and model sold both in the US and Europe. He settled on a Subaru Forester, narrow enough for the local roads, high enough for our not-always-dry riverbed road, and capable of climbing our twenty-degree driveway without complaint. The engine sold in the States as the Forester was sold as the Outback in Europe, so parts were available.

A prep school classmate of Aris told him about a company in Toronto that reliably transported cars to Greece. After driving the Forester heavily for a month so it qualified as a used car under the Greek law, we drove it to Toronto on Mother's Day.

Before going north, I stuffed it with everything I could squeeze into it—director's chairs, seat cushions for the dining chairs, matelassé coverlets in a seashell pattern for the twin beds, sheets, the rest of the China I'd been taking to the Island in suitcases, faux flowers, hypoallergenic bed pillows, a stereo receiver and speakers, brass cabinet knobs, tablecloths, a large wooden tray, and a plastic folding step stool, among other things.

The price for shipping the car to Piraeus (the port of Athens) was considerably less than the cost of having the shipping company handle customs. The customs service fee included providing "gifts" to the various customs officials. There was an art to managing the Greek customs office. Among other things, one needed to know the correct amount of the "gift" for each official.

Although we despise greasing the palms of government workers to get them to do their jobs, a friend's car was held hostage for weeks for lack of "gifts" and had four flat tires when it was finally released. After hearing that horror story, we weren't about to take a chance.

As if it knew we were on "Island Time," the ship with our car arrived in Piraeus at the end of July, nearly three months after we left it in Toronto, and just a week before we left Greece! Aris had to leave houseguests behind and go to Piraeus to collect the car. At various points in the customs process, he was encouraged to step out of the room. We assume this was done to provide plausible deniability for the bribes.

Finally, we had our own car here! The Forester has proven to be an excellent choice. It's given us no trouble at all for 14 years. It's still not an old car by Island standards.

When you own a car on the Island, you must accept that it will have scratches, scrapes, and dents. No matter how carefully you drive and park, others don't. Some park by playing bumper cars with the autos in front and back. Many park too close and ding your doors when opening theirs. And some roads are so narrow that cars going in opposite directions can pass only by inching to the edge of the road, where bushes and weeds, sometimes thorny, lurk, stretching into the roadway to scratch your car.

As with many other aspects of life here, getting around can be an adventure—one that's taught me not to rush.

CHAPTER THIRTY-NINE

On the Road

There are no traffic lights on the Island, which is just as well since Greeks regard red lights as mere suggestions, and seem to believe that honking is a suitable substitute for stopping. (Because of this, I don't recommend driving in Athens on your way to or from the Island—traffic there is the very definition of chaos.) Greeks display little reverence for stop signs either.

This cavalier attitude toward rules became such a problem at an intersection of three Island roads that the *dímos* built a roundabout there. Unfortunately, no yield signs are posted anywhere around the circle, and no one seems to remember the rules for entering and exiting, so this change may have been a step backward rather than forward.

Though there aren't many donkeys, sheep, or goats on the roads these days, traffic still gets snarled on the Island during peak season when the Island's full of tourists in rental cars. (In my opinion, they should limit the number of cars allowed here; some other islands don't allow any.)

Farmers, wearing hats or caps, long sleeves, and woolen vests—even in August—are now more often seen driving small three-wheeled trucks or ATVs than riding donkeys, but if you see one on a donkey, be sure to take a good look. The saddles here are made of wood, not leather. The farmers pad them and sit side-saddle, after finding a stone to step on to help them mount. The farmer's dog often trots alongside.

Even without animals on the roads, driving on the Island is not for amateurs. Most roads here are narrow, twisty, hilly, and badly built. Heedless, motorists often drive in the middle of the road, even on blind curves, making for frequent near misses. The roads rebuilt recently are much better, but the road conditions are still too poor and the drivers too reckless for me to be comfortable having Aris bicycle here.

Just the other day, a car rounding a curve in a hurry almost rode down a bicyclist wearing a proper white helmet and staying on the edge of his lane. Bicyclists are simply not expected here, so no one looks out for them. They barely look out for pedestrians! The rule here is "walker beware."

When traveling to an appointment, you need to allow more time than the drive actually takes, especially during peak season. Islanders traveling in opposite directions may stop to chat in their vehicles right in the middle of the road. They may also stop in the traffic lane to have a conversation with friends they see walking or sitting on the side of the road. And those driving construction vehicles sometimes stop right in the road to get a coffee! "Island Time," you know.

You also need to allow for delays caused by those who park in the street, temporarily (with flashers on) or longer-term, with their cars wholly or partially in the traffic lane. Cars "parked" like this on both sides of the road—not unusual on the road to the main village during peak season—pose a particular problem when a bus or truck comes along: You need to be prepared to get off the road to let the bus pass.

The road to our bay has four hairpin turns descending the hill, and sections of the road aren't wide enough for two cars of any size to pass unless one gives way and pulls over wherever a wider space may be found—before or after projecting rocks. That road is a bulldozed and paved donkey path, not ideal for motor vehicles.

Since most cars here are stick shifts, it's a traditional courtesy for the car traveling downhill to pull over at a likely spot and wait for the car traveling uphill to pass. This custom is observed by Islanders and Island regulars but isn't known to strangers. So, if I'm driving on the narrow part of the road to our bay, see a car coming from the other direction, and spot a place to pull over, I do, whether I'm ascending or descending. Even this is not enough for some people, particularly those who have no conception of the size of the vehicles they're driving.

One such visiting driver panicked over trying to pass me, even though I'd pulled over and there was more than enough space. She yelled that the Forester was too big, and I had no business bringing a car that size to the Island! The roads—and the drivers—here often cause me to wish that our car had a switch for retracting the side mirrors, as European cars do.

Here as elsewhere, people can get a bit crazed about their imagined privileges as drivers. Every year (except during the pandemic) there's been a wonderful, week-long program of classical music offered in various Island venues with performances by Greek and other artists. One of these events is held at the church of the Virgin Mary On The Mountain, a lovely venue offering a magnificent view of the wide bay, Platýs Gialós. The narrow road/driveway to that church was unpaved dirt and gravel and barely wide enough for two cars to pass carefully. One year, I took Cousin George's granddaughter and got her agreement to leave a little early to avoid a long wait to exit.

Cars were parked along the length of the driveway, and I passed them with care as I left. Just as I approached the junction with the road, a car entered the driveway. Passing was an impossibility, and I signaled the other driver to back up. He got out of his car and angrily insisted that I was on the road to his house and I was the one who had to back up.

I pointed to the long and growing line of cars behind me, which made my backing up impossible, and said, "*Den boró*" ("I can't"). The cars behind me started honking with impatience. His prudent female companion took over and moved his car, allowing me and the other concert attendees to leave.

I had a similar experience exiting the parking lot of the restaurant where we eat almost every day. The road to the parking lot is a narrow lane, with a stone and chestnut beam fence on the restaurant side and trees and a drop to the beach on the other. It's very unusual for me to drive there, but I was running quite late after taking Lira home and doing some shopping, and I was hungry! I left after lunch and was in front of the restaurant's fenced patio when a car came toward me. There were places where he could've pulled over, but nowhere I could.

I signaled for him to pull over. He refused and yelled at me to back up. I was contemplating doing that, even though I dislike backing up in such narrow spaces, when he yelled an epithet—the Greek word I hate most— *malákas*, which means "masturbator" (he wasn't an Islander; no Islander would have done that).

That did it! I pulled out my cell phone, turned off the ignition, and waited. I'd already eaten and guessed he hadn't.

Eventually, he did back up and let me leave, but he sure wasn't happy about it. Such is life in peak season.

This isn't a story about our Island, but it's such a very Greek experience that I'm sharing it anyway. We went to Crete in the '80s with good friends. One was carefully navigating the little rental car on a narrow road beside a walled town and tooting the horn before every turn, when a large truck approached. He tooted, edged over, stopped, and waited. The truck—evidently with bad brakes—slowed but kept coming and hit our rental car. It was a minor accident.

The truck driver, his companion, Aris, and one Greek friend exited their respective vehicles, and stood in the road, yelling. The trucker didn't deny his fault but wanted nothing to do with any sort of report. He kept throwing five-thousand-drachma bills (worth roughly $20 each at the time) and insisting that the offered sum was enough. The volume of the argument kept increasing. Until—suddenly—things were settled, at which point, everyone shook hands and left.

<hr />

Parking on the Island in peak season is perhaps even more interesting than driving. Greeks park everywhere! Inside a parking lot, people sometimes park perpendicularly six or seven feet behind your bumper and leave. It's possible to exit such a situation very slowly via repeated maneuvers with the help of a spotter, but it's a wicked thing to do to someone. I suspect that such occurrences account for many of the significant door dents so many cars here display.

A concert I attended in the main village was interrupted by an announcement asking whoever had parked a green Toyota

Camry, license number XXX0000, in the drive lane of the public parking lot to move it so that others could exit. They added that the performance would resume only after the car was moved. We had to wait a while, but it was moved eventually.

Some drivers here seem to think that parking illegally yields special privileges. While I was in the computer store patiently awaiting my turn to buy supplies, an acquaintance rushed in, insisting that she be served *amésos*—immediately—because she'd left her car in the street with her blinkers on! I held my tongue, letting her go ahead, but I couldn't resist saying, "*Geia sou*" (hi), when she turned to leave. She froze, her complacent expression instantly changing to embarrassment.

Island parking is perilous enough without discourtesy. When Faní parked her car next to a stone retaining wall in the main village, the wall collapsed and crushed it!

CHAPTER FORTY

Boating!

What is a Greek Island without a boat?

We bought our first boat in 2001. Named *Loráki* after me, and still going strong, it's a traditional sixteen-foot outboard motorboat that seats six, although it's mighty slow with six adults on board. We've circumnavigated the whole Island in this little boat in calm seas. It's perfect for traveling to undeveloped bays and coves, anchoring, diving in, swimming as long as we like, then going on to the next spot and diving in again. Such trips are idyllic.

But boating can be challenging too. We once took this boat from the main port to our bay in six Beaufort winds. Kóstas (formerly a ship's captain) was at the dock when we left and tried hard to persuade us not to go. It wasn't a pleasant ride, but we made it just fine, hugging the coast and going slowly.

Bumpy seas and high winds have caused us to make various unintentional gifts to Poseidon: several duck-billed hats each; a sunglass clip the wind pulled off Aris's glasses while he was wearing them; and two of Aris's prescription diving masks that bumped right off the seat of the boat into deep water as we were traveling.

I also unintentionally sacrificed my prescription sunglasses to Poseidon when I dropped them getting out of the boat in Vathí Bay. Three of us scoured the shallow water with masks on but couldn't find them in the seaweed.

My biggest unintended offering to Poseidon had nothing to do with the boat. I used to wear my wedding band to the beach (since Mána wore hers), thinking it was too tight to slip off. It did just that while we played volleyball in the shallows with Faní and Dimítris. Frantic searching with masks was unavailing.

I wonder if Poseidon enjoyed our gifts.

I *love* boating with the *Loráki*, but, as with all boats, we've had some misadventures with it. We learned to take potable water in the boat after we got stranded in an undeveloped bay for quite a while without any. We were rescued by the crew of a rental yacht. They gave us cold drinks, used their tools to get the motor started, and escorted us all the way back to our bay. We were very grateful for the kindness of those strangers.

We were stuck again the next year in a bay of the nearby un-inhabited island. After that, Aris convinced the mechanic who services the boat—a very decent fellow—that we *really, really* wanted him to throw the old gas out every year because it develops a crust over the winter that clogs the engine.

After a long day of swimming and boating, Aris once offered to drop me off at the little quay below the church on the rocky peninsula in our bay so that I could stay dry—a fine offer I eagerly accepted. Unfortunately, as I was leaving the boat (deboating?) with one foot on the quay and one foot on the bow of the boat, I remarked that the boat was very close to rocks.

Another mistake.

Aris immediately backed up. I did the splits and went *splunk!* into the sea—hat, sunglasses, towel, and all. It was like something out of a cartoon, and Aris couldn't stop laughing. I wasn't hurt and didn't lose anything—except my dignity—but it was a long, sloppy, salty walk home.

My hat did not recover.

CHAPTER FORTY-ONE

Keeping in Touch

When I first came to the Island in 1978, we communicated with the rest of the world via postcard, letter, or by lining up in the post office to use the community phone—briefly, of course, since others were waiting. To my recollection, there were no phones in private homes here at that time.

Phone service gradually expanded, village by village, but it was simultaneously expensive and of poor quality. I used to joke that if Americans had realized how superior our phone service was compared to other places, we'd never have broken up Ma Bell. Calling the States from a landline was extremely expensive here, and the landline at our house was dreadful. We still have to pay for *every* call we make with it, including calls to others on the Island.

The best thing that happened to telephone service in Greece was the advent of the cellular phone. That, too, was a slow process on the Island. When Aris and his colleague were both here in 2004 with their BlackBerrys, they couldn't get a signal at our home, but they could get one—one at a time—if they went down to the beach. Even now, we must often go outside to get a decent signal since we're in a narrow valley, against the stony side of a steep hill.

Not long after the turn of the century, a couple of internet cafés appeared on the Island for those who absolutely had to be connected. A houseguest in 2007 was among them. She was flabbergasted to learn that we had no internet access at our home. She paid almost daily visits via taxi to the internet café in town.

Assumptions that we had internet access back then led to some crossed wires. One incident involved my goddaughter, Nicole, who was arriving with a friend from a trip to Israel. I arranged for Leonídas to meet them at the ferry. Since he didn't have time to pick me up before going to get them at the port, I made a sign with Nicole's name on it for him to hold up. He drove to the port at the appointed time, turned down others who wanted rides, and waited . . . and waited. No girls appeared. Eventually, he returned home with an empty cab—something I heard about from his mother for weeks afterward.

Alarmed, I called Nicole's mom in the States. She said the girls had sent an email letting me know they'd changed their itinerary, never imagining that the message wouldn't reach me. They were duly retrieved the next day. We made it up to Leonídas—who refused to accept payment for the earlier trip to the port—by hiring him to take us all over the Island and tipping him generously.

Like everywhere else, internet cafés on the Island went the way of the dinosaurs when internet access became available in homes, hotels, restaurants, and even as a community service in the larger villages. I don't remember when it became available in our bay, but we subscribed to it in 2011.

We sometimes lose access over the winter due to dampness corroding the phone wire. When that happens, we have neither the house phone nor Wi-Fi until the electrician can get here to replace it. Fortunately, the restaurant on the beach below us—the one we patronize nearly every day—has Wi-Fi, and we can check our email there while waiting for the electrician.

Internet service at our home is maddeningly slow to this day. Download speed is only five megabits on a good day (it used to be three). This is much slower than in the main village, but it keeps us connected to the world. These days, like everyone else, everywhere else, we depend on it.

We use a VPN with a U.S. IP address to access our accounts at our banks and other financial institutions. We also use it to speak with friends in other countries and to attend board meetings virtually. And it's how I managed my elderly mom's finances, medications, and medical appointments, and called her every day until she died, without breaking the bank.

Once you've grown dependent on having internet access, its loss is traumatic. When I bought an iPhone in June 2020 from a wireless carrier, after our arrival here was delayed by the pandemic, I carefully explained that I would need to change the SIM card when I was in Greece. I was assured that the phone was unlocked.

Ha!

When we got here, I found it locked. I "chatted" with the carrier and was told that the price I paid for that iPhone was contingent on it being locked for *two whole years*! Like too many others, the salesperson who sold me the phone suffered from ignorance, apathy, or both. Aris to the rescue! He'd kept his old iPhone 5 and reset it for me to use with my Greek SIM card. Whew!

Because our house is reinforced concrete, the Wi-Fi signal doesn't travel very far—not to our bedroom or to the guest rooms. No one at our place can lie in bed surfing the web. But why would anyone want to when the brilliant Aegean Sea is waiting?

CHAPTER FORTY-TWO

Keeping Up Appearances

I never look as good at the end of the summer as I do when I first arrive—personal services here are limited. That reminds me of a conversation I had with one of Aris's cousins, who was quite lovely in her youth and had a fabulous figure. Now in her late seventies (or so), she's still very attractive—and stylish. She takes excellent care of herself and doesn't look her age.

Admiring her, I asked her about a facialist. She said there wasn't anyone on the Island she would trust, and confided that, after spending the summer on the Island, "I need *two* days in a spa to recover myself. One isn't enough." I see her point. There was a time when I was low maintenance, but that time has long passed. These days, I want all the help I can get!

A good resort hotel has been in operation on Vathí Bay since about 2004, and we enjoyed a wonderful stay there with a large group one September. If that hotel offered facials, I would get one there. The fact that it doesn't could reflect either a lack of demand by its guests or a lack of confidence in the local prac-titioners. I'm unwilling to take a chance.

And I'm unwilling to give up any of my time on the Island for a trip to Athens for a facial. So, I bring with me from the States four and a half months' worth of facial cleanser and mud masks, as well as hydrating masks, eye cream, moisturizer, and heavy sunscreen, which, of course, dooms us to always having to check one bag (I also bring cologne, but most of the time, my fragrance here is "*Eau de* Off!")

One summer, before I started bringing all those cleansers and masks to counter the effects of heavy sunscreen, I got a blemish so big I could see it just looking down—almost a second nose! And, wouldn't you know, that was the year a multimillionaire associat-ed with Aris's former business arrived on his 125-foot yacht with his family—the talk of the Island. Nothing like having a giant zit on your face, immortalized in lots of photos, to keep you humble.

If you spend more than four months on an Island, have short hair, and don't want the world to know just how much gray you have, you must either do it yourself or patronize a hairdresser. I can trim my hair a bit without making too much of a mess, but a full haircut is beyond my skill set. And I had a disastrous expe-rience with do-it-yourself hair color, so to the *kommotírio* I go.

This can be an adventure on the Island, and not always a pleasant one (Aris doesn't suffer this fate; I always cut his hair—but then, he doesn't have very much).

There's a very talented hairstylist here. She once gave me the best haircut of my life. But another time, despite sharing photos of the prior cut and asking her to cut "very little," she lopped off more than half my hair! Normally, I have it trimmed every four weeks, but that summer, I went twelve full weeks without a haircut.

Adding insult to injury, she managed to slosh shampoo in my eyes and down the front of my top. I left her salon, and suffered through dinner with friends, with extremely short hair, a wet blouse, and smeared mascara. Needless to say, I found someone else (a friend later told me that the same hairdresser also ignored her request for a trim and lopped off half of her hair too).

I next visited a stylist who paid attention when I asked her not to cut my hair very much—and she even did highlights! But I made the mistake of saying that my hair had bleached a lot in the sun from swimming. To compensate, she made my base color *two* shades darker.

Instead of looking like a natural dark blonde, I had dark hair, topped with very light blonde "frosting," and one side was significantly shorter than the other. It didn't look bad; it looked rather exotic—but certainly not natural. Far worse, she burned my hair. My hairdresser in the States speculated that she may not have taken into account that I have thinner strands than most Greeks. My over-processed hair was so dry and fragile that I slept with oil on it every night for the rest of the summer.

I then found a stylist who did a great job, without burning my hair, except once when she delegated coloring it to her assistant, who inexplicably dyed it dark brown. She was unembarrassed and breezily assured me that it would lighten in the sun and seawater. An American friend said that I should have refused to pay. I would never do that as word gets around, and I don't want it to be said that the *Amerikanída* cheated an Islander.

The good news about pedicures on the Island is that they're available. The bad news is that if there's a place on the Island to get anything approximating a spa pedicure, I've yet to find it. I contacted the resort hotel for the names and numbers of the nail technicians it used and went to one. When she quit working after having a baby, I went to the other one.

Both used the same process: They filled portable plastic tubs (which you fervently hope are properly sanitized) with water for soaking your feet. You then put your feet on top of a stool to have your rough skin removed—the sand here is not kind to feet— and your nails polished. The stools were so high that I wondered what older folks were expected to do. Eventually, my nail tech bought a chair with a footrest. Unfortunately, the mechanism to adjust the chair's height was broken (or never existed) so I had to climb into it using a stepladder. I'm still wondering how older, less agile customers managed.

My hairdresser engaged a wonderful nail tech last year, and I enjoyed her services the whole season. But she had another baby last winter and closed her shop—causing me to lose both her services and those of the nail tech in one blow. *Katastrofí* (catastrophe)! I went back to the second stylist, refraining from highlights. So far, so good—*chtýpa xýlo*, as the Greeks say for "knock on wood." With Lira's help, I located my nail tech. Yay! Life on a small island is never dull.

The sea, sun, and sand here are balm for the soul but aren't kind to hair, skin, or nails. So, as Aris's cousin said, we do the best we can while on this beautiful Island and "recover" when we return home.

CHAPTER FORTY-THREE

Water and Other Public Services

Water: Where, Oh Where, Did It Go?

Water on this arid Island is a huge issue.

There was no public water in the main village when I first arrived in 1978. I remember Babás hiring a water tank with a *very* long hose to refill the cistern of the village house when it was depleted by our usage. Some years later (in the early 1990s, I seem to recall), water pipes were laid on the edges of the stone-step streets in the villages. In country places like our valley, hoses—yes, hoses—about twice the diameter of a garden hose were laid.

I mentioned earlier that we have both public and cistern water at our house. We don't drink the water from either source, though we do brush our teeth with it. Access to both is essential. One winter, after we emptied the cistern to have it cleaned, there was very little rain and, consequently, little water in our cistern. Concerned about possibly exhausting our cistern supply, we started the summer using public water.

That lasted only a few weeks because the water in the faucets turned brown, generating bitter complaints around the Island. Aris was in Athens, so I had to undertake the switch to cistern water. It shouldn't have been hard—just four levers. One is on the pipe beside the meter down the driveway, simple enough to change. The other three are in the basement.

The engineer I married told me to "close the valve on the pipe to the public water system and open the valves on the pipes to the cistern." Perfect if you know how to do that. No help if you don't. Unfortunately, I didn't.

In the basement, I stared at the pipes, hoping for inspiration, which they stubbornly refused to provide. Finally, I moved the three red levers, leaving the four blue ones alone. That worked. Another Island lesson learned. I now keep photos of the correct lever positions for public and cistern water—eliminating the need for future engineering consultations.

Another reason for the dual water supply is that we can't use the cistern water if the pump doesn't work. We sometimes lose power in the summer when the heat causes the insulation on the power lines to crack, or it shuts off for other reasons. And the pump doesn't work without electricity.

You would think, would you not, that having duplicate water sources would be enough. Not quite!

One summer, when our cistern was full to the brim from a particularly wet winter, the pump failed a mere two days after we arrived. We switched to public water. Then it abruptly failed, too.

We suspected a broken water line, since service was restored within hours. Two days later, however, we lost water again—while I was in the shower with shampoo in my hair. Good thing we keep lots of bottled water on hand!

That interruption was due to an Islander down the road watering his pigs. Every single evening while the pump was out, we lost water for a while. When the plumber asked which replacement pump we wanted him to order, I voted for whichever would get here sooner!

The new pump arrived quickly, and the plumber promptly came with his father to install it. As is customary here, we offered refreshments when the job was done. While they were eating, the conversation turned to water issues. Having brown public water is a serious problem for those lacking adequate cistern water. You can drink and cook with bottled water, but how do you bathe and wash dishes and clothes when the water in the pipes is brown?

Like others who love the Island, the plumbers complained that the authorities—who don't live here—should stop allowing the construction of buildings without cisterns and of swimming pools, given the recurrent water shortages. We completely agree!

They also rightfully complained about foreigners who plant gardens unsuited to the Island, which require tons of water to maintain. Although our own plantings are not what anyone would call lush, Aris quickly explained that—except when we have no choice (for instance, when the pump is out)—we use only cistern water for our plants and everything else.

Speaking of water, water heaters are different here. They're much smaller, for one thing—which means no long, luxurious showers—and they're turned on only when needed, about 20 minutes in advance. Because of the 220-volt current, they're not left on while showering or bathing. If you stay in a bed and breakfast or a small hotel—here or elsewhere in Greece—expect instructions about turning the water heater on and off.

From ATMs to Amazon and the Case
of the Missing Step Stool

There are several ATMs on the Island, but only one staffed bank branch, located in the main village. It's open only on weekdays and only from 8:00 a.m. to 2:00 p.m. (And Americans think bankers' hours are bad in the States!)

The only post office on the Island is in the main village too. If you live there, your mail is delivered. But there's no postal service delivery to bays like ours. For many years, we had all our mail from the States—which takes 10 to 14 days to get here—sent in care of Faní to the village house, so we could get it from her, instead of lining up at the post office before 2:30 p.m. (on weekdays only) to retrieve it. I used to have packages sent in care of Faní too, but she now lives on another island when she's not in Athens, so we're reduced to retrieving our mail at the post office during the limited hours it's open.

A few years ago, Cousin George's granddaughter ordered something from Amazon.com (yes, from the U.S.) and it was delivered *to their house*—months later—but it *was* delivered! Inspired, I placed an order with Amazon Germany for printer ink. I directed it to be shipped to No. 10 River Road in our bay, a made-up but descriptive address.

The package was delivered to our front door—and it was only a few days late! I was very impressed. Emboldened, I ordered three items from Amazon Spain, giving the same address. My luck didn't hold. Two of the three, both small, were delivered to the post office, where we picked them up. The third, a plastic folding step stool, was MIA.

Chasing a missing package is never fun, but language issues make it harder here. The Amazon Spain site didn't offer an

English-language option. Thanks to Google Translate, I wrote my complaint in Spanish, as well as English. The representative replied that UPS confirmed delivery. I answered that Amazon Spain's site showed delivery to Athens—not here.

The rep then promised to investigate and asked for three days. While waiting, I checked with the local post office. Not there. I tried to "chat" with the UPS Spain site, but the chatbot knew only Spanish. The Greek UPS site reported "delivery in progress" and "address information needed"—offering no way to supply it on that site. I tracked down the phone number, called, and was told that a subcontractor had the package. I got its phone number.

After many unanswered calls—and just as I was about to give up—the subcontractor picked up, found the package, and told me I could get it at their office in the main village. Yay! I was sorely tempted to ask when they had planned to let us know that the package was available, but I restrained myself. I wanted to get it right away, but with the energy crisis arising from the war in Ukraine, Aris persuaded me that it was more responsible to wait until we went to the main village for other reasons.

Waiting was a mistake.

When Aris got there two days later, they said they'd been instructed to send it back (apparently, they had no intention of calling to let us know that either). So, more than a month after ordering it—and after a whole lot of effort—we still had no step stool. At least we got a refund.

I was all for ordering from Amazon Germany, but Aris found one on a Greek website. The color was unfortunate, but by that point I didn't care. It was delivered a week later! But—isn't there always a but?—it was broken. Aris informed the company, I repackaged it, and we shipped it back. To my surprise and delight, it was promptly replaced!

You're thinking that this is a lot of fuss and bother for a plastic step stool, aren't you? If we lived somewhere other than a small Greek island, you'd be right. But a lightweight folding step stool, which Lira and I both use often, is not to be found here.

I try to think of such inconveniences as a peculiar form of entertainment. They are a small price for the privilege of living on the Island.

CHAPTER FORTY-FOUR

Food Obsession

Food as Culture

Food is a really big deal in Greece. It's impossible to fully understand Greek life without appreciating both the food and the central role it plays in daily routines and relationships. It's a rare conversation that doesn't turn to food—what to eat, when, and where. Greeks eat a lot at the table, but obesity is much less common than in the States. I suspect it's because Greeks typically eat quality food at mealtimes and don't snack on junk.

Before the economic crisis, the typical table of a Greek family at a restaurant was packed with several appetizers (*mezédes*), salads, and multiple main courses, followed by fruit, dessert, or both. When dining at someone's home, seconds were a given.

On one of my early visits to Greece, we met several of Aris's prep school classmates and their wives for dinner. Multiple plates were passed around the table, and just when I thought I couldn't eat another bite, someone piped up with, "Children, what are we going to eat? It's getting late and we haven't eaten anything!" She wasn't joking—to Greeks, appetizers don't count.

Fruit!

Among the foods I most enjoy here are the delicious fresh fruits. In June, we gorge on cherries and apricots. When I was a kid, my folks had an apricot tree in the backyard, and I loved them. I hadn't smelled or tasted a real apricot in years—until I came here.

There are also wonderful peaches, donut-shaped (Saturn) peaches, and nectarines! The aroma is intoxicating. Later, the melons—similar to honeydews and oh so sweet—come into season, along with watermelons, cantaloupes, plums, pears, and grapes. The prize goes to figs, of course, but I've already told you about them.

Unique Offerings

Greece offers some unique cuisine. If you visit, be sure to find a taverna specializing in *kokorétsi* and *kontosoúvli*, both prepared on a rotisserie.

Kontosoúvli is grilled marinated pork and pancetta. When done well, it's rich and delicious. *Kokorétsi* is traditionally served at Easter feasts. Although some sources say that it was introduced to Greece by the Ottomans, others contend that it's a remnant of ancient Greek sacrificial feasts—the gods got the muscle meat, and the people ate the rest.

Kokorétsi is made of the seasoned internal organs of a lamb—liver, heart, kidneys, spleen, and sweetbreads—wrapped in seasoned intestines and grilled on a spit. I *know* it sounds nasty, but if you're adventurous, it's fabulous when prepared well. We like it with yellow mustard.

I made *kokorétsi* once and will *never* do that again. In Pittsburgh, before we retired, we prepared to celebrate Greek Easter one year by ordering a spring lamb. We dug a pit in our backyard and assembled a remarkable hand-turned spit created as a gift by engineers in Aris's department. We then rounded up guests to turn the spit and enjoy the results and eagerly awaited a delicious feast.

When we ordered the lamb, we asked for the internal organs needed for *kokorétsi*, but hadn't anticipated the stench and mess of thoroughly cleaning intestines. I can't imagine a worse job. Since we didn't know the tricks for preparing it properly, it wasn't very good—certainly not worth the effort.

Istanbul is still called Constantinople in Greece, even at the airport—a practice likely tied to the fall of the city to the Ottomans in 1453. While there, we eagerly searched for *kokorétsi*, thinking that it would be best at the reputed source. We were severely disappointed: It was boiled or steamed, and revolting. That experience gave us an object lesson in the difference between expectation and reality.

Babás used to tell a story about Mána, who was always skeptical of the cleanliness of other kitchens. One time, when they were eating *kokorétsi* with the King of Greece, one of the diners complimented the chef and asked what he'd done to make it so delicious, noting that his own cook had never been able to make it so well.

The chef asked, "Does he clean the intestines thoroughly?"

"Of course," the diner replied.

"Ah," said the chef. "That's the problem."

He was joking, of course, but Mána turned green and never touched it again.

On the Island, *mastélo* is a delicious alternative to the traditional Easter lamb on a spit with *kokorétsi*. This is lamb or kid meat washed in wine and cooked in a special unglazed clay pot—which looks something like a large canister laid on its side, though any unglazed ceramic roaster will do. Traditionally, the meat is placed on top of crosshatched sticks from the *skínos* bush. Since delicious *mastélo* is readily available here, I haven't made it myself. In case you'd like to try it, the simple recipe is in the Appendix.

Although it's debatable whether *kokorétsi* originated in Turkey, I have it on good authority that *soutzoukákia* (ground beef ovals in tomato sauce) did, and I've included my version of Mána's recipe in the Appendix, along with her recipe for a vegan dish, Artichokes Constantinople (*Agkináres à la Políta*). Enjoy!

The "Unmentionables"

Another unusual food is *amelétita*. On the Island, the term is used to refer to lamb's testicles—though it literally means "unmentionables." They may not sound appetizing, but like lamb kidneys, they're delectable when lightly floured, seasoned with salt and pepper, sautéed in good olive oil, and served with lemon wedges. I was introduced to them on my very first trip to the Island.

Aris and Babá thought it would be fun to play a trick on the *Amerikanída* from Kentucky—they ordered *amelétita* and didn't tell me what they were. When I'd happily eaten half a serving, they burst out laughing, and the truth came out. Having expected me to be revolted, they were dumbstruck when I blithely asked for more. The restaurant's owner was so impressed that he sent a whole bag of them home with me!

Weeds and Desserts

No discussion of Greek food would be complete without mentioning greens and desserts. Greeks eat a wide variety of greens, including arugula, dandelion greens, rapini, beet greens, and *vlíta*—which we believe to be sorrel greens, though some say that they are amaranth. Collectively, these are known as *chórta* (weeds). Instead of spinach pie, you may find delicious *chortópita* on offer—savory pie made with wild greens. (Some tavernas also offer savory onion, mushroom, or tomato pies.)

As to desserts, you probably know *baklavás*, one of the traditional baked phyllo pastry desserts made with chopped nuts (walnuts, pistachios, or almonds), soaked in a honey-based syrup with cinnamon and cloves. *Baklavás* and related desserts (like *kataífi*, made with a thin pastry like shredded phyllo) are available all over the Island and elsewhere in Greece, but there are many others.

There are marzipan-like sweets made with almonds (*amygdalotá*), an almond macaroon, Island biscuits with nuts, and *galaktoboúreko*—Greek custard (made from semolina, milk, vanilla, and eggs), baked in layers of crispy phyllo and covered with a syrup of sugar and lemon. *Bougátsa*—Aris's favorite—is made with creamy custard wrapped in crispy phyllo, sprinkled with melted butter, and garnished with confectioners' sugar and cinnamon.

And then there's a very special cookie, made on the Island, only in September, of ground almonds, spiced with cinnamon and cloves, and baked inside a pastry shell coated with confectioners' sugar. Friends beg us for these cookies. And we bring some back to the States!

Plenty of other confections are made here, too, including: *melópita*, similar to cheesecake, made with honey, soft cheese, and eggs in a pie crust; an absolutely devastating chocolate cake (oddly called a pie); a tangy orange pie; and my favorite, *pástes*. Similar to the small Northern Italian cakes, *pástes* are so light they practically melt in your mouth. Some Greeks insist that the Italians copied them! If you have a sweet tooth, be sure to visit a *zacharoplasteíon* (confectionery) when you come.

<hr />

To understand the Greeks, eat like them: not just the foods, but the noise, abundance, and joy of sharing a meal.

CHAPTER FORTY-FIVE

Getting Stoned (Benches and Tables)

On the Island, building is never one and done.

Ten years after we moved into the house, I was jolted awake at 7:30 a.m.—much too early, since we'd gotten home well after midnight. I desperately wanted to stay asleep, to hold on to my dream about my dad, who had died two years earlier (I almost always have vivid dreams here—I think it's the clean air). But no matter how I tried, I couldn't drift back to sleep—not with workmen smashing apart the concrete benches of the upstairs balcony right above our bedroom.

The only good thing about workers breaking concrete on the roof above my head was that they weren't using jackhammers!

The benches had to be demolished because, over the winter, the paint had peeled off our bedroom walls, a crack snaked along the wall toward the electrical conduit, and deep fissures had split open the upper outside corner of the house just below those benches. Once the stone tops of the benches were removed, their shoddy construction became obvious: Even though it hadn't rained in over two months, they were full of water!

After rebuilding the benches, parts of the eastern, southern, and western exterior walls above our bedroom had to be reconstructed too. The repairs solved the water problem, but the patches aren't perfect. They are quite visible to me and to the painters, though probably not to most people.

At least the paint stopped peeling completely off our bedroom walls.

<hr />

Several years later, we had another adventure with stone when we finally ended our ongoing debate and decided to have a round table built in the center of the circular part of our veranda we call the *alóni*. Until then, our only outdoor table was wooden, sixty inches long, and kept under the pergola outside the dining room. It was great for four, cramped for six, and impossible for more. After several episodes of dragging the indoor dining table outside to seat additional guests—and after repeated complaints by friends about how little we used the *alóni*, despite its stunning view—we surrendered.

Aris ordered the table to be two meters in diameter. This time, the builder paid attention, so the table is huge! Because it's so big, we usually sit with our guests on the side facing the sea and serve food buffet-style on the opposite side.

It took two workers the better part of three days to build it. Perhaps because he felt bad about the botched bathroom in the new guest suite, the builder personally supervised the first two days of the construction. The base was formed as a circular pillar of reinforced concrete, and covered with stacked, mortared stones. Wooden forms were custom-built for the reinforced concrete tabletop, including a hole for an umbrella.

After the concrete was poured—four inches thick!—and had cured for a while, we were told to water it daily for a week, which we did faithfully. When the week was up, slate stones were hand-chipped and carefully laid on top by Lira's brother, so precisely that plates and glasses don't wobble at all. Even with all that work, the table cost less than €800! Unwilling to wait until the painters could come to do it, I applied the stone sealant to the tabletop myself and painted its sides white.

Thrilled with the new table in the *alóni*, we decided to re-place the wooden table with another stone table in front of the *pentzoúles* under the pergola outside the dining room. Since that area is smaller, we chose a single slab of stone for the tabletop, as is customary on the Island. The slab was set on two stacks of ceramic blocks, covered in concrete and painted white.

The deliverymen recruited the Albanians working in the field across from our driveway to help carry the slab to its desti-nation on our back veranda—which they readily agreed to do. The tip of one corner broke off during transport, giving the table additional character. The surface isn't smooth enough to keep glasses and plates from wobbling, but it looks stunning in front of the *pentzoúles*, flanked by ceramic pots of Greek basil.

With the *pentzoúles*, the basil, and the plants we've man-aged to coax from the earth, the stone tables gave us lovely spac-es for entertaining friends and enjoying the slow progression of summer.

CHAPTER FORTY-SIX

New Appliances, Island Style

When your new refrigerator is delivered after 8 p.m., you know you're living on Island Time.

After twenty years with our original appliances, we were ready to replace the troublesome refrigerator (*psygeío*) and stove/oven—called a *kouzína* (literally, "kitchen"). Both were freestanding, not built in. I don't remember why we didn't choose built-ins, as we'd always done in the States, but in hindsight, it was a wise decision.

One of Aris's cousins put a built-in *kouzína* in her house, built a few years before ours, and when she tried to replace it, she couldn't do it without tearing the cabinets apart. So, she resorted to putting a small oven and a hotplate on top of the useless built-in—a fate we were determined to avoid.

Finding new appliances that would fit in the spaces between (and, for the fridge, also under) our cabinets wasn't too hard—except for the color. My small appliances are red, and I really wanted to get the new fridge and stove in red too. With white cabinets, gray stone floors, and gray tile on the backsplash and countertops, red would've been smashing! But no luck: We couldn't find the sizes we needed in red. We couldn't get both appliances in the same stainless-steel finish either, so we settled for white again (Maybe white will come back into fashion?)

It took the owner of the Island appliance store several days to confirm that he could get the models we'd picked. But once he did, I was amazed by how quickly delivery occurred. At eight o'clock one evening, as we were about to walk out the door to dinner with our visiting younger godson, the store owner called to say that they were leaving to deliver the refrigerator! Island Time strikes again! We frantically emptied the refrigerator and freezer into cardboard boxes—grateful that we had them and plenty of ice to keep things cold.

Just as we finished—a scant half hour later—the store owner arrived with a helper to haul away the old fridge and install the new one. Removal was incredibly messy: When turned off and tilted, the old fridge dripped rusty water all the way out the front door. Luckily, I'd retrieved the mop and bucket, anticipating some mess, though not that much. By the time the new fridge was installed and restocked, we were starving! We practically ran to the other restaurant in our bay, arriving just before the 10:00 p.m. cutoff for ordering. We inhaled that meal!

The installation wasn't quite right, though. After checking the manual, we realized the fridge was too close to the back wall. But when we pulled it forward, the left side was lower than the right. With stone floors, crooked happens. The store owner adjusted it when the stove was delivered some days later, propping the left back foot up with leftover ceramic tiles.

Finally—after twenty years—I have a refrigerator door that opens *toward* the work area of the kitchen!

Although most appliances sold in Europe come with thick manuals in multiple languages, the manual for the new stove—a product of Italy—is exclusively in Greek. I could read the words, but that didn't mean I understood them all. I knew that "air roasting" meant convection cooking but I had no clue what "moist roasting" meant. Neither did Aris. I recently consulted ChatGPT and learned it's braising. There was nothing in the manual on the subject of baking pitas, though it had pages and pages about baking pizza!

Illustrating the principle that "God sometimes punishes you by giving you what you ask for," I can't roast eggplants on the sleek glass stovetop, something I hadn't considered when we placed the order. A portable hotplate serves that purpose now. The very best part, though, is that the new oven radiates *much* less heat than the old one did—and, for the first time in twenty years, the broiler works!

The refrigerator and stove/oven were delivered and installed without our having signed anything or paid a single euro upfront. As Aris says, there are advantages to living on a small island where everyone's known you since you were five years old. He had to chase the appliance store owner to get the invoice and pay him—one of the many quirks I love about the Island.

Here, everything comes with a story.

CHAPTER FORTY-SEVEN

Panigýria (Saints' Day Celebrations)

On the Island, a *panigýri* isn't just a religious service, it's a community celebration.

The tradition is that there are 365 churches here, one for each day of the year. The real number, I'm told, is just under 300 churches, which is still quite remarkable for an island with fewer than 3,000 residents. Other than those in villages, churches here often perch atop hills and ridges and have stunning views. Many are tiny, deep in the countryside, and accessible only by foot, donkey—or, more recently, ATV—via narrow donkey paths (*monopátia*).

Even at the most remote churches, people come to these evening celebrations from all over. Strangers to the Island often display no reverence or respect for the liturgy and talk incessantly. But those from—or with connections to—the Island participate, greeting each other with the traditional "*voítheiá sas*" ("may it help you"). Saints' days are known to all Greeks, but I don't know how strangers to the Island find the churches in remote locations. Word somehow gets around.

The event includes the procession of the icon, and blessing the sponsors of the feast, their families, those in attendance, and the special loaves of bread—large, round, dusted with powdered sugar and stacked high—which are cut and distributed, first to the sponsors and then to everyone else.

After the service comes food and drink. The typical beverages are wine and water. At the larger events, where the churches have kitchen and dining facilities and there are more sponsors, everyone is served a full meal. Wine is poured and toasts are made to the sponsors (*panigyrádes),* the cooks, the servers, and everyone else. Diners bang their utensils on the plates and let out a yell, calling a blessing on the sponsors.

Delicious *revitháda* (chickpea stew) is served first with lemon wedges, followed by the equally delicious main course—roast kid or lamb with spaghetti or potatoes. The whole process is repeated until every soul has been fed. At the Saints' Day festival celebrating Prophet Elijah held at the top of the Island's highest peak, I've seen volunteers serve and clean up after 500 people with unmatched efficiency.

Local musicians may play traditional Island tunes on a lute and violin. If they do, the dancing starts. It's a lovely way to spend an evening under the stars.

Revitháda, served at *panigýria* here, is the traditional Sunday dish on the Island. In years past, special unglazed clay pots—individually called *tsoukáli* and shaped something like bee hives—would be filled with *revitháda* ingredients and carried to bakeries on Saturday to be cooked slowly overnight in the wood-fired ovens. The finished dish was picked up on Sunday.

There are many different recipes and traditions concerning *revitháda*, including debates about where the best chickpeas might be found. Bay leaves are often used, but some eschew them in favor of rosemary. Some use both. Some insist that this vegan dish must be cooked using only rainwater, in a *tsoukáli* placed in a wood-burning oven, while others maintain that slow roasting in any covered pot and oven is fine.

In any event, the recipe Aris uses to cook *revitháda* in our electric oven, without rainwater, but in a ceramic roaster, is in the Appendix. I hope you'll find it as delicious as I do.

One of the most celebrated *panigýria* on the Island takes place at the small church on the rocky peninsula we see from our verandas. Dedicated to the Virgin Mary, its icon is credited with many miracles. My favorite story tells of a miracle involving a young virgin, who, unaware that pirates were sheltering in the church, entered to light its candles. While running away from the pirates, the girl prayed to the Virgin Mary to save her. The peninsula then broke behind her as she ran—sending the pursuing pirates to their doom.

Normally, we arrive too late in the season for this event, but one year when it fell late on the calendar (the date is linked to Easter), I arrived at our house just in time. The church bells started ringing almost immediately and continued ringing off and on throughout the evening and into the night. It was hot and extremely crowded. Since I was tired from the trip, I attended only briefly.

Calling the event "crowded" is an understatement. The whole beach and our road were jam-packed with cars. Watching people trying to maneuver on our riverbed road was amusing. They displayed much less patience than one might expect from folks arriving to attend a holy service. Our bay was also filled with boats. I heard the services that night, and chants and liturgy the next morning, I was still hearing the services the next evening.

When I chose to arrive just in time for this event, I didn't think about the day being a holiday. I came home to a house that had been closed all winter and was devoid of food—and every store on the Island was closed! Kyría Évi to the rescue! I had dinner at the restaurant that night and she kindly gave me yogurt (which the restaurant doesn't sell) in a take-out container for breakfast. That held me over until the stores reopened the next afternoon.

The very first *panigýri* I attended was at *Mávro Chorió*, which means "Black Village" (no, I don't know how it got that name and neither does Aris). It's a celebration in late August at a church atop one of the tallest peaks on the Island, dedicated to St. John.

Aris, Faní, and I took off for it on foot on a donkey path in mid-afternoon. It was blazingly hot! Foolishly, we took no water, and we suffered for it. Aris still has a photo of me and Faní, red-faced, sweaty, and panting, sitting on the side of the *monopáti* trying to catch our breath. He couldn't stop laughing at us.

When we finally arrived at the church, I was desperate for water. But none was available except well water. Having heard Aris's stories of well water infested with leeches, I wouldn't drink it. There was wine, of course, but it was retsina. I know people, including Americans, who adore retsina, but I'm not one of them. It tastes like turpentine to me, but I drank it that night since there was no viable alternative.

Apart from the lack of potable water, it was an utterly charming evening. I didn't have enough Greek then to understand the liturgy or the chants, but I understood the spirit of the service, which was followed by the traditional feast. After the meal, came music and dancing. The evening and the walk back under the stars were enchanting.

The only rule about attire for Saints' Day events on the Island is to dress with a degree of modesty. Clothes suitable for hiking are fine. Local women attend in dresses or skirts and blouses. Local men wear blue jeans or trousers and shirts. Unfortunately, strangers sometimes show up, irreverently, in short shorts and strapless midriff tops—which feel incredibly out of place. Beyond dressing respectfully, men and women should remove their hats when entering the church, and it's customary to contribute a little money to its upkeep.

The *panigýri* in *Mávro Chorió* was my first introduction to Turkish toilets.

No one warned me.

CHAPTER FORTY-EIGHT

A Process of Elimination

When I first came to the Island, I never expected to learn new toilet etiquette, or the art and acrobatics of using a Turkish toilet.

In most of the Western world, one answers the call of nature with familiar flush toilets, with seats, that dispose of both waste and soiled paper. That wasn't the case on the Island. Until quite recently, except in the main port, there were no sewers here, only septic tanks. Since it's a dry and stony place, the contents of septic tanks break down very slowly, so toilet paper wasn't flushed anywhere except at the resort hotel and, thankfully, our house. Thank you, *agápi mou* Aris, for insisting on a giant septic tank.

One strange effect of Island living is that we were perpetually on the hunt for an acceptable quality of toilet paper. Much of what was available was rough, though not as dreadful as the infamous green recycled paper one used to encounter in public toilets in Germany. Some softer quilted versions were available, but they tended to ball up when wet.

So, if we came across decent toilet paper while traveling in Greece, we asked for the name of the brand (and, yes, we got a lot of strange looks). Unfortunately, we've had no luck with finding hotel brands on offer to the general public. I've been tempted to ship or carry Charmin toilet paper from the States—but doing that would land me in divorce court. And I've never been able to understand why facial tissues sold here as a purse pack are soft and wonderful, while those sold boxed for home use have much in common with the toilet paper.

Some Island restaurants have perfectly reasonable and even elegant toilet facilities, but many don't. One must become accustomed to missing toilet seats, overflowing and smelly trash cans, and the absence of hand soap, paper towels, or any other means of cleaning and drying your hands. It's a good idea to carry facial tissue and hand sanitizer into restaurant and public toilets, often marked "W.C." in the British style but known to Greeks as "*to méros*" (the place) or "*i toualéta*" (the toilet).

I'm deeply grateful never to have encountered, here or elsewhere in Greece, a restaurant offering only a Turkish toilet. In case you've never had the misfortune of experiencing one, let me explain: A Turkish toilet is essentially a hole, sometimes in a large porcelain tray, sometimes simply in the ground. Usually, there are slightly raised "footprint" areas in the porcelain tray or stones on the ground on either side of the hole for your feet.

Most men have little difficulty relieving their bladders into a Turkish toilet, but women confronted by an exigent need and only a Turkish toilet are glad if they wore a dress or skirt that can be hiked up. Those in slacks regret their choice of attire.

When confronted with a Turkish toilet while wearing slacks, a woman has limited choices. She can forego relieving her bladder, take her slacks and underwear off, wet herself, or attempt this gymnastic maneuver:

Step 1: Roll up your pant legs against errant spray.

Step 2: Plant your feet as far apart as the raised footprints or stones allow.

Step 3: Lower your pants and underwear and pull them as far away as possible while you squat over the hole.

Step 4: Hope to Heaven that your knees hold out and that no insect lands on exposed skin to cause you to jerk and spray your underwear and pants.

I'm sorry to say that I speak from sad experience.

Be forewarned that Turkish toilets are the norm in monasteries, both on islands and on the mainland. But you haven't truly experienced rural Greece until you've squatted over a hole while praying your knees don't give out.

———◇———

You may have noticed that I didn't mention a powder room among the rooms in our house. We don't have one. Aris thought a powder room would be pretentious in an Island house. More importantly to me, there wasn't a place to put one that didn't ruin each room's sea view, the open floor plan, or the symmetry of the space.

Instead, we made the master bathroom accessible from the dining room as well as the master bedroom and tucked the bidet inside the large shower behind glass block walls. When we entertain guests (other than houseguests), I hide our toothbrushes and other personal items, clean the sinks, empty the trash, and put out fresh guest towels.

Not that this does much good. Apart from Americans or Greeks who have lived abroad, it's rare that any guest takes advantage of the facilities. Some of Aris's male childhood friends have been known to answer the call of nature outdoors on the weeded areas of our property! Whether the others have capacious bladders or think it rude, I don't know.

Long before the pandemic, one of Aris's cousins was aghast that we lack a powder room and declined to use either our bathroom or those in our unoccupied guest suites. I'm *still* scratching my head about that.

Obviously, I haven't fully mastered toilet etiquette yet.

CHAPTER FORTY-NINE

The Evil Eye

In Greece, headaches and fatigue may not be ailments but the handiwork of the evil eye (*to máti*), a force as ancient as Greece itself. Though belief in *to máti* isn't unique to the Island, it has a strong influence here—stretching back to the days of classical Greece. Though sometimes described as a curse, it's actually a kind of malaise caused by too much admiration or by attracting someone's jealousy or envy.

To ward it off, blue-and-white "eye" tokens, featuring concentric circles, are worn, carried, and displayed everywhere—on the same chain as baptismal crosses, draped over personal icons, and dangling from the rearview mirror of nearly every cab.

Among her many talents, Mána could sense the presence of the evil eye and knew the secrets for removing it. One day, after being congratulated by old friends, Aris complained of a headache and fatigue. Mána told him it was *to máti*.

I'd never believed in the evil eye, but Mána shook my skepticism. She put a drop of oil in water and murmured a prayer no one else could hear, while crossing herself repeatedly. Eventually, both she and Aris began yawning profusely. *The oil dispersed, and Aris's headache vanished,* proving that the evil eye was vanquished—and that even scientific minds can fall victim to this mystic force.

CHAPTER FIFTY

Marriage

Island weddings are special.

From our veranda, we've seen many brides arrive at the church on the rocky peninsula to the music of pealing church bells. We've attended weddings there too, including one at which I discovered that the carpenter who installed our chestnut beam pergola was also a cantor. But one such wedding was special to us: the day Stélla, the youngest daughter of Kyría Évi and Kýrios Pétros, married Filippo under a blazing September sun.

Stélla is a lovely person in every way, and we'd also become fond of Filippo, her fiancé, an accomplished chef and Italian national. They visited us in Naples, Florida, the day after their unplanned civil wedding in Miami. A U.S. visa issue had changed their engagement into marriage overnight. Filippo was applying for an investor's visa in the States based on starting a catering business in South Beach. His lawyer advised that if they married before he applied, Stélla would be allowed to work in the States, but if they waited until afterwards, she wouldn't. That makes no sense to me. Then again, U.S. immigration laws have always been strange.

Their Island wedding, previously scheduled at the penin-sula church for early September the *following* year, couldn't be moved forward because the church was completely booked.

When we left Naples at the end of May in the year of the wedding, I packed what I thought would be appropriate for a September wedding on the Island. Unfortunately, that weekend wasn't cool and breezy; it was brutally hot, much too hot for the clothes I'd brought. I ended up buying something at a local store, which I rarely do since clothing here is much more expen-sive than in the States.

We walked to the wedding on the rough riverbed road, us-ing my umbrella as a shield against the relentless sun. I carried a pair of somewhat dressier shoes and changed into them after I navigated most of that road, leaving my flats at Cousin George's lower gate. And, for the first time ever, I used a Spanish fan a friend had given me years before, very grateful for her gift.

In keeping with Island tradition, the bride—wearing a gor-geous strapless floor-length gown—arrived by boat at the tiny quay below the church, greeted by shotgun fire. After disem-barking, she ascended the steps to the church and entered via the front walkway, heavily decorated with flowers. Filippo was waiting for her in a white linen suit, attended by his family. His mother wore a beautiful silk ensemble with a fascinator, which, like the rest of us, was drooping in the heat.

Guests' attire varied widely. Most of the younger women wore cocktail dresses—short, tight, low-cut, and/or backless—along with spike heels. How anyone can walk in stilettos on the unpaved and roughly paved areas around that church without breaking an ankle is beyond me.

Having arrived early, Aris and I entered the small church with its double barrel vault ceiling and thick columns. I didn't see much of the ceremony because I squeezed next to one of the tiny windows due to the heat. I heard part of it, but only part, because the guests never stopped talking! Not whispering, they spoke in their normal voices as if nothing sacred were taking place.

One of the most distinctive and charming moments in a Greek Orthodox wedding is when the bride and groom don flowered circlets connected by ribbons and walk around the altar together, symbolically taking their first steps as husband and wife. After the service, the crowd raised the traditional joyful shout. Then, as with other weddings, rice was thrown on the newlyweds to express wishes for their happiness together. Fireworks are often set off at this point, but Stélla and Filippo chose not to have them.

Everyone was delighted to leave the church, which was even hotter than being out in the blistering sun. We walked, dripping, under the umbrella the short distance from the church to Stélla's parents' restaurant, which had been transformed for the reception. The parking lot had become hors d'oeuvres stations and a dance floor. Since Filippo catered the event himself, we were treated to exquisite culinary creations.

After indulging in the delicious hors d'oeuvres, Aris and I found our seats, only to discover that we were alone at our table for ten. Despite formal invitations and RSVPs, none of the other guests assigned to our table showed up. One of these, an acquaintance, attended the wedding and ate appetizers at the reception but decided at the last minute not to stay for the dinner.

I knew that Island weddings are treated more casually than those in Athens. Even so, the disregard for the expense and time involved in arranging a large, formal wedding reception was a shock to me. Perhaps this reflected the old Island tradition—which continued into the 1970s—that everyone was welcome to weddings and the receptions after, even without invitation. Or maybe it was just the heat!

The family was dismayed that we were alone, though we didn't mind. We savored the food and enjoyed watching the guests dancing in a kaleidoscope of color to the music of a live band. We particularly loved hearing Stélla's sister, an accomplished vocalist, perform.

Nevertheless, other guests were sent to take turns sitting with us, and we met some interesting people. Having no desire to greet the sunrise, we left, well-fed and mellow, long before the party ended, taking with us the traditional wedding favor: sugared almonds in an elegant casing.

⸺⸺◆⸺⸺

A related, deeply rooted tradition is the dowry. Though outlawed in Greece since the 1980s, I'm told, dowries *(proíkes)* continue to be provided—and expected. Traditionally, it's a house or condo. On the Island, parents of limited means have been known to move into a hut, giving their home to their daughter on her marriage.

When a female relative married, she and her new husband moved into a fully furnished condo gifted by her parents, which (as was also common) was in the same building and on the same floor as her parents' place. Years later, she swapped apartments with her parents since theirs was larger. This often happens, and if the parents don't volunteer, they may be pressured to move. A friend unabashedly told us that she'd told her father to move out of the big house because he'd lived his life and it was her turn!

As we know from horrific stories of bride burnings in India, there are serious downsides to dowry systems, but from the wife's perspective, there's an upside: She can kick the husband out of the house, but not vice versa!

When Aris and I married, he didn't ask for a dowry—luckily for me—since all I had to bring to the marriage was a used 1968 Chevelle and a twelve-inch black-and-white portable television. I did, however, follow what was then the Greek tradition of taking both the possessive form of his first name and his surname. I found this new name much more interesting than the bland English name I was given at birth.

For years, Greece didn't recognize our marriage because we didn't marry in the Greek Orthodox Church. There was no separation of church and state then. When the law changed, I was registered as his wife and could finally apply for a Greek residency visa.

U.S. visa laws are not alone in being strange. The visa application process here was another . . . experience. On my third attempt, Faní argued with the official in charge, while I appealed to her subordinate. I said (in Greek), "My husband spent thirty-eight years with me in the States. Now that he's retired, he wants to be here, in his homeland, and he wants me to be with him. I don't need anything. I have money and insurance. I just want to be here with him, spending money, and bringing friends to do the same."

The subordinate thought a minute, then rummaged in a file cabinet and timidly approached her boss with a file. "I think we can do this," she said. "I think this is like this case we approved last year. I think it will be OK." Faní noticed that the file concerned an Albanian applicant and started to protest the comparison. I hurriedly shushed her.

After my application was accepted, no visa—or rejection—arrived. Ever. The U.S. Embassy assured me I could stay in Greece all year if I liked while the application was pending, and Faní was told it still was. I traveled with it freely for years. Luckily for me, no border agent ever bothered to check.

Eventually, we hired a lawyer who discovered the visa had been issued—and expired! That made the reapplication process complicated, but the lawyer prevailed, so I can be here, and in the Schengen Zone, as long as I like. The new visa came in the very nick of time. We left for the States right after I got it, and for the first time ever, a border agent flagged that I'd been here more than three months—proving, once again, that timing really is everything.

Of course, traditional wedding ceremonies can't change human nature. Even here, stories of adulterous liaisons are whispered, including one about a married grandmother found in bed with a priest! Some things are universal (it was quite wrong, of course, and a terrible scandal for her family, but I still felt a wicked urge to tip my hat to granny).

Weddings here are unforgettable and important milestones in life, and there's nowhere I'd rather celebrate them.

CHAPTER FIFTY-ONE

Birth and Baptism

Births here are celebrated with baptism, a joyful ritual leading to the lifelong pleasures of being a godparent.

Although Islanders tend to be socially conservative, small islands are the ultimate small towns—and as in all small towns, accidents happen. I first encountered an out-of-wedlock pregnancy here when I noticed that an unmarried Islander was quite far along. She and the father of her child did marry eventually. A friend told me the woman had confided that she'd gotten pregnant on purpose to drag her reluctant, long-term boyfriend to the altar.

I later learned of others who went down the same path, including a beautiful, well-educated young woman we'd tried to persuade to pursue her career in the States. Like many young Greek women, she prioritized family and declined. Her boyfriend (now husband) was obviously reluctant to commit, since they married less than a month before she gave birth. When a wedding is a shotgun affair, I often wonder how well the husband, wife, and in-laws get along afterward.

Baptism follows birth, and here, it's an event. Babies normally are baptized within a year. The godparents—there may be several—are called *nonós* (male) and *noná* (female). They baptize the child, promising to bring him or her up in the Church and to be spiritual role models. They purchase the baptismal clothes and an engraved gold cross with a chain, which is often worn with a pendant to ward off the evil eye. During the ceremony, the child is blessed with holy oil and carried all around the church by a godparent. As with other Greek celebrations, baptism is followed by a big reception, with plenty of food, drink, and sugared almonds.

My being godmother to our nephew, Spýros, was an issue when we baptized him since I hadn't converted to the Greek Orthodox Church and wasn't eligible, but—with an appropriate gift of money—I was allowed to participate anyway. Since we baptized him before his first birthday, I had no problem carrying him. (Our younger godson was nearly two and a half when he was baptized in a Greek Orthodox Church in the States, and he was heavy! I was very grateful that he was exhausted, and quiet. Had he wiggled, I might have dropped him!)

Aris and I have been long-distance godparents to Spýros, and our absence from events in his life was hard for him to understand when he was little. At four, he complained that we weren't around for holidays, his name day and other occasions, like other kids' godparents. Aris and I tried to explain how far away we lived.

He'd been on ferry boats and airplanes, and we told him that we lived so far away that it took a week on a boat and hours on a plane for us to reach Greece. We asked if he understood. "Uh-huh." The next day, we went to Platýs Gialós bay, a drive of maybe twenty minutes. When the bay came into view, Spýros eagerly asked, "Is this where you live?"

Though bright as a whip, the concept of a different language was understandably a puzzlement to him then. I was reading James Michener's *Hawaii* during our vacation, when Spýros dropped a comic book on my lap and asked me to read it to him. The writing in the speech balloons was in a cursive Greek script. I told him I was sorry, but I couldn't read it. He grabbed my thick paperback, threw it to the ground, and said, "You can read this big book, so why not my little one? You don't love me, *Noná*!"

When he was a little older, we took him all over the Island. I learned a couple of Greek tunes to sing with him. Aris taught him to swim. He learned English, both in school and from Dimítris, so I taught him the "The Ants Go Marching" song—and how to wiggle his ears. I also taught him to whistle the entire theme song to *The Andy Griffith Show*.

We got to have him with us in the States for weeks during the summers when he was twelve and thirteen. He later attended our alma mater and spent his breaks with us in Pittsburgh. He settled in Scotland, so we don't get to see him often now, but we love it when we do.

Here, baptism weaves a child into the godparents' hearts and lives in a way distance cannot unravel.

CHAPTER FIFTY-TWO

Aging

Aging on the Island can be gentler than in many other places. Islanders often continue to swim, walk long distances, climb onto donkeys, and work their fields deep into advanced old age. But some of our Greek friends simply decided that they're old—too old for even moderate physical activity.

When taking friends out on our little yacht, some surprised me by insisting they were too old to swim from the yacht to the shore and needed to be rowed instead. They were just Aris's age! One of Aris's high school friends, a lovely woman who endeared herself to me forever by visiting Mána weekly for well over a year after Babás died, stayed with us once. She descended our steps slowly, clinging to her husband's arm, and declined to walk the path to Fáros Bay, saying she was too old for that.

We've made some concessions to age ourselves. Aris doesn't free dive as much anymore. I take trek poles when we hike any distance, and we've put risers under the feet of our low-slung living room furniture.

Faní took more drastic action. She sold the village house, where she'd been living most of the year with Dimítris, and bought a place on a larger island. She said she needed a place where she could live year-round that had decent healthcare services.

Islanders couldn't understand her decision at all. When several said, "I guess Faní doesn't like us anymore," I always explained the healthcare concern.

Then they'd ask, "Is she ill? Is Dimítris ill?"

"No, no," I replied, "she's just thinking ahead."

Inevitably, I'd hear some version of, "I can't understand her—she wants to be near a hospital when she's not even sick."

CHAPTER FIFTY-THREE

Death

Babás died on July 11, 2007. It was the first time anyone really close to me died, and it hit me hard. Babás had enjoyed being coddled and petted and I had loved doing that, so I'd been a favorite. Not long before he died, he said that I was the only person who truly loved him. Aris said that meant I'd have a long life.

Babás died in Athens. I was on the Island, and Aris was in Japan. Fortunately, Aris had seen Babás just two days earlier and I'd spoken with him the day before. I learned of his death when I called that morning as usual, and the woman who'd been taking care of him and Mána told me.

We didn't have internet in the house then and Aris's BlackBerry didn't work in Japan anyway. Worse, I didn't have his itinerary. His assistant undoubtedly sent it to me, but with no internet I had no access to it. So, I counted the hours until 8:00 a.m. Eastern Time when I could call his assistant in the States and get a number where I could reach him.

Before that happened, Aris called me, and I gave him the sad news. He immediately began arranging to return to Athens.

Meanwhile, Faní left the Island for Athens to make funeral arrangements.

I was stuck here, unable to leave because we had houseguests en route. I could have gone to the internet café and tried to alert them to the situation. But even if they'd received the message, it would have been next to impossible for them to find alternative accommodations in July on short notice, and being alone in our relatively isolated house would also have been very difficult. So, I said nothing to them and stayed, unhappily, put.

A lot is said about comfort food. I have comfort books, and when Babás died, I reread *The Lord of the Rings* straight through. What better book to remind us that even the darkest of times will pass?

The next day, I went to the main village to see Dimítris, who'd stayed on the Island to tend to the store he and Faní had opened when they retired. An older woman who'd started one of the Island's souvlaki shops noticed that I was dressed all in black and asked me about it. When I told her, she went through the streets calling out, "The grandfather died."

Though told that I needn't wear black, I chose to wear it for a while. I *felt* black. I didn't wear it for forty days, which I understand is the custom in Greece after the deaths of relatives other than a spouse. In the past, widows in Athens wore black for at least two years, then eventually changed to gray and lavender. On this Island, many widows wore no color but black for the rest of their lives. This has changed. The recently widowed women I know have not worn black except immediately after their husbands' deaths.

In addition to the funeral, Islanders remember the dead with a memorial service on the fortieth day after the death and on each anniversary. Those who are particularly devout also commemorate the death after nine days and after three and six months. We returned to the States before the fortieth-day memorial service, but we held a dinner in Babás's honor on the anniversary of his death the following year.

My etiquette book advised that thank-you notes were owed to those who sent expressions of sympathy. It took me months to write those notes after Babás died. Every time I'd start writing one, I'd break down in tears. Writing those acknowledgments felt like putting nails in his coffin.

Almost three years after Babás's death, Mána died. We'd effectively lost her before her death due to her dementia, but amazingly, when Aris called her the Sunday before she died, she knew who he was for the first time in months. We didn't get to Greece in time for her funeral, but we were on the Island for her fortieth-day memorial service.

I wish I'd known that people can speak at such services; evidently, the priest hadn't known Mána well and didn't understand how wonderful she was. He said words to the effect that she was a good person. I was quite upset by how little he said about her, but Aris found the traditional service comforting, and I was glad for that. After the service, as is the tradition, those in attendance were invited for coffee, brandy, and Island biscuits (cookies) at a nearby café.

Since the priest didn't say much about Mána, I will. I never met a smarter, more selfless, kinder, or more generous person. Her life was all about pleasing others. Mána did no needlecraft at all until she found out that I liked handmade linens. She then learned needlepoint, crochet, and embroidery to make things for me—and later for others. She made many beautiful embroidered table scarves, as well as needlepoint pillows, dining chair seat covers, and a tapestry for me.

The most amazing of her gifts was a crocheted bedspread that she spent an entire year making. That project had its genesis in a shopping trip while she and Babás wintered with us in Pittsburgh. We were in a furniture store and a four-poster bed, like mine, was displayed dressed in a lace coverlet. I admired it, but Mána disparaged it for being machine-made. When I protested that handmade versions were not to be found, Mána said I should wait and let her see if she could find one in Athens.

Instead of finding it, she created it, one square at a time, over the course of a year. When she returned to Pittsburgh, she conspired with my cleaning woman to get it washed and bleached after she stitched it together. It now adorns our bed on the Island, and every time I make that bed, I think of her.

Mána was very intuitive. She told an American friend of mine that she was pregnant before my friend even suspected it herself. She was also a keen observer of people, and a master of the excruciatingly polite, but utterly devastating, put-down. After observing how nasty another American friend's mother-in-law was to her, Mána confided that she wished she spoke better English so that she could tell her off.

Before she married, Mána held a responsible management position—very unusual for a Greek woman at the time. And she never criticized me for having a career.

I heard her directly contradict Babás only twice. Once, when he started to offer an opinion about a disagreement Aris and I had, she insisted that it was not their business and that neither of them would ever comment—even if asked—about any disagreement between us. The other was when he said Faní shouldn't return to work and leave their year-old grandson with her mother-in-law. Mána told him he had no idea what it was like to be out in the world with a productive job and then to be home with only an infant for company.

A perfectionist who spoke impeccable French, Mána had tremendous patience with me and others. She cooked to give us pleasure, and she loved Harlequin romances, socializing, playing cards, and her family. She was an angel and one of the best friends I ever had. I still miss her.

───────◆───────

It wasn't until Theía Flóra later died—at nearly 106 years old!—that I attended a funeral on the Island. Theía Flóra was a teacher, and during the cruel Nazi occupation of Greece in World War II, when everyone was starving, she walked miles from her home to teach, and hug, Island children without pay. Dozens of Islanders turned out for her funeral and several, in addition to her daughter, spoke movingly about her.

After the service, we and other mourners walked behind the hearse to the cemetery for the interment in the tomb and then walked back for the reception. In Island tradition, mourners are offered brandy, coffee, and cookies, while the family is also served fish soup and the boiled fish used to make it. (Mána's recipe is in the Appendix.)

───────◆───────

I've experienced other deaths while on the Island. I was here when my older sister died, and again when her son and our mother died several years later. Leaving the Island for the States is a process, entailing a three-hour ferry trip to Piraeus and two flights.

When my older sister became critically ill, I asked my younger sister, Lesa, a physician, to email a note on her letterhead or prescription pad documenting her critical condition. I wanted to try to change my tickets on a hardship basis to leave early to see her. But our sister died before Lesa could send the note.

Years later, when our mom was ninety-three years old and very frail, my nephew died suddenly of cardiac arrest just shy of his fifty-second birthday. Mom had raised him for about a dozen years, and Lesa and I feared that her death would soon follow. I left the Island to be with Mom at and after his funeral, giving Lesa a much-needed vacation. I stayed with Mom for ten days, during which we spoke a lot about her youth, and I reassured her that she'd been a good mother, wife, grandmother, teacher, and friend. It was clear that she was dying, and I requested hospice care.

When you book an international flight at the last minute during peak season, you take what you can get. The flight to the States wasn't bad, but I picked up a virus—not COVID, thankfully—which kept me masked and at a distance from Mom throughout my visit with her. The return trip took twenty-six hours, which is miserable when you are ill. My recovery was slow, and I canceled a planned visit to our elder godson, Spýros, and his wife and baby son in Scotland because I just wasn't up to another trip.

Mom died five weeks after I returned to the Island. Except for a few days near the end, she was lucid, and I spoke with her at least once every day. As Lesa and I had agreed before the trip— and as Mom had requested—I didn't go back for the funeral.

Thanks to the internet, I was able to help Lesa remotely. I had scanned Mom's funeral and burial contracts into my computer and helped with those arrangements. I also managed financial, estate, and some personal property disposal issues from the Island. But I was sorry not to be with Lesa.

I wore black, reread *The Lord of the Rings*, and wept alone.

CHAPTER FIFTY-FOUR

The Little Yacht that Owned Us

Because we loved the outboard motorboat so much, it was easy to decide to buy the little yacht—a cabin cruiser capable of traveling to other islands and parts of the mainland. We dreamed of overnight adventures, sleeping on board, and carefree island hopping.

We're still dreaming.

It's said that the two happiest days in a man's life are the day he buys a yacht and the day he sells it. That perfectly sums up my love-hate relationship with the little yacht. Our dream turned into a nightmare of bureaucratic battles and the humbling realities of yacht ownership.

Aris bought the yacht in gently used condition. His agent did a fine job getting everything taken care of and checked the records certifying that all taxes had been paid. Nevertheless, Aris was sued, along with the former owners, by the government for unpaid taxes.

He won both the initial decision and the appeal, but the government still refused to verify that he owed no taxes. We were lucky that this lawsuit didn't take forever. Someone we know waited about ten years for a decision on his challenge to the government's refusal to let him finish building a house.

When Aris bought the yacht, he took and passed the test for his captain's license—as expected. But he had to wait weeks to get it. We worried that it wouldn't come at all because, the year before, he'd applied in June for a bird hunting license that hadn't arrived by October. He'd been told then that, due to the economic crisis, the government hadn't paid the company from which it purchased its stamps, and the company refused to supply any more. Since there were no stamps, no licenses could be issued!

Aside from the license, there was the issue of where to dock. For the first few days, we docked in the main port. We were set to head out one day, but they warned us that they couldn't hold our spot if we left (it *was* very crowded). The marina in the next bay over from ours had no available space either. Although Greece was in a depression, there were no vacancies at the marina or the port!

Aris decided to solve the problem by sinking an anchorage (a one-meter cube of concrete with a metal eyelet for a chain) into our bay. But that took a while too because someone else's yacht was tied up to the end of the dock—right where it needed to be dropped into the sea. A very kind fisherman from Fáros, Giánnis, towed the anchorage from Fáros to our bay and sank it exactly where Aris specified.

After he refused any compensation whatsoever, Aris asked Fisherman Giánnis's cousin how we could thank him without insulting him. The cousin recommended that we patronize his excellent fish restaurant. That's always been easy duty!

Anchoring the yacht in our bay solved the problem of where to dock but caused the boat to always be filthy. Dirt from the hills and a black salt film coated everything. I needed to clean it every time we took it out. Once, we even had to contend with—and clean up after—birds that flew into the yacht's salon through a window we'd left open a bit too wide.

Traveling to other islands presented unexpected challenges too. When we decided to visit Santorini one September, Aris checked in with the harbor master before we left. He assured us that we'd have no problem docking. But when we got there, we had to tie up three boats out, too far for water or electrical connection. Aris didn't want to run the generator, so we had no air conditioning and couldn't shower. Worse, another yacht tied up on the other side of us, blocking the breeze. And it was noisy!

In the morning as we walked up the hill, we paused to book a table for dinner right on the edge of the caldera at sunset, before spending the day walking in the heat and sun. When we returned for dinner, I did my best in the restaurant's restroom to rinse off the sticky sweat and arrange my sweaty hair, with limited success. The view was truly spectacular, but I would've enjoyed it more had I been cleaner. Dinner and bed while sticky with sweat was not the salt life I'd envisioned.

Another time, the harbor master of an island we wished to visit assured Aris that we could dock. However, when we arrived, we were told that not only could we not dock, due to a race in progress, but we couldn't anchor in the bay either! Aris took us to another, lightly developed bay on that island, where we dropped anchor.

He rowed us to the shore in the "dinky dinghy" (the tender). We did some exploring, had a delicious meal, filled a water bottle with local wine, and took it back to the yacht. We drank it under the stars while Aris enjoyed his cigar. An enchanting evening!

But when dawn was still pale in the morning sky, the yacht started rocking—a lot. Defying predictions, the weather changed for the worse and we had to yank anchor and hightail it back to the Island. A poor ending to an otherwise idyllic experience.

I could go on about docking issues, but you get the picture.

There was also a First Mate issue: You see, I was the First Mate, and not a skilled one. One dock master called me *áchristi* (useless) because I didn't know how to do something no one had ever shown or explained to me. I was good at retrieving the rope tied to the float at the anchorage with a very long pole that had a hook on the end, but the rope and chain were too heavy for me to pull up from the sea.

Early on, I squatted low to pull up the rope and chain—and was feeling quite pleased that I could squat like that—when part of the meniscus of my left knee tore off. I learned that squatting is a common way of tearing the meniscus.

What happens when you tear your meniscus on a small island? Well, like anywhere else, the knee and leg swell up and trying to bend it produced red-hot poker pain. Had I been in the States, I'd have gone to a doctor. Here, I chose not to as we were leaving in a month. From what I read online (later confirmed by an orthopedist in the States), there was nothing to do short of surgery, other than rest, ice, compression, and elevation. I did that for a week until houseguests arrived.

There was only one *panigýri* (saints' day celebration) during their visit and the church where it was being held was accessible only via a rugged path. I didn't want our guests to miss the experience, so I wore my knee support, took my trek poles to take the strain off my knee, and, however foolishly, I went.

I did get better as First Mate over time. Once, when we were docking at Pollónia in Milos, I tied the rope to the yacht's dockside front cleat, coiled the excess over my shoulder, climbed over the railing, and jumped with the rope onto the dock, ready to tie the yacht up. I was so proud of myself!

However, Aris decided that the waves were too big and backed away, leaving me on the dock, the rope dragging in the sea, and him without any help. At that point, there was no way for him to dock, so he dropped anchor in the bay instead.

That brings us to minor yacht calamities.

We went to Pollónia in Milos at that time for an overnight trip because neither of us had seen any part of that island except its shoreline and that small port. We anchored in the bay for the reason just described, untied the new tender, and lowered it into the sea. I don't know why, but Aris suggested that I get in first. I got both feet in, but before I could get the rest of me into the tender, it shot away—and I was left hanging onto yacht ropes with my feet in the tender and my rump outside, trying desperately not to get wet.

I failed.

Aris was laughing too hard to help, and I ended up with my backside in the drink before I could recover. I had packed just one pair of pants and had no way to clean and dry them, so I spent the evening walking around the little port town looking as though I'd wet myself! The Greek gods must have taken notice of my earlier hubris and decided to take me down a peg!

Because the tender to the yacht had no motor, we often used the Loráki, the outboard motorboat, as a tender while in our home bay. We'd take it to the beach, load it up, and then take it to the yacht at its anchorage. One time after I'd hooked the Loráki to the yacht with the boat clip at the end of its rope, the clip unaccountably came loose and—before we realized it was gone—the little boat drifted across our bay until it bumped up against the rocky peninsula with the church.

I almost had a heart attack when I saw what had happened! Thank goodness Aris is a strong swimmer! He raced after it and caught it before it could drift out of the bay to another island.

While raising the yacht's anchor one day, I didn't release the button for the motor soon enough and it hit and stuck to the prow. We didn't have a mallet, and pushing at it did nothing, so there was nothing for it but to return home to our bay. And once, the motor to raise the anchor refused to work at all, leaving us to limp back to our bay.

Like so many things in life, the little yacht was wonderful in idea, but problematic in reality. We enjoyed taking friends for day trips to other islands and loved cruising the lilac sea while sitting on its flybridge, but in the end, the negatives outweighed the positives.

CHAPTER FIFTY-FIVE

Mediterranean Cyclone!

In 2018, our little yacht became a stranded casualty of the first Mediterranean cyclone in seventy-five years.

Fisherman Giánnis continued to be a *very* good friend. He dredged the yacht ropes and chains out of the sand before we arrived every year and checked them. He even bought new rope when it needed to be replaced and installed it. But his greatest service came after the yacht was beached during the Mediterranean cyclone.

The storm had been predicted before Aris left for France, but the winds were supposed to come from the north. That had me worried because the house has functioning shutters everywhere except on the north side. Perforce, we have those windows covered with boards for the winter, but that wasn't going to get done before this storm. I brought everything movable inside and tied down the things I couldn't move, like the *kioúpia* (large ceramic pots).

Our bay faces south and is a very safe harbor in northern winds, so after consulting multiple sources, Aris decided to leave our boats in place. But the weather proved to be unpredictable, even here. While he was gone, it was determined that the winds would actually come from the south—which was not good at all.

Aris couldn't get back; all forms of transport had shut down due to the coming storm. He spoke with Island friends who are also licensed and experienced boat captains, and they graciously agreed to take both the yacht and the outboard motorboat to the neighboring marina.

They did not succeed.

As the storm moved in, the sea became increasingly rough. Just getting to the little yacht was a challenge for our friends. Given the urgent need to get both boats to the marina quickly, they tied the little boat to the back of the yacht to tow it. Unfortunately, in the angry sea, the tow rope tangled in the propellers and the yacht's engines shut down. It was nothing short of a miracle that the yacht ran aground on a sandy—rather than rocky—part of the beach in our bay.

The outboard motorboat capsized, but our friends, the captains, dove into the cold, rough water and recovered its seats and life preservers. We urgently contacted one of the fuel suppliers to drain the diesel from the yacht, in case the tank was damaged, to prevent leakage into the sea. The mechanic who services the outboard motorboat came with his truck, took charge of that boat, and helped secure the yacht by tying it to trees on the beach against the expected winds.

Several others of Aris's childhood friends also showed up to help. It was cold and wet, and everyone was exhausted and shivering miserably. Kýrios Pétros and Kyría Évi offered hot coffee and tea to all.

A few days later, after Aris returned, Fisherman Giánnis came with his boat to tow the yacht from the beach. He couldn't do it the first time he tried—it had sunk into the sand, and his tow ropes broke. A hoist was hired to lift the yacht from the beach. The hoist machine made a messy trench in the beach, and lifting the yacht probably bent the propeller shaft and blades. But eventually, the yacht was towed away, and we hired workers to restore the beach immediately.

To make a long story shorter, no one was injured, the environment was unharmed, the house was untouched, and the boat damage was reparable—expensive, but reparable. The yacht had to be towed elsewhere for repairs—another expensive proposition—and the episode was no one's idea of a good time.

The weirdest thing about this whole ordeal was that the Coast Guard called Aris in for a meeting after seeing photos of the beached yacht online and told him that he should have gotten a permit to beach the boat, as if this had been planned! But the Coast Guard official was a decent guy and didn't impose a fine.

This harrowing experience endeared our Island friends to us even more but also led to Aris's decision to sell the little yacht. Our new plan for island-hopping adventures is to rent a boat!

The Rest of the Story

Life on the Island is idyllic—until you encounter a vicious Doberman or otherwise need medical care. These stories reveal the hidden downsides of living on a small island in Greece.

Dog Bite

Very late one evening at a friend's home, his brother's Doberman Pinscher bit my arm without provocation and without so much as a growl, bark, or bared teeth. I've been around dogs all my life, and we loved our own large dogs. That dog was crazy; I was his tenth bite.

The dog got onto the veranda and stuck his nose into my crotch. I moved my arm with the idea of nudging him back, but he bit me before I even touched him. We washed the wounds well and applied hydrogen peroxide, alcohol, and a bandage, but they ached and seeped throughout the night. First thing in the morning, we headed to the medical clinic (which is part of the social medicine system) for treatment and a tetanus shot.

The clinic physician, a fairly young man, showed up over an hour after we did. He got around to me after noon and chided us for not having come in earlier, saying it was almost too late for a tetanus shot to be effective. Aris pointed out that we'd been there, waiting, for hours. The doctor then claimed that we hadn't properly described the problem when we registered. Aris replied that we'd reported a dog bite. I guess we were supposed to report a *bad* dog bite.

The doctor didn't care and started scrubbing the wounds roughly. I told him in Greek, "I'm dizzy" (*zalízomai*). "I'm almost finished," he replied, still scrubbing away. Too late—I passed out cold.

I had low blood pressure and fainting made it even lower. That scared the doctor, who then tried—unsuccessfully—to start an IV. I came to, so he gave up on the IV, but he refused to prescribe an antibiotic. "I cleaned the wounds so well, there's no need for antibiotics," he insisted.

As you've probably guessed, he was wrong. The next day, I had cellulitis, which made my lower arm and elbow swell. They were warm and extremely sensitive to touch. Back to the doctor. After another long wait, he gave me an antibiotic, but too little, too late. One wound abscessed.

When I returned to the States a couple of weeks later, my internist gave me the choice of taking a massive dose of antibiotics or having surgery. I chose the antibiotic. Prescribed in the dosage for Anthrax, it had lots of unpleasant side effects, including, oddly, dermographia. Lesson learned. Since then, my internist in the States annually prescribes antibiotics for me to bring here. I also carry four-plus months' worth of my regular medicines, as some are not available here at any price.

The friend's wife asked me to report the dog because it had also bitten both of her older children, and she feared it would bite her six-year-old daughter in the face. We informed the local police. They shrugged.

The cellulitis wasn't enough to keep me home—not with excellent conditions for boating. Now, as anyone who's ever ridden with Aris while he was driving a car or operating a boat knows, he likes to go fast! On a day of choppy seas, he was enjoying bucking the waves.

I turned to ask him to slow down just as we hit a wave.

I slid right off the seat—*smack!*—onto the bottom of the boat, hitting my wounded arm on the anchor, temporarily stowed there. Aris started to laugh until he realized what had happened. He felt so badly about it that, when we returned to Athens, he bought me a beautiful necklace in the Empress Theodora style. I call it my "dog bite compensation necklace."

Sore Throat, Aching Ear, and Healthcare Options

For those who didn't care to be treated by the doctor at the medical clinic, there was a private physician who provided services for cash. It wasn't just *xénoi* (foreigners) like me who paid; locals did too, though he treated some Islanders for free.

I went to see him when I got an ear infection. I wasn't impressed. He first prescribed non-antibiotic ear drops, which did nothing. The infection got worse.

When I went back, he prescribed an antibiotic without asking me about allergies. Once I realized what it was, I told him I was allergic to it and asked for a different antibiotic—one I'd taken before that the FDA website listed as effective for ear infections. Fortunately, he agreed to prescribe it, and my aching ear was relieved a few days later.

In 2019—pre-COVID—I picked up a nasty bug that gave me a high fever and the worst sore throat of my life. I could barely swallow water and lost five pounds. Aris was away. After several days with no improvement, I started taking an antibiotic I had brought from the States. Coincidentally or not, I began to recover.

Faní brought me juice and lozenges and scolded me for not having gone to the doctor. But after the earache experience, I didn't trust him, and I already had the antibiotic.

———◆———

In August, some medical specialists came to the Island and offered services for a few hours in the morning in exchange for cash. Now, there are other physicians here. For emergencies, there's a helipad for medical evacuation via helicopter to a hospital in Athens.

I don't know what the situation is now, but some years ago, a friend whose husband died in a hospital in Athens told me that the only way to have round-the-clock care was to hire your own night nurse. During the economic crisis, people were advised to bring their own sheets, towels, and syringes to the hospital with them.

Obviously, there are significant gaps in the social medicine system here.

Bad Tooth

I'd hoped that the abscess from the dog bite would be my last on the Island, but this was not to be. During August several years ago, a four-root molar abscessed, requiring a root canal. Having unfortunately had many, I knew what was happening even before I saw the Island dentist. She did some root canals, she said, but a partially calcified four-root molar was beyond her capability.

Most professionals in Southern Europe vacation in August, and no endodontist was to be found in Athens. The Island dentist told me I could go to a hospital there and have the tooth extracted or take antibiotics and wait to see an endodontist in September. I chose the latter route and took Amoxicillin and Ibuprofen for over three weeks.

Aris worked his network of friends. One, who'd lived in the States for many years and had had several root canals, recommended his endodontist. We booked an appointment in September.

I was tempted to trust the antibiotics to kill the infection and wait to get the root canal in the States, but I knew that dental abscesses could migrate to the brain because that happened to my dad and caused a stroke! Good thing I didn't wait: The endodontist told me that, despite the weeks of antibiotics, the root and adjacent bone were badly infected.

My prior root canals generally took forty-five minutes, even for four-root teeth, and with one exception, had been painless. This one took a grueling *six and a half hours in the chair*—four for the first three roots, and, later, two and a half for the last. It was a form of torture.

The whole approach was quite different than in the States. The endodontist was in the room for maybe five minutes at the start of the procedure and another couple of minutes at the end. The rest of the time, other staff, who seemed to be in no hurry, worked on my tooth, while I listened—hour after hour—to their social plans and boyfriend issues. After the first procedure, the tooth throbbed, and I was very swollen. I looked like I had the mumps on that side. Throbbing meant infection, so I had to take still more antibiotics.

That root canal cost a small fraction of what it would've cost in the U.S.—we paid cash directly into the endodontist's hand—but I *never* want to go through that again.

A Greek physician from Athens who practiced medicine in the States for thirty-eight years used to say that the best hospital in Greece was the Athens airport. Let's just say that, while summer life on the Island comes close to being paradise, its beauty hides its limitations, and it's best not to have a medical or dental problem here.

CHAPTER FIFTY-SEVEN

Departure

All good things come to an end and summer is no exception. The end of summer on the Island is always bittersweet. It's startling how quickly the summer Aegean sky, with its intense color and brilliant, sparkling light, changes to a sky not much different from Pittsburgh's with significant cloud cover. Rain isn't unusual in the fall, although in some years we wait for it in vain, wanting to enjoy the way the earth smells after the first rainfall in months.

With the fall, foods change. Figs disappear, but pears, grapes, plums, and pomegranates ripen. Spinach pies give way to zucchini and pumpkin pies (savory, not sweet), and sometimes pies made with mushrooms! *Zargánes* (garfish) and *atherínes* (small, smelt-like fishes) become abundant, lobster disappears, fresh squid becomes available, and so do red mullets so small you can eat them whole in two bites.

With the Fall come heavier foods, such as Greek Pot Roast and Stifádo. (Mána's Recipes are in the Appendix.) It's also a lovely time for walking and hiking on the Island if it's not raining, and the sea is often dead calm in September, making it perfect for boating. Typically, the sea is also warmer, inviting long swims. Most restaurants stay open through at least September 10; those in our bay stay open longer. Service is faster and more relaxed.

Fall also brings the Food Festival, a celebration of the foods of this and other islands, with demonstrations and samples. A reenactment of an old-fashioned Island wedding (not too dissimilar from the Sicilian wedding in *The Godfather*) also typically occurs.

When it's time to leave, all outside movables are brought inside or tied down. Unless we've had good rain, the roofs need to be washed so the rainwater collected in the cistern isn't full of dirt. And we dismantle the house.

Starting with the guest suites, all fabrics—bed coverings, curtains, sheets, towels, table scarves, etc.—as well as lamps and accessories, are stowed away among silicon packets and lavender sachets. The cushions of the sofa and chairs are wrapped or covered in fabric, as are the wooden furniture, TV, printer, and microwave. Electronics are disconnected and stowed.

All shutters are closed, one window in each room is vented, and chemical dehumidifiers are placed in the closets, which are left open. The refrigerator and cabinets are emptied of all perishable foodstuffs. The doors of the dishwasher, refrigerator, and washing machine are propped open. The electricity to the house is shut off too. After we leave, plywood will be screwed over the shutterless windows and doors on the North side of the house.

I get depressed looking at the dismantled rooms with the furnishings covered and the windows shuttered. But then I go outside, gaze at the magnificent Aegean Sea, and begin to dream of next summer when, once again, my heart will warm as I see the Island come into view.

APPENDIX OF RECIPES

(ALPHABETICAL, WITH SERVING SUGGESTIONS;
VEGETARIAN RECIPES ARE STARRED)

1. *Artichokes Constantinople (*Agkináres à la Políta*), Kikí's

INGREDIENTS:

- 1 pkg. (21 ounces) frozen Egyptian or Greek artichoke bottoms, defrosted and cleaned (or you can clean fresh artichokes—a tedious job).

- 3 medium golden globe or Yukon Gold potatoes, peeled and cut into wedges or an equivalent amount of small golden potatoes.

- 1 cup olive oil

- ½ lb. carrots, preferably baby carrots. If using large carrots, slice them.

- ½ cup fresh dill, chopped

- 12 or more green onions (white part only), sliced

- 5 small yellow football-shaped onions, whole. (These should be 2-3 inches long and 3/4 inch or so in diameter. If larger onions are used, they must be quartered but will fall apart.)

- The juice of one lemon

- Salt

  Optional: 1 cup green peas

PREPARATION:

- Sauté the green onions in oil with some of the dill.

- Add the carrots and the yellow onions (and any peas) and continue sautéing them until they're tender, but not soft.

- Add about one cup of water (enough to semi-cover the artichokes), let it boil, and add the artichokes, potatoes, the rest of the dill, the lemon, and salt.

- Cook together for 60 to 75 minutes until the vegetables are well-cooked and no water remains.

    Serve with good bread, Greek olives, and feta cheese.

2. *Caper Salad (*Kaparosaláta*)

INGREDIENTS:

- 100 grams (3.5 ounces) of dried caper buds
- 800 grams (28.2 ounces) or more of sliced red onions
- 250 ml (8.8 ounces) good olive oil
- 100 ml (3.5 ounces) red wine vinegar
- 50 ml (1.75 ounces) thick balsamic vinegar or Island vinegar
- 1 bay leaf

PREPARATION:

- Soak the dried caper buds in water overnight. Drain.
- Boil a pot of water and blanch the capers for two minutes. Drain and repeat twice with fresh water.
- Heat the oil in a large sauté pan and add the onions and capers. Sauté until well wilted.
- Lower the heat and add the vinegar and bay leaf.
- Remove from heat when all liquid except the oil has evaporated.

  Remove the bay leaf and serve at room temperature with good bread.

3. *Chickpea Stew (*Revíthada*), Aris's

INGREDIENTS:

- 1 lb. chickpeas, soaked overnight in warm water with salt and baking soda, then drained
- Twice as much water as chickpeas
- 1 large red onion, roughly chopped
- Approximately 1/2 cup olive oil
- Bay leaves, salt and pepper

PREPARATION:

- Place all ingredients in a covered pot and cook in the oven at 350°F for one hour.
- Reduce the heat to 300°F for one more hour, then cook for seven to nine hours at 250°F until thickened. Check after seven hours.

  Serve warm with lemons to squeeze into it and have a pepper mill at hand. Offer it with Greek olives and feta cheese.

4. Cuttlefish in Wine and Ink (*Soupiés Krasátes me Meláni*)

INGREDIENTS:

- 5 lbs. cleaned cuttlefish

- Squid or cuttlefish ink—two to three packets of purchased squid or cuttlefish ink (about 1.5 tbsp.) dissolved in water

- At least 1 cup olive oil

- 2 large yellow onions, sliced

- 1+ cup red wine

- 3 tbsp. tomato paste

- 4 bay leaves

- salt (lightly)

- pepper

PREPARATION:

- Remove the mouth, cartilage, and other tough bits.

- Cut the eyes, remove the skin, and cut the body into pieces about 2x2 inches and wash them well.

- Place the pieces in a dry, hot pot (or split into two pots) and let it cook until all of the water it makes is gone.

- Add the olive oil and the onion.

- When the onion is soft, add the ink and water mixture, the wine, bay leaves, salt, and pepper.

- After 15 minutes, add the tomato paste.

- Add water from time to time as needed.

- Cook for 1.5 to 3 hours until it cuts easily with the side of a fork and all water is gone.

The sauce should be oily, black, and orange. It looks like sin but tastes like heaven.

Serve it with green salad and good bread.

5. Eggplant Casserole (*Mousakás*), Kikí's

TO BUY:

- 6 lbs. purple eggplants, preferably small and with narrow bottoms, sliced about 1/3" thick

- 2.25 lb. lean ground beef (or ground lamb, or a mixture of ground lamb and beef)

- 1 can evaporated milk

- 1 small can tomato sauce

- ½ lb. grated kefalotýri (a hard sheep's milk cheese) available at Greek groceries, or grated Romano cheese

- *Manoúra*, or aged parmesan, grated

- 1 large yellow onion, finely chopped

- 3 eggs, lightly beaten (2 eggs separated from the other one)

- ½+ cup red wine

- Butter, preferably butter ghee, generally offered in the same aisle of the grocery as cooking oils

- Olive oil (lots)

  From Your Cupboard: Allspice, nutmeg, cinnamon, salt, pepper, flour, one 10" by 16" baking pan, and two large frying pans.

PREPARATION:

- Soak the sliced eggplants in salted water for at least eight hours (preferably overnight). Completely cover them with the salted water and weigh them with a heavy plate.

- Squeeze out the excess water (I use old dish towels) and sauté the eggplants in olive oil until soft and brown. Alternatively, you can baste the eggplant slices with olive oil and broil them, but the result won't be authentic.

- In 2-3 tbsp. of butter, sauté the chopped onion until soft and clear, but not brown.

- Add the ground meat and sauté it until brown, then add the red wine and tomato sauce, as well as salt, pepper, allspice, and cinnamon to taste. Continue sautéing until the meat is cooked.

- Remove from heat and add 1/3 of the cheese.

- Correct the seasonings, then add one egg, lightly beaten.

- Melt 2-3 tbsp. butter.

- Layer 2/3 of the eggplant slices in the baking dish, trying to make an even surface.

- Spread the meat sauce over the eggplant slices. Layer the remaining eggplant slices evenly, then spread béchamel sauce (see below) evenly on top.

- Pour the melted butter over the béchamel sauce and sprinkle the remaining cheese on top.

- Bake at 350°F on a rack in the middle of the oven for 1 to 1.5 hours. The top should be golden brown.

BÉCHAMEL SAUCE

- Melt 8 ounces of butter in a large frying pan.

- Add to it "as much flour as it will take," stirring constantly. [According to Julia Child, the traditional ratio of butter to flour for béchamel sauce is equal amounts of each. You want this to be thick. If it's too thick, add more butter. If it's too thin, add more flour. Start with 1 cup.]

- Sauté this until golden, but not brown.

- Add the evaporated milk, nutmeg, and a little salt, stirring constantly.

- Add "as much water as it will take," and continue cooking until the sauce is thick and almost ready to boil. [Add water or more milk or both, bit by bit, to thin the sauce, and continue cooking until the sauce is the consistency of cream cheese frosting.]

- After it thickens, add a mixture of two beaten eggs, warmed up by slowly adding some of the sauce to the eggs, and then add 1/3 of the cheese.

  Serve with green salad and good bread.

6. *Eggplants *Imám Bayildí*, Laura's

TO BUY:

- 2 lbs. small, narrow purple or oriental eggplants, cut lengthwise into wedges closely equal in size—roughly an inch and a half wide

- 2 lbs. red onions, roughly chopped

- 2 lbs. ripe tomatoes, roughly chopped

- 6 substantial cloves of garlic, chopped

- 1 green, red or yellow pepper, chopped

- 2 tbsp. tomato paste

- 1/2 cup finely chopped fresh parsley

  From Your Cupboard: 1+ cup olive oil, salt, and freshly ground black pepper

PREPARATION:

- Salt the eggplants thoroughly and soak in water for at least eight hours.

- Squeeze the water from the eggplants (I use old dish towels) and sauté them in olive oil until soft and browned on all sides.

- Arrange them skin side down in a baking pan. Reserve the olive oil used to sauté them.

- Preheat the oven to 350°F.

- Scorch the tomato paste in the same olive oil, then add the onions and sauté until soft.

- Add the garlic.

- When the garlic is golden, add the tomatoes, fresh pepper, parsley, salt, and black pepper, and cook until no water remains. Add water if needed—the vegetable mixture should be thick.

- Spoon the vegetable mixture over the eggplants. Pour in the olive oil and add a little water.

- Bake in the oven for 45 minutes to one hour until the water is absorbed.

  Serve with good feta cheese, Greek olives, and crusty bread.

7. *Eggplant Salad (*Melitzanosaláta*), Laura's

INGREDIENTS:

- 2 lbs. small, narrow eggplants
- 1/4 to 1/2 cup olive oil
- 1/4 cup balsamic vinegar
- 1/2 cup red onion
- 1/2 cup fresh parsley
- 2 or more large cloves garlic
- 1 small tomato, peeled and deseeded
- salt to taste

PREPARATION:

- Pierce the eggplants once, then grill them on all sides—and the bottom—until blistered and soft. (If broiling, spray them lightly with olive oil and pierce once.)
- Immediately after roasting, insert the eggplants into Ziploc bags and seal them to loosen the skin.
- When cool enough to handle, immediately skin the eggplants. (If not skinned promptly, the flesh of the eggplants will turn dark.)
- Remove the seeds.
- While the eggplants are roasting, purée the other ingredients in a food processor, reserving some of each liquid.
- Add the skinned eggplants and purée them with the other ingredients.
- Adjust seasoning.

  Enjoy with good bread.

8. Fish & Soup with Egg-Lemon Sauce & Fish with Mayo (*Psarósoupa Avgolémono & Psári Magionéza*), Kikí's

INGREDIENTS:

- The head(s) of a fatty fish, such as grouper, or about 3 lbs. of grouper, cod, or sea bass, cut into pieces
- 1/2 cup or more olive oil
- 2 medium potatoes, cut into wedges
- 1/2 lb. baby carrots
- 3 stalks celery with leaves, cut into pieces
- 5 small whole yellow onions
- 1/4–1/3 cup short grain or arborio rice
- 2 eggs at room temperature
- juice of 1 or more lemons
- salt
- freshly ground black pepper

PREPARATION:

- Add about 6 cups of water and the olive oil to a large stock pot and bring to a boil.
- Add the vegetables, salt and pepper, bring to a boil, and simmer, covered, for about 30 minutes.

- Add the fish.

- Bring to a boil, reduce the heat, and cook for about 30 minutes until the fish is done. Watch this closely as you do not want to overcook the fish.

- Remove the fish to a platter and remove the vegetables to a bowl.

- Strain the stock through a fine sieve into a clean pot.

- Bring to a boil and add the rice. Stir and simmer until the rice is soft.

- Beat the eggs lightly and slowly add the lemon juice while continuing to beat the eggs.

- Slowly ladle hot broth into the egg-lemon mixture while continuing to beat it until the egg-lemon mixture is as hot as the broth.

- Pour the egg-lemon mixture into the broth, stirring constantly, then remove from heat immediately to prevent curdling.

- Clean fish bits from the boiled vegetables and clean the boiled fish from the bones.

Arrange the fish meat into the shape of a fish. It may be served plain, surrounded by the vegetables, or covered with mayonnaise, preferably homemade. If covered with mayonnaise, it can be decorated with half slices of raw carrot, capers, and thin slices of pepper, arranged to imitate a fish head and scales.

Serve the fish with the soup, and lemon wedges.

9. *Garlic & Potato Spread (*Skordaliá*), Kikí's

INGREDIENTS:

- 2 large russet or golden globe potatoes
- 1/2 head of garlic
- 2/3 cup olive oil (possibly less)
- 1 lemon (possibly less or more, depending on its juiciness)
- 3 tsp. wine vinegar
- salt
- 1/2 tsp. sugar (optional)
- 1-2 tbsp. warm water
- 1 egg yolk—optional

PREPARATION:

- Salt and boil potatoes until flaking apart. Do not scorch.
- In a food processor, mix all liquids except the egg. Leave some of the olive oil and lemon aside and adjust for taste after adding everything except the egg yolk.
- Add the solids and mix well, then add the egg yolk, if desired.

  Serve with boiled beets, boiled haricots verts, thinly sliced fried zucchini or eggplants, fried cod, fried skate wing, or fried baby shark.

10. *Giant Greek Baked Beans (*Gígantes*), Aris's

INGREDIENTS:

- Three 16 oz. cans of Joan of Arc butter beans (We cheat and do not use fresh butter beans—these are just too easy and good. But if you choose to use fresh butter beans, be sure to boil them with baking soda!)

- One 8 oz. can tomato sauce

- 1/2 cup olive oil

- Three bay leaves

- 1/4 tsp. ground nutmeg or to taste

- 1/4 tsp. ground allspice or to taste

- One heaping tsp. Greek oregano

- One large red onion, quartered and sliced

  From your cupboard: Salt, pepper, 8"x14" Pyrex baking pan

PREPARATION:

- Mix all ingredients and bake for one hour at 350°F.

- Stir. Bake for an additional 45 minutes to one hour. The dish should have a red-golden color and be fairly thick.

  Remove the bay leaves and serve at room temperature with Greek village salad.

11. Greek Meatballs (*Keftedákia*), Kikí's, with Laura's tweaks

INGREDIENTS:

- 1.5 lb. ground beef
- 1 lb. dried bread without crust, soaked in water, or 0.5 lb. plain breadcrumbs, softened with water, and drained well
- ¼ cup fresh mint
- fresh parsley (I use 1/4 cup or more; Mána used less)
- 2+ tbsp. marjoram (Mána didn't use it)
- 1 smallish tomato, peeled and seeds removed
- 1/2 tsp. baking soda, dissolved in very little water
- 1 medium onion, finely grated (Mána used a small onion)
- 2 or more cloves of garlic, minced (Mána used one)
- 1/4 cup ouzo
- 2 tbsp. red wine vinegar
- 1 egg
- salt and freshly ground pepper
- flour
- olive oil

PREPARATION:

- Purée the vegetables and herbs in a food processor. Add them and the drained bread to the ground beef and mix well.

- Then add the remaining ingredients (except the flour and oil) and mix well.

- Form meatballs, less than an inch in diameter, roll them in flour, and fry them in HOT olive oil in a frying pan, browning them on all sides.

   Serve with weeds, like rapini, or Greek Village Salad.

12. *Greek Village Salad (*Choriátiki Saláta*) (in the text at page 97)

13. Lamb with Artichokes (*Arní me Agkináres*), Kikí's

INGREDIENTS:

- 3 lbs. lamb shoulder with bone, or lamb rib chops, or a mix of both
- Cleaned, frozen Egyptian or Greek artichoke bottoms (10+ artichokes), defrosted, tough parts removed, and quartered (or you can clean fresh artichokes—a time-consuming chore)
- Fresh dill (3 tbsp. or more), finely cut
- 16 green onions (white parts only), sliced
- 1 large yellow onion, sliced and quartered
- Juice of one lemon
- 2 heaping large spoons of butter ghee
- 1 tsp. flour dissolved in 1 tbsp. warm water
- Salt
- Freshly ground pepper

For the Avgolémono:

- 3 eggs at room temperature
- Juice of one lemon

PREPARATION:

- Pat the meat dry, then salt and pepper it and sauté it in the butter with the onions and dill until nicely browned.

- Cut the meat into portions and transfer it to a large pot.

- Add about a cup of water and cook until approaching tender, about 40 minutes. Stir regularly.

- Add the artichokes, lemon, salt, pepper, and dissolved flour, and cook covered for about 1/2 hour until the artichokes are fork tender. Move the meat around to allow the artichokes to cook. Stir regularly.

AVGOLÉMONO:

- Whisk the room temperature eggs well. Gradually add the lemon juice to the eggs and whisk well until smooth.

- Very gradually add some of the hot liquid from the pot with the meat to the egg mixture and whisk well. Slow down if you see signs of curdling!

- Keep adding the hot liquid until the egg mixture is at the same temperature as the liquid in the pot with the meat.

- Add the egg mixture to the pot and shake well to mix. Remove from heat immediately. Allow it to set for about five minutes before serving.

  Serve with good bread.

14. Lamb or Kid Roasted with Wine and Dill (*Mastélo*), generic, untried recipe

INGREDIENTS:

- 6 lbs. lamb or goat or both, cut into portions
- 1 large bunch of fresh dill, roughly cut
- Rosemary sprigs—optional
- Salt and abundant freshly ground pepper
- 1/2-quart strong rosé wine—though some use white wine

PREPARATION:

- Wash the meat with the wine and reserve the wine used.
- Put the meat in a covered roasting pan, ideally ceramic, on top of cross-hatched sticks or another support.
- Add all of the ingredients except some of the wine.
- Turn the meat over with your hands.
- Add the rest of the wine.
- Cover the top of the roasting pan with aluminum foil and seal it well.
- Put the roasting pan in a preheated oven at 425°F.
- After an hour, reduce the temperature to 300°F.

  Check from time to time, but it should be ready in about four hours.

  Serve with green salad and crusty bread.

15. Octopus (boiled) with Vinegar (*Chtapódi Xydáto*) (in the text at page 177)

16. Onion Stew with Beef, Hare, or Pheasant (*Stifádo*), Kikí's

TO BUY:

- 2 cleaned rabbits or pheasants, cut up, or 2 lb. tip sirloin, cut into cubes of an inch or so square

- 3 lbs. small yellow, football-shaped onions

- 1 large yellow onion, sliced

- 2 tsp. fresh parsley

- 5-6 cloves garlic

- At least 1/2 cup red wine

- 1/2 tsp. cinnamon

- 2 heaping large spoons butter ghee

- olive oil

- 14-ounce can of whole plum tomatoes

- 3-4 tbsp. tomato paste

    From Your Cupboard: Salt, freshly ground pepper, 1/2 tsp. ground allspice, 6 cloves, 5 bay leaves

PREPARATION:

- Parboil the small onions whole briefly, peel them, and fry them whole in olive oil until golden.

- Separately, sauté the sliced onion in the butter until soft.

- Pat the meat or birds dry, then salt and pepper it, add it to the pan with the sliced onion and butter, and sauté until nicely browned all over.

- Add everything, except the small onions and olive oil, along with enough water to cover the meat or birds and cook for about one hour.

- Then add the small, sautéed onions and all of the olive oil they cooked in and cook until tender.

  Serve with green salad and plenty of good bread.

17. Pot Roast & Mashed Potatoes (*Moschári Kokkinistó me Pouré*), Kikí's

TO BUY:

- 1 large yellow onion, peeled and left whole
- Garlic (2 large cloves, peeled and slivered lengthwise—not fine, the pieces must be stiff)
- 2.5 lb. eye of round beef roast, trimmed
- 2 tbsp. butter ghee
- 1 28-ounce can whole plum tomatoes
- 2 tbsp. tomato paste
- 1 carrot, peeled and quartered
- 1 stalk celery, roughly cut

  From Your Cupboard: 10 whole cloves; 12 whole allspice; 2 bay leaves; 1/2 tsp. cinnamon; 1/2 tsp. sugar (optional); 1/2 cup olive oil; 1/2 cup red wine; salt; freshly ground black pepper.

PREPARATION:

- Stuff the onion with 10 whole cloves.

- Roll the slivered garlic in salt and pepper, stab the meat all over (roughly, every inch and a half), and stuff the holes with the coated garlic.

- In a large pot, sauté the stuffed onion and the stuffed meat in 2 tbsp. of butter until well browned on all sides.

- Add all of the other ingredients to the pot, with 1.75 cups of water, and cook at medium heat for 30 minutes. Turn the roast over and continue cooking for another 30 minutes.

- Remove and slice the meat, about 1/3 inch thick.

- Remove the bay leaves.

- Blend all remaining ingredients—except the meat—in a food processor.

- Layer the meat in the pot, add the pureed vegetable sauce, and continue cooking at low heat for 1 to 1.5 hours until the meat is tender and has begun to stick to the pot. Shake the pot periodically to reduce sticking.

Serve with green salad and Greek mashed potatoes (*pouré*).

Greek mashed potatoes (*pouré*): 4 to 6 golden globe potatoes, peeled, quartered, and boiled until tender; 1/2 to 1 can evaporated milk; 4 to 8 ounces sweet butter; salt; freshly ground black pepper; and hard-grated Romano cheese to taste. Mix in a mixer until well blended and serve hot.

18. Shrimp with Tomatoes and Feta Cheese (*Garídes Saganáki*), Laura's

INGREDIENTS:

- 20 large shrimp, preferably with heads and shells. If heads are used, cut off the antennae.

- 16 or more sliced green onions (white parts only)

- 2 or more cloves of garlic, minced

- 1/4 to 1/3 cup of fresh parsley, finely chopped

- Oregano to taste

- Freshly ground black pepper to taste

- Salt to taste

- 1/2 cup ouzo

- 6-8 plum tomatoes, peeled and roughly chopped (do not use canned diced tomatoes; they do not break down well)

- 1/2 lb. (or more) feta cheese, cut into small cubes

- Olive oil

PREPARATION:

- In a large, heavy frying pan, heat the olive oil and sauté the onions until translucent, then add the garlic and sauté briefly.

- Add the parsley, pepper, salt, and oregano and continue sautéing for a couple of minutes.

- Add the ouzo and shrimp and sauté for 2-3 minutes per side, until opaque. Do not overcook! Remove the shrimp, then de-shell and devein it if necessary when they cool.

- Add the chopped tomatoes and cook for about 10 minutes.

- Then add the feta and simmer until the water is gone and the feta has melted.

  This can be prepared to this point and left overnight. If left, heat the sauce, then add the cleaned, de-shelled shrimp back into the pan and warm thoroughly.

  Offer with green salad and Risotto alla Milanese or good bread.

19. Spicy Ground Beef Ovals in Tomato Sauce (*Soutzoukákia*), Kikí's (Laura's tweaks)

INGREDIENTS:

For the meat ovals:

- 1.7 lb. ground beef
- 1 lb. stale bread, crust removed (or 0.5 lb. breadcrumbs), thoroughly moistened in water or in a mixture of water and red wine
- 2 cloves of garlic, minced
- 1 egg
- salt
- pepper
- cumin—1/2 tbsp.
- allspice—1/2 tsp.
- fresh parsley, minced—5 tbsp.
- 1/4 cup or more olive oil

For the Sauce:

- 2 tbsp. tomato paste
- 2 large (28 ounce) cans peeled whole tomatoes, chopped
- 2 large tbsp. butter ghee (clarified butter)
- cinnamon
- 2 tsp. sugar (optional)

PREPARATION:

- Heat the butter and add the tomato sauce. Sauté for a bit and add the tomatoes, the cinnamon, any sugar, and some water. Simmer until the tomatoes break down.

- While the tomatoes are cooking, mix the other ingredients together. Form the meat mixture into 2-inch-long ovals, less than an inch wide.

- Fry the meat ovals in hot olive oil.

- Add the meat and the oil they fried in to the tomatoes and cook until done, shaking the pot, not stirring, to avoid breaking the meat ovals.

  Serve with French fries or spaghetti and green salad.

20. Spinach-Leek-Cheese Pie (Spanakoprasotirópita), Laura's

TO BUY:

- 4 lbs. fresh spinach, roughly chopped, or frozen chopped or cut leaf spinach

- 36-42 green onions, depending on thickness, thinly sliced (white parts only)

- 4 leeks, sliced (and quartered if the leeks are thick)—discard all green parts and all woody parts

- 2 lbs. feta cheese, crumbled, preferably, or cubed

- 1/2 cup or more fresh dill, finely chopped

- 2 eggs, lightly beaten

- 1 large pkg. phyllo dough—do not freeze (if frozen, allow to defrost in the refrigerator)

  From Your Cupboard: Olive oil, salt, black pepper, cayenne pepper, ground nutmeg. One large stock pot or pasta pot. One 14"x11" baking pan, or a cookie sheet and parchment paper for triangles. A pastry brush or oil sprayer.

PREPARATION:

- Preheat oven to 375°F.

- Boil the spinach with a little salt until soft and drain it VERY well.

- Pour about 1/3 inch of olive oil into the pot. Sauté the leeks in the olive oil and add the onion when the leeks start getting soft. Continue sautéing the onions until soft, and golden, but not brown.

- Add the well-drained spinach and sauté it as well. Then add the dill and sauté the mixture until no water remains. Do not scorch.

- Turn off the heat and add 1/2 to 1 tsp. black pepper, 1/4 tsp. cayenne pepper, and 1/2 tsp. ground nutmeg. Stir well.

- Mix in the feta cheese. Taste and adjust seasonings; add salt if desired. Leave on the burner to allow the fluid from the feta cheese to evaporate.

- Add the lightly beaten eggs. If making triangles rather than a pan, skip to "triangles" below.

- Spray or brush olive oil on the baking pan.

- Moving quickly, place four to six layers of phyllo dough, one at a time, in the bottom of the baking pan, spraying or brushing each layer with olive oil.

- Spoon in the spinach mixture, being careful not to disturb the phyllo.

- Quickly layer four to six more sheets of phyllo dough, one at a time, on top of the spinach mixture, spraying or brushing between each layer, and spraying or brushing the top layer with olive oil.

- Trim or fold the phyllo to fit the pan.

- Put the pan on a lower (but not bottom) rack for the first 15-20 minutes, then move to a middle rack.

- Bake at 375°F for 50 minutes to one hour until the phyllo is golden.

TRIANGLES:

- Cut the phyllo into equal strips about three inches wide. Return all but one section of the strips to the refrigerator, wrapped in plastic, to keep them from drying out.

- If it's thin phyllo, place three strips on top of each other. If its thick phyllo, layer one or two strips.

- Place about two tbsp. of the spinach mixture in one corner at one end of the strips in a triangular shape and begin rolling the mixture into the strips. Put a dab of olive oil on the end to secure it.

- Once made, you can freeze the triangles for later, but the phyllo may flake. If you freeze them, separate the layers of the stuffed triangles with parchment paper.

To cook frozen triangles:

- Preheat the oven to 375°F.

- Place parchment paper on a cookie sheet.

- Arrange the triangles on the parchment paper, brush or spray them with olive oil, and place them in the hot oven on a middle shelf for about 45 minutes. They should have a nice golden color. Check after 35 minutes.

  If you cook the triangles without freezing them, prepare them the same way, but check them after 25-30 minutes.

  Serve as an appetizer or with Greek village salad, feta cheese, and Greek olives.

21. Stuffed Grape Leaves with Egg-Lemon Sauce (*Dolmádes me Avgolémono*)

INGREDIENTS FOR THE STUFFED GRAPE LEAVES:

- 1 lb. grape leaves
- 2 lbs. ground beef or a mixture of ground beef and ground lamb
- Beef broth, about 3 cups
- 1/2 cup+ fresh parsley, minced
- 1/4+ cup fresh mint, minced
- 1/4+ cup fresh dill, chopped (optional)
- 16-20 green onions (white parts only), finely chopped
- 1 large yellow onion, finely chopped
- 1/2 cup starchy short grain rice, such as Carolina or Arborio, uncooked
- Juice of one lemon (1/4-1/3 cup)
- Salt and freshly ground pepper
- Olive oil (1/2 cup)

Avgolémono Ingredients:

- 3 egg yolks at room temperature
- salt, pepper, juice of at least one lemon
- at least 2 tbsp. cornstarch (preferably) or flour
- 1/4 cup water or less
- 1/2 cup evaporated milk or cream

PREPARATION:

- Wash the leaves in water, then boil water and carefully add the leaves. Boil gently at high heat for 3-5 minutes until tender. Drain and rinse with cool water.

- Trim the leaves to remove the stems and thick veins. Save any damaged leaves for the bottom and top of the pot.

- Rinse the rice in water. Soak the rice for 20 minutes in hot water or sauté it with the onions.

- Sauté the onions (and rice if you wish—I do) in olive oil until the onions are translucent, but not brown.

- Mix the onions and rice thoroughly with the meat, herbs, and seasoning.

- Oil the pot lightly and place damaged leaves in the bottom of the pot.

- To stuff the grape leaves, place them shiny side down and place one tbsp. or so of the meat mixture in the center of each leaf at the stem end, fold the sides over it, and roll them up, tucking in the sides as you go. Do not roll them too tightly; the rice needs room to expand.

- Place the stuffed grape leaves snugly, but not tightly, leaf ends down, into the pot on top of the bed of empty leaves.

- Place any extra leaves on top and put a heavy plate on top of them to keep the stuffed grape leaves from opening while cooking.

- Boil the broth. Pour the boiling broth, the lemon juice, and the rest of the oil over the grape leaves.

- Cover, bring to a boil, then reduce heat and simmer for 40-50 minutes until liquid is reduced by 1/3 to 1/2 and the rice is cooked. Check after 30 minutes.

- Keep the extra liquid for the avgolémono sauce. There should be about two cups. Add water or broth if necessary. Keep it hot but not boiling.

AVGOLÉMONO:

- Whisk the room-temperature egg yolks well. Gradually add the lemon juice to the eggs and whisk well until smooth.

- Dissolve the cornstarch in warm water and whisk it.

- Add the cornstarch mixture to the egg-lemon mixture and whisk continuously over low heat.

- Very gradually add some of the hot broth to the egg mixture and whisk well. Keep adding broth slowly while whisking and simmer until thickened.

- Remove from heat and add the evaporated milk or cream, whisking well.

  Serve the avgolémono immediately over or beside the stuffed grape leaves and offer them with Greek village salad.

22. Tomatoes, Eggs and Cheese (Strapatsáda) (in the text at p. 96)

23. Tomato Sauce with Ground Beef/Greek Spaghetti Sauce (*Sáltsa me Kimá*), Laura's

INGREDIENTS:

- 1/3 cup olive oil
- 1 large onion, diced
- 2 cloves garlic, minced
- 1 lb. freshly ground beef
- 1 28-ounce can whole peeled plum tomatoes, roughly chopped
- 2 tbsp. tomato paste
- 3 tbsp. finely chopped fresh parsley
- Allspice, nutmeg, salt, and freshly ground black pepper to taste

PREPARATION:

- Heat the oil in a frying pan, then add the onion and cook until soft, but not brown.
- Add the tomato paste and scorch it.
- Add the garlic and sauté lightly
- Add the meat and spices, except the parsley, and cook until brown and cooked through.
- Add the chopped tomatoes and parsley and simmer for about 1 hour until thick.
- Toss with spaghetti.

  Serve with grated *manoúra*, or aged parmesan cheese, or both, and green salad.

24. Pink or White Caviar Spread (*Taramosaláta*), Kikí's

INGREDIENTS:

- Taramá—available at Greek grocers—about nine ounces

- Fresh lemon juice, at least 1/4 cup, possibly more

- Olive oil, 1/2 to 3/4 cup

- White onion, grated, about 3/4 cup rounded

- White bread, crust removed and allowed to go stale, broken into pieces and moistened with water, OR plain, white breadcrumbs, moistened with water, enough to form two balls the size of a tennis ball

PREPARATION:

- Puree all ingredients except the oil, in a food processor or blender, then drizzle in the olive oil, and adjust for taste.

Serve as an appetizer with crusty bread and Greek olives.

25. *Yellow Split Pea Purée (*Fáva*), Kikí's

INGREDIENTS:

- 1 pkg. (17.6 ounces) of Greek cut *fava* (dried split peas), thoroughly washed
- 1 large red onion, peeled, sliced and quartered
- Salt and freshly ground black pepper
- Olive oil
- Balsamic vinegar

PREPARATION:

- Boil the *fáva* and red onion with salt and pepper until very soft and mushy, and no water remains. Skim off the scum periodically.
- Purée in a food processor. Add olive oil and balsamic vinegar to taste.

  When ready to eat, add capers, minced red onion, and chopped fresh tomatoes.

  Serve with Greek olives and feta cheese.

26. *Yogurt & Garlic Spread (*Tzatzíki*), Kikí's

INGREDIENTS:

- 6 ounces of plain Greek yogurt
- 2-3 cloves of garlic, minced
- 1-2 tsp. red wine vinegar
- Approximately 2 tbsp. olive oil
- 2 inches of peeled cucumber, seeds removed and grated
- Fresh dill to taste if desired (not in Kikí's recipe)

PREPARATION:

- Blend thoroughly.

  Serve with crusty bread and boiled octopus, fried zucchini slices, or fried eggplant slices.

A FEW ISLAND PHOTOS

ACKNOWLEDGEMENTS

Asking someone to review a draft book is asking for a gift of their time and thought—a gift I value highly. I'm deeply grateful to Susan Francis, Cathy Hackney (deceased), Julietta Karoli, Linda Pool, and Susan Yohe, who read drafts of *Greek by Osmosis* and offered encouragement and thoughtful feedback. As well as to George Psacharopoulos, who contributed colorful Greek expressions and corrected many of my transliterations, and Barbara Mohajery, who painstakingly reviewed the draft layout. I'm especially indebted to:

- Carol Light, author of the Windy City and Southern Secrets mysteries, who read an early draft, offered insightful suggestions for reorganizing the book, and encouraged me to expand the background section and pursue publication. She also reread and edited a later version!

- Jane Shropshire, who went above and beyond—providing thoughtful, detailed comments, suggesting edits in tracking and otherwise, and reviewing multiple drafts.

I thank them all from the bottom of my heart, not only for their contributions to this book, but for the great gift of their friendship.

I'm also grateful for the assistance of OpenAI's ChatGPT with recent editing, including some Greek transliterations and fact-checking, and to copy editor Fotini Pipi, who caught several glitches, as well as historical errors, and mis-transliterations.

Finally, I thank the people of the Island, who welcomed this *xéni* into their special world.

ABOUT LAURA A. CANDRIS

Originally from Louisville, Kentucky, Laura is a graduate of Transylvania University—in Lexington, Kentucky, not Romania—where she met Aris, the charming and brilliant Greek student she married at age nineteen. Like many who love writing, she chose law school, earning her degree from the University of Pittsburgh School of Law. She spent most of her life in Pittsburgh, a seriously underrated city.

Laura practiced labor and employment law for thirty-four years, all but two of them in Pittsburgh, and became a mediator late in her career. She was a full equity partner in two Pittsburgh law firms and held leadership roles in both. Listed in *Best Lawyers in America* and other peer-reviewed publications, she also held leadership positions in several nonprofit organizations and the local Bar Association and served on the faculty of the Pennsylvania Bar Institute educating fellow attorneys. Additionally, she often spoke to business and HR organizations and published articles on legal topics.

Laura was also a corporate spouse: Aris rose from Senior Engineer B to become President and CEO of Westinghouse Electric Company—and she never got a nickel of legal work from it.

They loved everything about Pittsburgh—except the weather and the roads. The climate drove them to retire to Naples, Florida, for the months they're not on the beloved Greek island. In Naples, Laura serves on two nonprofit boards, volunteers in the community, participates in four book groups, cooks, and writes.

www.ingramcontent.com/pod-product-compliance
Lightning Source LLC
Chambersburg PA
CBHW030358130626
46549CB00004B/1541